MADAME DE LAFAYETTE
AND
'LA PRINCESSE DE CLÈVES'

by

Janet Raitt

GEORGE G. HARRAP & Co. LTD
London   Toronto   Wellington   Sydney

First published in Great Britain 1971
by GEORGE G. HARRAP & CO. LTD
182/184 High Holborn, London, WC1V 7AX

© *Janet Raitt* 1971

ISBN 0 245 50389 7

*Composed in Garamond type and printed
by the Pitman Press, Bath
Made in Great Britain*

CONTENTS

page

INTRODUCTION   9

PART I
Her life   15

PART II
1   Love romance before 'La Princesse de Clèves'   63

2   The moral theme   91

3   Technique of psychological analysis   120

4   The historical setting   147

5   Form and style   169

SELECT BIBLIOGRAPHY   189

ILLUSTRATIONS

Madame de Lafayette, 1634-1693
  (Antoine Hoerse)   Frontispiece

Madame de Sévigné
  (G. Staal)   facing page 32

Gilles Ménage
  (Rob. Nantueil)   33

François, duc de La Rochefoucauld   48

Henriette d'Angleterre, 1644-1670   49
  (Pierre Mignard)

Henri II, roi de France   facing page 112
  (François Clouet)

Jacques de Savoie, duc de Nemours   113
  (François Clouet)

François de Clèves, duc de Nevers   128
  (École des Clouet, vers 1540)

Catherine de Médicis, reine de France   129
  (École des Clouet, vers 1549)

INTRODUCTION

La Princesse de Clèves appears to be an isolated phenomenon, the first modern psychological novel, written three centuries ago, with no predecessors and no immediate descendants. Whereas the plays of Racine and Corneille, despite their uniqueness and their splendour, belong firmly within a classical, theatrical tradition which stretches from the sixteenth to the early nineteenth century, Mme de Lafayette's novel seems a work on its own. We find in it a human truth, a moral complexity and a formal beauty, even a poetry, of which there is no hint in any other novel of the century.

Yet it is of course not possible for any literary work to erupt out of a void; it will always have affiliations, however slender, with the works which precede and accompany it; an author cannot remain uninfluenced by the ideals, attitudes and techniques of his century. So it is with Mme de Lafayette. *La Princesse de Clèves* owes something first to the pastoral and chivalric romance of the early seventeenth century, and then to the *nouvelle*, especially the *nouvelle historique*, which replaced the romance in the public's taste in her own time. For every aspect of the novel, we have tried in this book to ascertain exactly how much its author owes to the literary tradition in which she was writing and we have then attempted to define and analyse Mme de Lafayette's own original contribution, her peculiar genius. We may thus perhaps explain why it is that to read her masterpiece remains even now a unique experience. In making this distinction between what is borrowed and what is original, a study of the author's other fictional works in which her genius is latent but still submerged has also been made when necessary for any enlightenment it might provide.

It seemed useful, before embarking on an analysis in depth of *La Princesse de Clèves* itself, to attempt a survey of the literature of love from the Middle Ages to the seventeenth century so that, however sketchy this must of necessity be, we might explain with more exactness the attitudes to man and his passions which lie behind the literary genre to which it belongs. There seem to emerge from this survey two distinct philosophies of love, each belonging to a different tradition. The first is primitive and fatalistic; love is irrational, irreversible and destructive. It appears for example in the French Middle Ages, in the various versions of the legend of Tristan and Isolde. The second is sophisticated and optimistic; it holds that love can strengthen and purify, and it is embodied in the medieval ideal of *amour courtois* and its later Platonic adaptations. The seventeenth century saw illustrations of both these traditions; the second dominated the early part of the century, in *L'Astrée* by Honoré d'Urfé and in a more complex form in the plays of Corneille. The first gained in importance after this as classical Greek and Roman literature became more fashionable; it reached its highest and purest expression in the plays of Racine in the 1660s and '70s. Although chronologically Mme de Lafayette's works belong to this second period, she had been brought up on the literature of the first, and thus the moral themes of her novels have a dual philosophical inspiration. Moreover, since these two attitudes to love and duty in fact contradict each other, this duality leads to a moral complexity, an ambiguity which has power to interest as well as move us still today.

It is in *La Princesse de Clèves* that this ambiguity is most effectively expressed. It appears also in Mme de Lafayette's other works, especially in *La Princesse de Montpensier* and *Zaïde*, since it was obviously central to her own thoughts about man and his behaviour, but there it is less fully developed. In the character of Mme de Clèves and secondarily in that of her husband, the first, the fatal idea of love is embodied with all the anguish and disaster it inevitably brings with it. Mme de Lafayette's description of her heroine's gradual descent to catastrophe and despair has a subtlety and a realism which rival that of the most complex of more modern novelists, Flaubert or even Proust. She too shows how incapable man is of controlling his own desires and even his actions, try as he may, how obscure and irrational are his motives, and how helpless and hopeless his plight. The belief in discipline and order of the later seventeenth century in France was only superficial. It hid a frightening awareness of confusion and futility underneath, and in this aspect of her novel, in her description of *amour passion*, Mme de Lafayette is very much a contemporary of Racine, Pascal or La Rochefoucauld.

But Mme de Clèves's attitude to this love which devours her,

her guilt and her resistance, belong to an earlier period, to an age which believed that men and women could control their weaknesses, could direct their destinies towards their greatest self-fulfilment, the age of D'Urfé, Descartes and Corneille—although even here Mme de Lafayette has not remained uninfluenced by the pessimism of her contemporaries. The Princesse is strong enough to want to resist, but not strong enough to be able to do it. She needs support, and when her mother dies she gradually turns to the protection of her husband to whom, at the climax of the novel, she confesses her guilty love. This appears as the triumph of her virtue and his generosity. M. de Clèves' jealousy, however, now gradually overwhelms him until his suspicions kill him, and his wife is left tired and empty, able only to run away as she has always run away. The sterility of Mme de Lafayette's idealism is in the end even darker than the irrational violence of the Racinian Hermione's devotion to passion.

In this combination of two opposing contemporary attitudes within one work lies Mme de Lafayette's greatest originality, in the unique conflict with which it endows the heroine, unable to resist yet unable also to yield. Chapters 3, 4 and 5 of the second part of this book will study Mme de Lafayette's technique in presenting this central moral theme, comparing at each stage her practice with the practice of her immediate forerunners and contemporaries in the genre, and her success in *La Princesse de Clèves* with her lesser achievement in her other fictional works. It will, we believe, emerge from this how far at almost every point Mme de Lafayette's masterpiece surpasses all the other novels of the time in subtlety and aesthetic perfection. For as well as being a great psychologist she was a great artist; she knew instinctively how best to present her material for it to achieve the richest effects. The minuteness of her analysis of the conflicts of her main characters is precise and convincing, and she links it throughout with the historical, courtly setting in which the drama plays itself out. The novel is satisfyingly, almost dramatically constructed and the author's style has not only the abstract clarity and concision characteristic of most of the later seventeenth century, but also occasionally a muted tragic poetry of a kind we find nowhere else.

At every stage then we can see how Mme de Lafayette has borrowed, altered and immeasurably improved upon the technique of her contemporaries. We hope that this analysis of the exact nature of these improvements will have gone some way towards explaining why it is that *La Princesse de Clèves* is still read and re-read today while the *nouvelles* of Mme de Villedieu, or Saint-Réal and even the romances of D'Urfé and Mlle de Scudéry have long lain in neglect.

*   *   *

The detailed study of Mme de Lafayette's work is preceded by a biographical chapter. This is intended to throw some light on the complex personality who produced such a masterpiece as *La Princesse de Clèves* almost, as it were, by accident, while playing her full part in the rich daily life of her century.

PART I

HER LIFE

The external facts of Mme de Lafayette's life offer little excitement in themselves, for outwardly she led the conventional existence of a great lady in the French seventeenth century. Yet beneath these facts one can discern a character full of complexities and apparent ambiguities, melancholy and sensitive on the one hand—this is the Mme de Lafayette made famous by Sainte-Beuve[1]—active, lucid and materialistic on the other, admired by almost all but loved only by a very few. It may be that these contradictions are real, or it may be that they only appear as such to the modern reader who wants to define a literary personality in a single and necessarily over-simple formula. Was Mme de Lafayette simply sharing in all the various preoccupations of the seventeenth century, scorning nothing which brought new interest to her active mind, however incongruous the combination of these activities might now seem to us? And is this why she wrote novels, definitely not the kind of enterprise expected of her? What importance did she herself attach to her literary work and how does it compare with the importance she attached to her friends, her duties at Court, her children? A brief account of the main facts known about her life may provide tentative answers to these questions.

Marie-Madeleine Pioche de la Vergne was born in Paris in 1634. Louis XIII was then king but, finding little interest in governing, from 1624, he had vested much of his power in Cardinal Richelieu. Marie-Madeleine's father, Écuyer Marc Pioche de la Vergne, became tutor in 1630 to the young Marquis de Brézé, son of the Maréchal-duc de Brézé and nephew of Richelieu, and was established in the Petit Luxembourg, a palace in the rue de Vaugirard belonging to Richelieu, where his pupil lived. De la Vergne came from the lower reaches of the aristocracy but by his intelligence and his knowledge, especially of military theory, had won the favour of the great Richelieu. His task as tutor was a difficult one, since he had to prepare for a military career a young boy whose shyness and awkwardness hardly fitted him for the great things expected of him. Marc Pioche acquitted himself well, however, and thus rose yet further in Richelieu's esteem.

Also living at the Petit Luxembourg was Mme de Combalet, later the duchesse d'Aiguillon, Richelieu's niece, and among her ladies-in-waiting was a young girl called Isabelle Péna. Mlle Péna came from an illustrious although socially inferior family of scholars and doctors—her father, uncle and guardian had all been the king's doctor—but she herself had little interest in learning. She seems to have been gay and lively, and was described thus by one of her contemporaries:

> Cette Mme de la Vergne étoit honnête femme dans le fond, mais intéressée au dernier point et plus susceptible de vanité pour toute sorte d'intrigue, sans exception, que femme que j'aie jamais connue.[2]

She also had patrons of high social rank—notably the duchesse d'Aiguillon, the Princesse de Condé and Richelieu himself. Since they were both living at the Petit Luxembourg and both came from approximately the same social rank, it is easy to see how M. de la Vergne and Mlle Péna met and became engaged, although de la Vergne was probably somewhat older than his betrothed since he had already had a wife. They were married in February 1633 and a year later, in March 1634, their first child, Marie-Madeleine, was christened at the Petit Luxembourg, with the Maréchal-duc de Brézé and Mme de Combalet as her god-parents.

Mlle de la Vergne spent most of her childhood in a large, pleasant house and garden built by her father in the rue de Vaugirard near the Petit Luxembourg. The de la Vergnes were obviously loth to move far from the protectors who supported them financially and upon whom they depended for their place in society. Yet Marie-Madeleine's parents also had friends of their own who frequently visited the house in the rue de Vaugirard, and some relatives too—a cousin of Marc's and a sister of his wife's, who resided there for a while: they seem to have had a strong sense of family. Most loyal and affectionate perhaps among the friends was a certain Jacques le Pailleur, a *bon viveur* and erudite eccentric, who had been banished from the Court for his independence of mind. When he was not singing songs, inventing poems or playing games for the benefit of the small Marie-Madeleine, he was talking of mathematics, in which he was passionately interested, with his learned friend, Marc de la Vergne. Other visitors included the abbé d'Aubignac, occasionally Voiture, the popular society poet and grammarian, and Mlle de Scudéry and Mme de Sablé, two of the greatest literary ladies of the time. In 1635 and 1636 two more babies were born to Marc and Isabelle de la Vergne.

Thus Marie-Madeleine apparently lived her early years in a gay and stimulating household full of talk and laughter, and in the midst of it we catch one glimpse of the little girl accompanying her mother, in a poem sent by Le Pailleur to his friend:

> Il me dit que ta chère femme
> Est une bonne et belle Dame
> (Oyseau rare en cette saison!)
> Qu'elle garde bien la maison,
> Entretient bien la Compagnie
> Avec sa petite Ménie,
> Qui de son côté vaut beaucoup,
> Surtout quand elle fait le loup
> Son devanteau dessus sa tête.[3]

Meanwhile, France's military situation was deteriorating. She had been at war with Spain and Austria since 1635, and in 1636 the Spanish were advancing on Paris. The young Marquis de Brézé was given his own regiment with his tutor, de la Vergne, as captain, and in 1636 they were sent off to see to the defences and renew the fortifications at Pontoise. After the first panic and when it became clear that the Spanish were still far from Pontoise, de la Vergne was joined by his family and they remained there for some months. Eventually de la Vergne was involved in some successful action against the enemy and everyone returned triumphantly to Paris. But from now on Marie-Madeleine's father was increasingly absent from his home as his pupil was sent on various missions connected with the war in order to gain military experience. He was away in 1639 and again in 1640 and 1641. Then in 1643, since the Marquis de Brézé now needed him no longer, he was given another pupil, also a nephew of Richelieu, Armand Jean de Vigneron, and in 1645 he departed on a naval mission during which his bravery was much praised. In 1646 Mme d'Aiguillon made him 'Lieutenant du gouvernement' at Le Havre and from then on he spent several months a year there.

During all this time Marie-Madeleine was left largely to the care of her mother, whose social ambitions were growing as the favour of Richelieu made her husband and herself increasingly prosperous. She not only proved herself an expert manager of her own house and garden but also supervised efficiently the buying of more property. She obviously attached great importance to material success, both financial and social, and probably taught her young daughter many lessons on its acquisition and on its management—lessons which were later to bear fruit. Yet Marie-Madeleine probably suffered from the absences of her father, better fitted in mind and spirit to be her intellectual companion. Living constantly with her practical and frivolous mother, she may have been forced into that liking for solitude and thought, that mental reserve which later characterized her.

Richelieu died in 1642 and Louis XIII in 1643. Richelieu's collaborator, Cardinal Mazarin, took over power and governed in the name of the Regent, Anne of Austria, Louis XIII's widow and mother of the young Louis XIV. The rule of the Italian diplomat and the Spanish queen was not altogether a popular one: the war against Austria and Spain continued until the treaties of Westphalia in 1648, and caused misery and resentment in Paris. These were exploited first by the 'Parlement', the *noblesse de robe*, in the 'Fronde Parlementaire' of 1648, then by the nobility proper in the 'Fronde des Princes' of 1650-52—both attempts to wrest power from the royal authority, though their complete defeat by 1652 only made it more secure.

In 1648 M. de la Vergne and his family were in Le Havre and in 1649 he was made 'maréchal des camps et armées du roi' under the threat of the Fronde. The duc de Longueville, a prominent *frondeur,* had taken over the whole of Normandy except Le Havre. De la Vergne resisted all attacks on his city and eventually counter-attacked at Honfleur and successfully drove the *frondeurs* away from the region. He then returned to Paris with his family but in December 1649 quite suddenly died. The year had been an eventful one for the young Marie-Madeleine, then fifteen. In Le Havre she must have known panic and bloodshed, and the horror of this was to be followed immediately by the shock of her father's unexpected death.

Exactly a year later, Mme de la Vergne was married again, to the Chevalier Renaud-René de Sévigné, a brave, impulsive and chivalrous partisan of the Fronde. In thus allying herself with a grave enemy of the Crown, she was not only in a sense betraying the memory of her first husband but also risking that favour of Richelieu and then of Mazarin which had given her all the prosperity and reputation she now enjoyed. Yet her yearning for a place in the highest ranks of the aristocracy made the risk seem worth taking. The Chevalier de Sévigné came from an ancient noble family and enjoyed the prestige of an illustrious heredity. In marrying him, Mme de la Vergne's social ambitions were at last completely satisfied.

What were her eldest daughter's feelings at her rapid re-marriage? Gossip had it that Marie-Madeleine was in love with the Chevalier de Sévigné herself and was greatly disappointed when he chose to marry her mother instead of her:

> Mais cette charmante mignonne
> Qu'elle a de son premier époux
> En témoigne un peu de courroux,
> Ayant cru pour être belle
> Que la feste seroit pour elle,
> Que l'amour ne trempe ses dards
> Que dans ses aymables regards
> Que les filles fraîches et neuves
> Se doivent préférer aux veuves
> Et qu'un de ces tendrons charmans
> Vaut mieux que quarante mamans.[4]

Whether this rumour was true or not, experience was already making Mlle de la Vergne independent and resourceful, teaching her not to show her emotions and to rely on no one but herself.

After 1650, when she was sixteen, Marie-Madeleine began to take her own place in society. She occasionally visited the famous precious *salons* of Mme de Rambouillet and Mlle de Scudéry, those centres of refinement and sophistication where great lords and ladies and men of letters gathered together to read and converse. She probably learnt here a certain poise and elegance of manner, and certainly acquired a taste for contemporary literature, for she now began to read Mlle de Scudéry's long romance, *Le Grand Cyrus*. The *salon* of Mme de Rambouillet, however, had been partly broken up by the Fronde and never regained its old prestige and importance, so that Mlle de la Vergne can only have appeared there a few times. In fact throughout her life she remained impervious to the excesses of the *précieuses*, while fully sharing their preoccupation with the casuistry of love, contemporary literature and society gossip. Her judgement was too fine, her sense of the ridiculous and the insincere too acute for her not to deplore the absurd refinements in costume, language and behaviour in which some of the less sensible of her contemporaries indulged. She herself can be called a *précieuse* only in the most general sense of the word, as it describes a certain way of life, centred on *salon* society.

As a result of her mother's second marriage, Marie-Madeleine made the acquaintance of the now famous Mme de Sévigné, whose husband (killed in a duel in 1651) was her stepfather's nephew. Mlle de la Vergne was probably attracted by her new friend's gentleness and charm, and by that gaiety which no domestic grief could quite quench. The two of them shared the attentions at this time of the abbé Gilles Ménage, a society poet and philologist, highly thought of in the *salon* circles that he frequented. He was something of a dandy, rather vain and pretentious, and his work was second-rate, but he could be witty and amusing and his attachment to the two young ladies was obviously genuine. Marie-Madeleine was very proud of having such an admirer and of finding her name celebrated in some of his poems. "Me voilà une manière de Madame Laure", she was to write to Ménage in 1656.[5] She may even have been a little jealous of her rival for his attentions, although Mme de Sévigné, older and more experienced, never really responded to Ménage's advances, and he quickly chose to concentrate his admiration on his other friend. Yet although she liked to be adored, she always kept her adorer at a certain distance, played with his affections, encouraging him and then waxing indignant when she thought he had become too bold. It is to her he refers in these lines:

> Ce portrait ressemble à la belle,
> Il est insensible comme elle.

Their relationship was indeed more a literary than an amorous one. It was born and grew as they read and discussed poetry and romance together, and Ménage expressed his feelings probably more in elegies and rondeaux than by word of mouth. While not formally her tutor, he was undoubtedly pleased by her intelligence and her fresh interest in literature, and did much to form her literary taste.

Ménage and his poetry did not, however, take up all Mlle de la Vergne's time during these years, 1650–53. Through the influence of the duchesse d'Aiguillon, her godmother, she became lady-in-waiting to the queen, Anne of Austria, thus rising a step further up the social ladder and receiving her first taste of that Court life which was to form the subject of almost all her work. The Court at this time was not the gay, cultural rendezvous of

great lords and ladies that it became some years later. Louis XIV
was still too young to have any sort of power and his mother
was growing old and disapproved of frivolity and entertainment.
There are hints in the *Histoire d'Henriette d'Angleterre*, written
fifteen years later, that Mlle de la Vergne did not particularly
admire her royal mistress:

> . . . elle n'avait pensé qu'à mener une vie douce, à s'occuper à ses
> exercices de dévotion, et avait témoigné une assez grande indifférence
> pour toutes choses.[6]

We do not know how often she appeared at Court at this time;
but there is no doubt that it is the atmosphere of the Louvre ten
years later that she describes in her great novels.

Mlle de la Vergne probably found more to amuse her at her
house in the rue de Vaugirard, for there now lived next door to
her a most charming and attractive young lady called Catherine-
Henriette d'Angennes, demoiselle de la Louppe. With her new
neighbour Marie-Madeleine soon formed a friendship close
enough for a door to be pierced in the wall that separated the
two gardens so that they might visit each other more easily.
Mlle de la Louppe was prettier and more worldly than her friend
and together they learnt much about the attractions and dangers
of a young lady's life. Indeed, it has been suggested that under
the influence of her friend, who, after she married the comte
d'Olonne in 1652, became a notorious flirt, Mlle de la Vergne
indulged in a few amorous escapades with daring and unscrupu-
lous gentlemen. Not only, however, would this have been quite
out of character but all the evidence we have points rather the
other way. There is a passage in the *Mémoires* of the Cardinal de
Retz in which he describes a planned seduction of Mlle de la
Louppe but his advances were firmly resisted and indeed he
praises the young lady's virtue and modesty. Elsewhere Retz is
joined by the duc de Brissac, who evidently preferred Mlle de la
Louppe's friend, Marie-Madeleine:

> . . . la principale de ces parties de divertissement vint du commerce
> que le duc de Brissac avoit avec Mlle de la Vergne. . . . Cette
> demoiselle, qui étoit fort bien faite, avoit pour voisines Mlles de la
> Louppe, dont l'aînée étoit une des plus belles personnes de France;
> et, comme il y avoit une porte de communication d'une maison à
> l'autre, Mlle de la Louppe étoit à tous moments chez Mlle de la
> Vergne, où le Cardinal et le duc alloient souvent la nuit entretenir
> les deux demoiselles.[7]

What happened during these evening conversations nobody knows, but we cannot infer that they were anything but quite harmless.

The full and interesting life which Marie-Madeleine had been leading for the last two years was now to come to an abrupt end. In 1652 the Cardinal de Retz was arrested for his part in the Fronde and soon after, the Chevalier de Sévigné, Marie-Madeleine's stepfather, who had fought with him against the Crown, was exiled to his estate at Champiré in Anjou. He probably complained bitterly of loneliness and boredom, for he was soon joined by his wife and stepdaughter, first for a few months in 1653 and then for the whole of 1654. Mlle de la Vergne must have had a melancholy year and a half: she cannot but have missed the entertainments, the friends, the conversations of her Parisian life in the lonely, dilapidated castle of Champiré where she had only her stepfather, downcast at his plight, and her mother for company. Once again, as at the time of her father's death and mother's remarriage, she was driven back on her own resources and forced to make her happiness herself.

She was much helped in this by the faithful Ménage, who wrote to her regularly and not only amused and flattered her by his exaggerated admiration but also kept her supplied with the social and literary gossip of her friends in Paris. His courtship was growing more and more ardent: he sent presents, wrote poems full of extravagant praises of her intellect and beauty, then paid her a visit in Anjou and read Italian poetry with her. Marie-Madeleine's letters to him were playful and intimate, as she encouraged his literary efforts—

> Je suis bien aise que vous remontiez sur le Parnasse : il y a si peu de presse présentement et les Muses ont si peu de gens à qui donner leurs grâces, que je croy qu'elles augmenteront celles qu'elles ont accoutumé de vous faire. Voilà de si grands mots, au commencement de ma lettre, que j'ay envie de ne la pas faire plus longue ; car, quand on a parlé des Muses et du Parnasse, l'on ne peut pas se rabaisser à parler d'autre chose.[8]

—or scolded him for being too generous to a stranger:

> Il faut que je commence tout ce que j'ay à vous dire par une belle et grande réprimande de la folie que vous avéz faite de prester quatre cents pistoles à un Suédois. Il n'y a que vous au monde qui alliéz chercher des gens du Nord pour leur prester vostre argent.[9]

She clearly values above all else the pleasures of friendship.

She rebukes Ménage when his professions of love become too ardent, then draws him back to her when he, perhaps disappointed in her feelings for him, seems to withdraw his affections:

> Vous ne m'aiméz plus comme vous avéz fait. . . . Je vous aime et vous estime autant que j'ay jamais fait; tant que j'ay esté à Paris, je n'ay point négligé de vous voir; présentement que je n'y suis plus, je ne négligé point de vous escrire; enfin vous ne scauriéz vous plaindre avec justice.[10]

Thus, although still immensely flattered by his admiration, she is clearly afraid of committing her heart as yet—she is too independent and reserved to give herself easily: "Je suis si persuadée que l'amour est une chose incommode, que j'ay de la joye que mes amis et moy en soyons exempts",[11] she says elsewhere.

Marie-Madeleine had another faithful friend whose visits and regular letters to her relieved the tedium of life at Champiré. He was a provincial cleric with a taste for literary disputation, named Costar, to whom she had first written in Paris through the intermediary of Ménage. Like Ménage, he was a pedant and a man of letters but had little of the wit and charm of his friend. His letters to the young Mlle de la Vergne are full of hyperbolical praises of her mind and her complexion which in her lonely exile she took quite seriously. She valued too highly her literary reputation, her complacent image of herself as idol and queen of contemporary poets, to laugh with her usual good sense at such compliments as these:

> J'ay tâché seulement, Mademoiselle, de vous faire bien remarquer sur mon visage et dans toutes mes actions l'extrême joye que je recevois de vous voir si belle, si spirituelle, si raisonnable et, pour vous tout dire en un mot, si semblable à l'excellent portrait que l'on m'avoit fait de vos grâces à ma mémoire et à mon imagination.[12]

At the end of 1654 Retz escaped from his prison in Nantes, a crime in which Sévigné was implicated since he had seen him in captivity a short while before. Soon after this, the latter's wife and daughter left for Paris, primarily in order to work for his release but also, one can assume, because they were anxious to return to their former interesting life.

Marie-Madeleine was now twenty-one. There are no portraits of her at this age—all that we have show an older woman already weakened and disfigured by ill-health. There, however, several witnesses of her beauty, more or less sincere, so she must have had a certain attraction. She was clever, though not a scholar, and keenly interested in contemporary literature. She shared her mother's social ambitions and was pleased with every mark of esteem and respect shown to her. She was reserved, even cold, and she was already eminently *raisonnable*, the adjective that friends and critics most often use to describe her. Her long months in exile during her most formative years away from the full and often frivolous life of the capital did much to mould her character, to teach her the joys of a rich mental life as well as the value of a friendship which remained constant through vicissitude and separation. It was Costar who, after her marriage, wrote perhaps the best appreciation of her qualities:

> Mais Madame, vostre douceur, vostre modération, vostre sage et judicieuse conduite produiront infailliblement dans vostre âme des plaisirs tranquilles et des contentements tout purs, qui vous cousteront que ce qu'ils valent et qui n'auront point de fâcheuses suites.[13]

When she was back in Paris at the end of 1654, Mlle de la Vergne visited the convent of Chaillot, founded by Henriette de France, daughter of Henri IV and exiled wife of Charles I of England, to house herself and her young daughter, together with another young girl, Jeanne-Baptiste de Nemours. The superior of this convent was Louise-Angélique de Lafayette, with whom Louis XIII had once been in love and who had been forced by political pressures to retire to a convent to prevent the king from forming an inopportune liaison with her. Louise-Angélique's eldest brother was François, comte de Lafayette, a widower who was looking for a wife. What more fitting than that he should marry Marie-Madeleine de la Vergne, who was still unmarried at twenty-one? His family was of a much higher social rank than hers, and since he was the eldest of the family he owned all the Lafayette estates in Auvergne, although the family debts made his possession in some cases a little dubious. Marie-Madeleine, on the other hand, although her name was not illustrious could bring with her a substantial dowry, her two sisters' shares having been added to her own on their entering a convent. The marriage was good business for both sides: Marie-Madeleine's money would help Lafayette to recover his property; to belong to so old and noble a family would satisfy those yearnings felt by both Mlle de la Vergne and her mother for a secure position among the highest ranks of the aristocracy. Marriages in the seventeenth century were frequently thus arranged not to suit the inclinations of individuals but to add glory to a wealthy but inferior family or riches to a high-ranking but less affluent one.

A meeting was arranged between the two parties very early in 1655 and this must have been successful for they were married only a month or so later, on 14th February of that same year. There has been much speculation as to why the marriage was so hasty—it had obviously not been thought of before the return of Marie-Madeleine and her mother to Paris in December 1654. Even contemporary Parisians were surprised. But the fact was that, at twenty-one, Marie-Madeleine was already growing old by seventeenth-century standards; her mother, needing to return to Champiré to her husband, was anxious to establish her quickly; since François and Marie-Madeleine were agreeable, there was no reason to wait. The comte de Lafayette was now thirty-nine, considerably older than his wife, and had already been married once, for a short time, between 1641 and 1644, to Sibylle d'Amaulry, lady-in-waiting to the queen. He seems to have been a good, gentle man, perhaps rather shy, more interested in administering his land than in the literary gossip of Paris. He had spent some of his youth at the Court and had observed the mean intrigues of Richelieu and his followers which had forced his sister into a convent, although he had refused to take any part in them. He had successfully held a command in the army for some years but in 1644 had given up his military and social career to return to his castles in Auvergne where he now lived a peaceful country life. He was in every way different from his wife. Indeed the differences were prophetically described in a comic song of the period:

> La belle, consultée
> Sur son futur époux,
> Dit, dans cette assemblée
> Qu'il lui paraissoit doux
> Et d'un air fort honnête—
> Quoique peut-être bête;
> Mais qu'après tout pour elle un sot Mari
> Était un bon parti.
>
> De la jeune Lisette
> On approuva l'avis;
> une dame discrète
> Aussitôt repartit:
> Il vivra dans sa terre,
> Comme Monsieur son Père,

Et vous ferez des romans à Paris
Avec les beaux esprits.[14]

Soon after their marriage, the new Mme de Lafayette left Paris with her husband to live in Auvergne, in the castle of Nades. The change must have been bewildering. The journey was long and uncomfortable; Mme de Lafayette was already pregnant. The castle itself was lonely and forbidding, so different from her lively, fashionable house in the rue de Vaugirard—and here Marie-Madeleine was to spend the rest of her life! How much she now needed that inner strength, those resources against loneliness which she had cultivated in exile at the castle of Champiré! Quite quickly she resigned herself, and formed her own moderate view of happiness, founded on peace and sober contentment rather than on ecstasy and delight. She was somewhat disillusioned, but no less practical for that. She took simple pleasure in talking to her neighbours, in the beauty of the countryside and the calm solitude of her home:

> . . . il est vray aussi que nous avons des hommes, icy autour, qui ont bien de l'esprit, pour des gens de province. Les femmes n'y sont pas à beaucoup près si raisonnables; mais aussi elles ne font guère de visites: et ainsi l'on n'en est pas incommodé. Pour moy, j'aime bien mieux ne voir guère de gens que d'en voir de fâcheux, et la solitude que je trouve icy m'est plutost agréable qu'ennuyeuse. Le soing que je prends de ma maison m'occupe et me divertit fort; et, comme d'ailleurs je n'ay point de chagrin, que mon espoux m'adore, que je l'aime fort, que je suis maîtresse absolue, je vous asseure que la vie que je fais m'est fort heureuse et que je ne demande à Dieu que la continuation. Quand on croit estre heureux, vous scavéz que cela suffit pour l'estre et, comme je suis persuadée que je le suis, je vis plus contente que ne font peut-estre toutes les reines de l'Europe.[15]

Another reason for her melancholy resignation lay in her increasing ill-health. In August 1655 she had a miscarriage and so began various uncomfortable symptoms which persisted to the end of her life. She was never to feel quite well again. All her later pregnancies and confinements tired and weakened her considerably and she sometimes complained of feeling unwell. Her famous cry: "c'est assez que d'être", expresses a philosophy born of disappointment and suffering.

Mme de Lafayette's great solace during these early years in Auvergne was her regular correspondence with the faithful Ménage. Their feelings for each other, in spite of constant misunderstandings, complaints and re-affirmations, remained the same as ever. She depended on him entirely in her exile for books and information about the outside world; but besides this she genuinely liked and esteemed him, and enjoyed his literary adulation. Although she was by nature reserved, finding it difficult to show her feelings, she needed her friend all the more because of the solitude in which she was now living. Thus she was possessive and jealous of other women in his life or in his poems:

> Je suis comme jalouse qu'elles (his works) s'advancent si fort en mon absence et j'ay dans la teste que quelqu'un vous aide au lieu de moy; mandéz-moy sincèrement ce quy en est; et au moins, si je ne suis celle quy vous aide, que je sache quy elle est.[16]

Ménage occasionally rebelled against this bondage which seemed to bring him so little—on the whole, however, he was resigned to have her only as a correspondent and his literary inspiration.

Ménage's main rôle at this time was to keep his exiled friend in touch with the capital, to tell her all the social gossip and to send her the new works of society poets and novelists, including his own. She pressed him urgently to procure for her the poetry of Sarasin, a contemporary precious writer, and the last elegy of the comtesse de Suze, but it was for the second volume of Mlle de Scudéry's *Clélie*, the work which reflected her own life in Paris, that she asked most persistently. She enjoyed this long, heroic novel thoroughly when finally it arrived, although she criticized the lack of historical *vraisemblance* of its Roman setting:

> Mais songéz aussi que le bel esprit des Romains tournoit du costé d'une générosité extraordinaire et d'un amour infiny pour la patrie, et qu'il n'alloit pas à disputer des questions tendres et galantes comme elles sont dans *Clélie* . . .[17]

She is original in thus attacking Mlle de Scudéry's too obvious use of her historical setting as a cover for contemporary revelations, for *vraisemblance* to most of the seventeenth century meant the image they themselves formed of another period by projecting their own ideals into it, rather than fidelity to the real truth. Yet at other times Mme de Lafayette judged her century with less detachment: she was delighted by Ménage's weak and trivial poems—perhaps largely because they were often dedicated to her —and was also as anxious as anyone to discover the keys to the portraits of contemporaries in which *Clélie* abounds.

After a few years of marriage Mme de Lafayette became active in another sphere. She began to help her husband in the lawsuits in which he was involved over possession of some of his property in Auvergne, and eventually she took them in hand almost completely. Litigation was to take a large part of her time throughout much of her life and although it was usually forced on her by circumstances, by the complications ensuing from her mother's will or by her husband's difficulties, she seems to have enjoyed the mental activity it involved. Here is another aspect of her character which nineteenth-century critics found it difficult to reconcile with their image of the melancholy invalid fashioning jewels of artistic pessimism. Yet it is not at all mysterious if one forgets any preconceived image and places Mme de Lafayette in the context of her daily life with all its inevitable pressures and demands. She had always been materialistic and practical, grasping at every advantage that life offered her. Now she threw herself heart and soul into the unravelling and solving of the complex cases which were threatening her husband's and therefore her own property. For a while she did nothing else:

> Par exemple, je n'ay plus dans la teste que les sentences, les exploits, les arrests, les productions; je n'escris presque que pour mes affaires; je ne lis que des papiers de chicane; je ne songe non plus ny aux vers, ny à l'italien, ny à l'espagnol, que si je n'en avois jamais jamais ouy parler. . . . C'est une chose admirable que ce qui fait l'intérest que l'on prend aux affaires: si celles-cy n'estoient point les miennes, je n'y comprendrois que le haut allemand; et je les sçay dans ma teste comme mon *Pater* et dispute tous les jours contre nos gens d'affaires des choses dont je n'ay nulle cognoissance et où mon intérêt seul me donne de la lumière.[18]

With that frank honesty which so many of her contemporaries commented on, she was not afraid to admit that it was her self-interest which made her so tenacious. She was indeed a highly competent disputant—her active, lucid mind, used to analysis and discussion, equipped her well for the task. Later on she was to help others, La Rochefoucauld and Charles Sévigné, with their affairs.

It was largely these legal cases which brought the Lafayette couple to Paris on several occasions between 1656 and 1659— Mme de Lafayette also came to give birth to her sons, Louis in March 1658 and Renaud-Armand in September 1659, in the capital where she would be assured of expert attention. They came first in 1656 when Mme de Lafayette's mother died, in order to work out the details of the will with the widower, the chevalier de Sévigné, now returned from exile. They returned in January 1658 for a few months and then again in January 1659, when they lived first in a house of theirs in the rue Férou and then, from September, when the chevalier de Sévigné retired to the Jansenist foundation of Port-Royal, in Mme de Lafayette's old home in the rue de Vaugirard. On each of these visits Mme de Lafayette resumed her old place in society: she met her friends, visited the Court, heard or read the latest literary production as soon as it appeared. On their last visit the Lafayette couple remained for over two years in the rue de Vaugirard and when the comte de Lafayette finally returned to Auvergne in November 1661, he left his wife behind. No quarrel accompanied their separation; M. de Lafayette continued to stay with his wife in Paris at intervals until his death in 1683. She kept constantly in touch with him, largely through the intermediary of the faithful Ménage, who wrote to him on her behalf, and she showed concern for his well-being: "J'envoye à Paris pour sçavoir des nouvelles de Mr. de Lafayette dont je suis en peine",[19] she writes to Ménage on one occasion when she was out of Paris and her husband staying in her house.

One can give reasons for their separation. Mme de Lafayette wanted to remain in Paris so that she could supervise more closely the conduct of their lawsuits, and so that her sons might receive a good education; but no reason is really necessary. After a few years' trial, the couple had found that their interests and tastes were different and gradually accepted that they should both live their own lives while remaining on perfectly friendly terms with each other. It is doubtful whether either at first intended the separation to be definitive, but as Mme de Lafayette became ever more involved in her life in Paris, a renewed exile in the country with her husband must have struck her as unthinkable. Because no documents have come down to us and because our conventions are different, the separation appears mysterious to us now. But in the seventeenth century the marriage tie was much less close, since so many unions were arranged by third parties, usually by parents when their children were still young, and thus were entered into without real love. Each party to it kept his or her separate individuality; the woman often retained her maiden name and there was not automatically the same community of property. Indeed in the *salon* society in which Mme de Lafayette moved, marriages were regarded by some as an inferior tie which the noblest women scorned. What the feminist *précieuse* really desired was a pure attachment between a man and woman (in which the woman was the dominant partner), the spiritual nature of which would inevitably be sullied by the gross intimacy of marriage.

Mme de Lafayette's three most famous stories, *La Princesse de Montpensier* (1662), *La Princesse de Clèves* (1678) and *La Comtesse de Tende* (not published until 1724), are all based on a marriage into which the lady had entered without profound enthusiasm and which ended disastrously. Can we see in Mme de Lafayette's own experience with her husband a source for this recurring situation in her work? Only, it would appear, in its external characteristics, for how remote the two are in all their essentials! It was not an overwhelming passion for another man which separated Mme de Lafayette from her husband in 1661—it was the practical convenience of her continuing to live in Paris. She can have felt neither remorse nor guilt towards him for she was working in her old home as much for his advantage as for her own, and indeed went on seeing him for the rest of his life. While his love may well have gradually declined, he obviously continued to respect and admire her as she assumed his responsibilities in Paris. There is indeed little resemblance between this peaceful bond and the guilt-ridden, jealous relationship of the Princesse de Clèves and her husband. That material which Mme de Lafayette took from her life she could just as well have taken from countless other lives around her; her own marriage was characteristic of her age and it is her age that she is portraying in her work, not her personal experience. This merely formed in her a certain attitude of mind which made her view the passions and behaviour of others with that critical and melancholy spirit which pervades her best work.

In 1659, then, Mme de Lafayette settled in the house built by her father in the rue de Vaugirard and began again her life in Paris. She had no family left, since her mother had died and her stepfather had now retired to Port-Royal, but she was active and had influential connections. The most important of these was Henriette d'Angleterre, who, having fled from England with her mother, Henriette de France, after the defeat and execution of her father, Charles I of England, by the Roundheads, was brought up from an early age in the convent of Chaillot, where, as we have seen, Mme de Lafayette had occasionally visited her before her marriage. She and her mother were poorly lodged and neglected by the Court of France and Henriette was doubtless grateful for the friendship which Mme de Lafayette then showed her.

In 1661, however, Cardinal Mazarin died; Louis XIV, now twenty-two, assumed authority and the young Henriette d'Angleterre, whose brother, Charles II, was now king of England, was given to the king's brother, the duc d'Orléans, called Monsieur, in marriage. Henriette's strict, retired upbringing under the absolute authority of her mother and in the peaceful, religious atmosphere of a convent, had made her sensitive and spontaneous. Had she been brought up at Court, she would have learnt early what standards and what behaviour were expected of her and would bring her most success, and she would probably have had little of the freshness and sincerity which conquered the Court on her appearance there in 1661. She was only seventeen at the time of her marriage and, not having led a very joyful existence till then, was intoxicated with the delights and excitements of Court life. She loved pleasure and threw herself into everything, the balls, the literary entertainments, the love affairs, that came her way. Her husband was selfish and frivolous, and rather effeminate, and she probably found him an uncongenial companion from quite early on. Indeed, soon after her marriage she and the king played at being in love and were probably only prevented from entering into a serious relationship by reasons of state. The king then preferred to her one of her ladies-in-waiting, Louise de la Vallière, and she on her side soon began an affair with the charming comte de Guiche.

In the midst of all this, Madame, as she was called, now an important and popular figure at the Court, did not forget her former friend, and for the nine years between Henriette's marriage and her death, Mme de Lafayette was very often to be seen at Court beside her, not as a lady-in-waiting but rather as an intimate and loyal companion. For Henriette was not only gay and attractive, she was also intelligent and interested in literature. She seems to have appreciated Mme de Lafayette's qualities of wisdom and integrity and to have treated her more serious, reserved friend, nearly ten years her senior, as counsellor and confidant. We see from Mme de Lafayette's letters to Ménage of this period how frequently she spent an afternoon or an evening with Madame at Court:

J'ay esté tout le jour chez Madame, à faire ma cour.[20]
Vendredy, je seray à vous jusques à trois ou quatre heures, que j'iray chez Madame.[21]

In April 1661 Mme de Lafayette accompanied Madame to Fontainebleau and remained there with her several days, and in describing this visit Loret mentioned her and Guiche as being Madame's great intimates:

> La Reyne mère d'Angleterre
> Anne et Thérèse nos deux reines
> Monsieur et Madame
> La Fayette et le jeune Guiche.

We have the best evidence of their friendship in a narrative by Mme de Lafayette—the *Histoire d'Henriette d'Angleterre*, written between 1665 and 1670—which describes the Princess's life after her marriage and in particular her relations with the king and Guiche. Mme de Lafayette apparently wrote it all down as Henriette told it to her in retrospect and we see the trust which Madame evidently felt in her confidant:

> J'eus toutes les entrées particulières chez elle, et, quoique je fusse plus âgée de dix ans qu'elle, elle me témoigna jusqu'à la mort beaucoup de bonté et eut beaucoup d'égards pour moi.
> Je n'avais aucune part à sa confidence sur de certaines affaires; mais, quand elles étaient passées, et presque rendues publiques, elle prenoit plaisir à me les raconter.[22]

The narrative ends with Henriette's sudden death in 1670, in the telling of which Mme de Lafayette is almost as great a literary master as anywhere in all her work. The pathos of all the small, homely details which she includes and the absolute simplicity of the style are full of a contained yet powerful emotion which the reader can still feel keenly:

> . . . Lorsque le roi se fut retiré, j'étais auprès de son lit; elle me dit: «Mme de Lafayette, mon nez s'est déjà retiré.» Je ne lui répondis qu'avec des larmes, car ce qu'elle me disait était véritable, et je n'y avais pas encore pris garde. On la remit ensuite dans son grand lit. Le hoquet lui prit: elle dit à M. Esprit que c'était le hoquet de la mort. Elle avait déjà demandé plusieurs fois quand elle mourrait, elle le demandait encore; et, quoiqu'on lui répondit comme à une personne qui n'en était pas proche, on voyait bien qu'elle n'avait aucune espérance.[23]

How great is the contrast between the tragedy here and the futile

G. *Staal*

Madame de Sévigné

Rob. Nanteuil

Gilles Ménage

(Bibliothèque Nationale, Par

frivolity of the preceding narrative of Henriette's worldly life at the Court! This was surely not lost on Mme de Lafayette.

Louis XIV had deliberately made of his Court a place of brilliance and refinement, a centre of culture and fashion, overwhelmingly attractive to the nobility but a drain on their wealth and their time. The magnificent palace of Versailles was being built and after 1669 the whole Court moved there to live in an artificial atmosphere of pleasure and frivolity, thinking of nothing but the endless entertainments provided for them, or of the complicated intrigues of love or ambition in which they were ceaselessly involved.

Through Henriette d'Angleterre, Mme de Lafayette had acquired a certain prestige at the Court, and from her observations of life there she drew much of her material for the settings of her novels. What exactly did she think of the person and policy of the king and the behaviour of the courtiers? There is no doubt that, besides her affection for Henriette, she was anxious to secure a good position for herself there, and once she had secured it to maintain it. She had won the favour too of Mme de Montespan, the king's mistress, and was later to have frequent dealings with Louvois, the minister for War. We find her in 1661 present at the royal festivities at the palace of Vaux, owned by Fouquet, the financier, which were so magnificent that they aroused Louis XIV's jealousy and Fouquet was disgraced forever. Some years later, Mme de Lafayette was distinguished by the king personally as she paid her respects at Versailles. Elsewhere she thanked him in the most flattering terms for the present of a benefice which he had accorded to her elder son. She undoubtedly possessed a certain worldliness of spirit, that practical sense of her own advancement and of that of her sons, which we have already noted, and which led her to accept at least superficially the values accepted by all her contemporaries: that is, to covet as the highest mark of success a position at the Court and the favour of the king. It is also of course true that the entertainments and conversations at the Court were brilliant and distinguished, not to be missed by a sophisticated lady of the time.

Yet, while apparently participating wholeheartedly in contemporary activities, Mme de Lafayette was forming in her mind a biting judgment of them. Even in the *Histoire d'Henriette d'Angleterre*, begun in 1665, when her position was still to be consolidated, she allowed herself an occasional dig at the great

c

personalities of the Court—at Monsieur, for example: "son amour-propre semblait ne le rendre capable que d'attachement pour lui-même"[24]—and even the rash conduct of Henriette herself she depicted tactfully but frankly. In the *Mémoires de la cour de France*, for the years 1688 and 1689, written when Mme de Lafayette's life was nearly over, she was less discreet in expressing an independent judgment of the king's behaviour and policy, criticizing for example the injustices of the royal system and the hypocritical religious atmosphere of the Court under the auspices of the king's new mistress, Mme de Maintenon: ". . . à l'heure qu'il est, hors de la piété point de salut à la cour, aussi bien que dans l'autre monde."[25] Her criticism is implicit in a different form in her novels too, in her depiction of the futile complications of the many intrigues at the Court and their potentially tragic consequences. Indeed, *La Princesse de Clèves* can be seen as a long indictment of life at the Court where all true values are dead.

Here then Mme de Lafayette found confirmation for her disillusioned attitude to love and human integrity, and material for its eventual embodiment in a work of art. It was probably in her *salon,* and in the *salons* of others, that she developed the fine literary taste and the sense of form to which *La Princesse de Clèves* and her shorter novels owe much of their success. She frequented especially the Hôtel de Nevers, presided over by Mme de Plessis-Guénegaud, and in the summer its country equivalent at Fresnes. The *salon* of the Hôtel de Nevers in many ways continued the traditions of the *Chambre bleue* of Mme de Rambouillet, and was visited by some of the same people. Their activities were typical of most precious *salons* at that time—they listened to the latest literary production, they played word games and above all, they cultivated the art of conversation by talking wittily and endlessly about politics, the latest romance, the newest scandal, fashions in clothes and hair styles.

The Hôtel de Nevers had, moreover, a special reputation as a literary centre: we know for instance that Racine read his *Alexandre* there in the presence of Mme de Lafayette and Mme de Sévigné, and Boileau his *Satires*. Although she does not mention such experiences (we know of them from Mme de Sévigné), Mme de Lafayette can have missed few new literary happenings. She must have heard too a certain amount of criticism of the Crown, for the Hôtel de Nevers had been a centre for political agitation, especially against Mazarin's régime. Mme de

Plessis-Guénegaud, having thus lost her favour at the king's Court, built up a small court of her own to which were welcomed such people as Fouquet and Pomponne. Indeed, Mme de Plessis-Guénegaud's own husband, as Secretary of State, was compromised in Fouquet's downfall and temporarily imprisoned as a result. Mme de Lafayette, in spite of the favour in which she was held at Court, knew well these people whom the king would on no account have received and perhaps heard them attack her masters. She, however, remained detached from all political factions: her reason and practical materialism told her to seek only her advantage, interest and amusement in the places she frequented, not a cause to which to sacrifice herself.

Mme de Plessis-Guénegaud also felt sympathy for the heretical Jansenists of Port-Royal, a Catholic sect which believed in grace and predestination and whose views were not accepted by the Established Church, and she sometimes used her *salon* to propagate Jansenist doctrine. Thus it may have been here that Mme de Lafayette first came into direct contact with the Jansenist attitude to life. We have evidence of her interest in Jansenist moralists, in the *Essais de Morale et Instructions théologiques* of Nicole, and Pascal's *Pensées*. Its fatalistic pessimism, its belief in man's predestination to sin and suffering, unless he be one of the few saved by grace, had much in common with the philosophy of life she had developed already, apparently independently. Her greatest works give us a picture of man's weakness in the face of passion similar to the one we find in Racine's plays, probably more directly influenced by Jansenism. In her visits to the unorthodox Hôtel de Nevers, between 1660 and 1670, Mme de Lafayette found an interest and an excitement which were not present in the other *salons* of the time.

What of the people whom Mme de Lafayette received in her own house? Her *salon* too had a reputation as an intellectual and literary centre—Saint-Simon says of it: "c'était un tribunal pour les ouvrages d'esprit"—and even as far back as 1658, she was held in high esteem: "C'est une femme de grand esprit, de grande réputation, où une fois du jour on voit la plupart des polis et des biendisants de cette ville. . . . Enfin c'est une des précieuses du plus haut rang et de la plus haute volée."

It is clear that Mme de Lafayette was respected by her contemporaries as a clever and cultured woman; in 1675 she was included in a model of a room, called the Chambre du Sublime, given as a present by Mme de Thianges to her nephew, Louis-Auguste de Bourbon, in the illustrious company of La Rochefoucauld, Bossuet, Boileau, Racine and La Fontaine.

Mme de Lafayette's greatest friends between 1660 and 1670 were not on the whole such outstanding and well-known figures. She rather attracted around her men of letters of an inferior social rank for whom she was a kind of patroness as well as an interested friend and correspondent. Ménage was still foremost among these, although Mme de Lafayette seems to have used him more and esteemed him less than when she was younger and more in need of friends. She would summon him whenever she had a job for him: it was he who wrote to her husband for her, he who ran errands in connection with her lawsuits, he who taught her Latin, he who escorted her on her walks and her visits; and if she found something better to do, she did not hesitate to put him off with the slimmest of excuses:

> Je vous prie de me venir voir demain de bonne heure; nous estudierons et puis nous irons nous promener.[26]
> Je vais demain disner à Chaliot. Si vous voulez y venir avec moy, trouvez-vous céans à dix heures et demye; si non, vous ne me verrez point encore demain, et vous aurez dimanche de mes nouvelles.[27]
> Si vous n'avez point d'affaire aujourduy, vous m'obligeriez tout à fait de vouloir voir Mr. Le Chancelier pour demander un rapporteur pour un gentilhomme des amis et des parens de Mr. de La Fayette. . . . Si vous ne pouvez le voir aujourduy, vous le verrez demain.[28]

Her attitude may seem cruel. She appears to assume that all Ménage's time is at her disposal, that whenever she calls on him he will be free to reply. Yet though he occasionally rebelled, she always won him back with renewed affirmations of her affection for him. There is no doubt that beneath all her dominating ways, her demands and her angers, she truly cared for him and missed him when he was away not only for what he could do for her but also for what he was to her:

> Je n'ay jamais veu escrire si seichement aux gens qu'on ne les aime plus et je n'ay jamais veu une amitié mourir si subitement que la vostre. Je croye qu'elle n'est qu'esvanouye et je ne consentiray pas à son enterrement que je ne sois bien asseurée de sa mort. C'est pourquoy je vous prie que je vous voye demain; je ne sortiray point encore.[29]

Another literary friend of Mme de Lafayette's in the 1660s was Paul-Daniel Huet, to whom she was probably introduced by

Ménage, although later on Ménage became jealous of him and attempted to break off relations between his two friends by not passing on messages which Huet wrote to him to give to Mme de Lafayette. When his treachery was discovered, a direct correspondence was established between Huet at Caen and Mme de Lafayette in Paris, and they saw each other whenever Huet visited the capital. He was a scholar and philosopher of some standing, with perhaps a deeper and broader intelligence than Ménage although, since he was not on the spot, Ménage remained the favourite. Mme de Lafayette had great respect for Huet's knowledge and asked him to correct the style of *Zaïde*, her first novel. Indeed, he was enthusiastic enough to contribute a treatise on the novel, the *Traité du Roman*, as a preface for it. He also offered to teach her Hebrew but she never took up his proposal seriously—she was not interested in arid learning for its own sake: "J'aime mieux laisser détruire toute ma science que de construire des phrases."[30]

Mme de Lafayette also saw something of Segrais, a charming man of letters and poet in the service of Mlle de Montpensier, when he was in Paris. She even lodged him in her house for a while when he was dismissed from Mademoiselle's service in 1671. It is with him that she joined in the composition of her long, chivalric romance, *Zaïde*, published in 1669 and 1670, not for details of language—these she sought from Huet—nor so much for help in the supervision of its publication—as she used Ménage for *La Princesse de Montpensier* in 1662—but rather, as we shall see later, in the devising of the plot and even in the actual writing of parts of it. The novel appeared under his name and for a long time was thought to be his since he also had written some works of fiction.

The relationship between Mme de Lafayette and these scholars and poets was a curious one: they talked and wrote mainly of literature and language but the tone in which they wrote was something more than merely intellectual. Mme de Lafayette teased Huet about his reproaches to her for not writing more often:

Il est vray que vous avéz tort; ne penséz pas le dire en plaisanterie: je vous le maintiens sérieusement. Quoy, monsieur, vous m'auréz escrit une lettre et vous bouderéz parce que je n'y auray pas fait responce? Ne sçavéz-vous donc point qu'il faut pour le moins trois lettres de Caen pour une de Paris? Vous vous arrestéz à la premiére.[31]

—or about his love affairs:

> Je ne sçay si je me trompe; mais je treuve que les cœurs de campagne bruslent à bien plus grand feu que ceux de la cour, et il me semble mesme que ceux de la cour bruslent mieux à la campagne qu'à Paris.[32]

She continues by wittily pitying Segrais in his exile with Mademoiselle:

> Ce pauvre Segrais aura tout loisir de brusler à Saint-Fargeau. Il ne luy manquera que du feu; mais je ne croy pas qu'il en puisse trouver là pour allumer une allumette.

Indeed, Huet seems to have been half in love with Mme de Lafayette himself. They obviously all of them enjoyed the ambiguous nature of their relationship; such harmless bantering forms a pleasant and amusing contrast to the more solemn parts of their correspondence.

It is time now to say a few special words on the profound and enduring friendship between Mme de Lafayette and Mme de Sévigné. As we have seen, it began before the former's marriage but only became the close tie of which we find proof in the latter's letters after Mme de Lafayette had resettled in Paris in 1659. It was at this time that she composed her portrait of Mme de Sévigné to be included in a collection of portraits which appeared under the auspices of Mlle de Montpensier in 1659; it was Mme de Lafayette's first published work. It follows the tradition of the time in concentrating far more on moral than physical characteristics, but avoids the hyperbolic insipidity of most of the other pieces in the collection, perhaps because Mme de Lafayette chose to do a portrait of a friend and not her own. In it we see the shrewdness and yet the depth of an affection which both saw and excused faults, and which felt all the charm and all the goodness of its object:

> . . . le brillant de votre esprit donne un si grand éclat à votre teint et à vos yeux que lorsqu'on vous écoute, l'on ne voit plus qu'il manque quelque chose à la régularité de vos traits, et l'on vous croit la beauté du monde la plus achevée. . . . Enfin la joie est l'état véritable de votre âme, et le chagrin vous est plus contraire qu'à personne du monde.[33]

This is one of the earliest examples of Mme de Lafayette's lucidity and sensitivity in psychological analysis.

Indeed it is true that at first sight an intimacy between the two women which after 1670 was to bring them together nearly every day may seem unexpected since they had such different temperaments—the one gay, resilient and impulsive, the other reserved, critical and among the profoundest spirits the seventeenth century produced. Probably, however, each was attracted by the opposing qualities of the other—they were consistently devoted throughout their lives. Mme de Lafayette listened patiently to Mme de Sévigné's interminable praises of her daughter and even joined in, although, despite Mme de Sévigné's pathetic attempts to bring them together, the friend and daughter really felt little sympathy for each other. Mme de Lafayette also materially helped her friend's family, particularly her son Charles de Sévigné, by using her influence at Court. Then, when they were both growing old, she showed a protective, almost domineering concern for Mme de Sévigné's health. We can see from her description of her friend which of her qualities were particularly attractive to her— her gaiety, her charm, her affectionate nature, her generosity— and added to these as the years passed by must have been her fidelity in friendship.

The very strength of Mme de Sévigné's affection for Mme de Lafayette blinded her both to some of her friend's qualities and to her faults. She gives us the picture in her letters of a wise and disillusioned invalid, standing slightly aloof from the world, whom she could admire and pity, whereas Mme de Lafayette had a practical realism and a shrewdness which this sentimental view ignores. Thus Mme de Sévigné describes her as quite broken at the time of the death of La Rochefoucauld, her friend, companion, perhaps lover of long standing:

> . . . la pauvre Mme de Lafayette ne sait plus que faire d'elle-même; la perte de M. de La Rochefoucauld fait un si terrible vide dans sa vie, qu'elle en comprend mieux le prix d'un si agréable commerce: tout le monde se consolera, hormis elle, parce qu'elle n'a plus d'occupation . . .[34]

This was no doubt true, but in fact, a month after his death, she was engaged on diplomatic missions between the Courts of Savoie and France, of which her friend knew nothing, just as she knew nothing of Mme de Lafayette's literary works until after they were finished. Indeed, to judge from her agreement with Bussy-Rabutin's unfavourable and misguided judgment of *La Princesse de Clèves*, she understood little of what Mme de Lafayette was attempting to do.

Undoubtedly the most important person in Mme de Lafayette's life was the duc de La Rochefoucauld. The date of the beginning of her friendship with him is not absolutely certain but should not be fixed before 1665, although she had already known him for up to ten years as an occasional social acquaintance: as early as 1656 she talks in a letter to Ménage of "la belle sympathie"[35] between them. They probably began to meet more often as Mme de Lafayette frequented the *salon* of the Hôtel de Nevers of which La Rochefoucauld was an habitué. At this time Mme de Sablé, a famous *précieuse* who since 1659 had retired to Port-Royal but still held her *salon* there, was La Rochefoucauld's most intimate friend. Her disillusioned melancholy, akin to his own, and the good food served at her table probably drew him to her. There are several letters in the years 1663, 1664 and 1665 written to Mme de Sablé by Mme de Lafayette, showing a growing familiarity and a pressing desire to see her:

> Je ne voulois rien que vous voir, Madame. Mais je me plains bien que vous ne me regardiéz que comme une personne qu'il ne faut voir que dans la joye et quy n'est pas capable d'entrer dans les sentiments que donne la perte d'une amie.[36]

Then:

> Je suis résolue à avoir l'honneur de vous voir, quand vous seriéz ensevelie dans le plus noir des chagrins. . . .[37]

or:

> Vous ne songéz non plus à moy qu'aux gens de l'autre monde et je songe plus à vous qu'à tous ceux de celuy-ci. Il m'ennuye cruellement de ne vous point voir.[38]

Do these urgent phrases express only Mme de Lafayette's affection for Mme de Sablé, or had she not perhaps a hope of meeting La Rochefoucauld at her friend's house as well as at the Hôtel de Nevers? In 1664 had come the publication of La Rochefoucauld's *Maximes* and here is what Mme de Lafayette says of them in a letter to their mutual friend:

> Ha, Madame, quelle corruption il faut avoir dans l'esprit et dans le cœur pour etre capable d'imaginer tout cela! J'en suis si espouvantée que je vous asseure que, si les plaisanteries estoient des choses sérieuses, de telles maximes gasteroient plus ses affaires que tous les potages qu'il mangea l'autre jour chéz vous.[39]

Is there not here a more than natural concern for La Rochefoucauld's character on Mme de Lafayette's part and a hint that he

on his side is already trying to win her favour? Is not her shocked
dismay at the *Maximes* excessive precisely because of an interest
in their author? In *La Princesse de Montpensier*, she herself had
expressed a view of man not much more encouraging.

The most open confession by Mme de Lafayette of her affection
for La Rochefoucauld she made involuntarily in a letter to Mme
de Sablé, probably at the end of 1664 or the beginning of 1665.
She had received a visit from the comte de Saint-Paul, an illegiti-
mate son of La Rochefoucauld's, who had obviously teased her
on her relationship with his father:

> J'ai bien veu que Mr. le Comte de St. Paul avoit ouy parler de ces
> dits-là; et j'y suis un peu entrée avec luy. Mais j'ay peur qu'il n'ait
> pris tout sérieusement ce que je luy en ay dit. Je vous conjure, la
> première fois que vous le verréz, de luy parler de vous-mesme de
> ces bruits-là. Cela viendra aisément à propos, car je luy ay donné les
> *Maximes* et il vous le dira sans doute. Mais je vous prie de luy en
> parler bien comme il faut pour luy mettre dans la teste que ce n'est
> autre chose qu'une plaisanterie. Je ne suis pas asséz asseurée de ce
> que vous en penséz pour respondre que vous diréz bien et je pense
> qu'il faudroit commencer par persuader l'ambassadeur. Néanmoins,
> il faut s'en fier à votre habileté: elle est au-dessus des maximes
> ordinaires; mais enfin persuadéz-le. Je hay comme la mort que les
> gens de son âge puissent croire que j'ay des galanteries. Il me semble
> qu'on leur paroist cent ans dès que l'on est plus vieille qu'eux et ils
> sont tout propres à s'estonner qu'il soit encore question des gens.
> Et de plus il croiroit plus aisément ce qu'on luy diroit de Mr. de la
> R. que d'un autre. Enfin, je ne veux pas qu'il en pense rien, sinon
> qu'il est de mes amis . . .[40]

Mme de Lafayette becomes more and more agitated as the letter
proceeds and this very agitation seems to prove that the rumours
about her relationship are not unfounded and that it is a fear of
their mature friendship being ridiculed by young wits that moves
her most. In fact, by this time, their intimacy was an open secret
and it gradually became acknowledged and accepted by their
friends and acquaintances.

There has inevitably been much discussion on the nature of
their intimacy. It is unlikely that it was a violent, physical passion
that brought La Rochefoucauld and Mme de Lafayette together
in the first place: they were neither of them in the prime of youth
and Mme de Lafayette, to judge from portraits of her, was not
a great beauty. More probably they were first drawn together by
a feeling of intellectual and spiritual sympathy, by certain affinities
in their view of people and their weaknesses, and by their common

interest in literature. Life had taken from them most of their
illusions: La Rochefoucauld's rebellious ambitions had failed
with the failure of the Fronde, and his former love affairs were
finished; Mme de Lafayette had not found in marriage the
companionship she desired. Moreover they were both forced to
live in semi-retirement because of ill-health. It is natural that they
should gradually have spent a large part of each day together
talking, reading and writing. Most of their friends assumed their
friendship to be a respectable one; Mme de Scudéry wrote to
Bussy-Rabutin:

> M. de la Rochefoucauld vit fort honnêtement avec Mme de Lafayette;
> il n'y paroit que de l'amitié. . . . Elle est sa favorite et sa première
> amie. Rien n'est plus heureux pour elle que cela, ni plus honnête
> pour lui.[41]

Then, two years later, rather unkindly she says in talking of
La Princesse de Clèves:

> M. de La Rochefoucauld et Mme de Lafayette ont fait un roman des
> galanteries de la cour de Henri second, qu'on dit être admirablement
> bien écrit; ils ne sont pas en âge de faire autre chose ensemble.[42]

Mme de Sévigné, who probably knew them most closely and who
frequently mentions them and the conversations they had
together in her letters, never hints at anything beyond a gentle
friendship of kindred minds, which grew up gradually and which
depended much more on mental than on physical communion.
Here is how she describes it on the occasion of La Rochefoucauld's
death:

> . . . où Mme de Lafayette retrouvera-t-elle un tel ami, une telle
> société, une pareille douceur, un agrément, une confiance, une
> considération pour elle et pour son fils? . . . rien ne pouvait etre
> comparé à la confiance et aux charmes de leur amitié.[43]

Were Mme de Lafayette not the author of *La Princesse de
Clèves*, one would enquire no further. As it is, however, whether
or not she became La Rochefoucauld's mistress could be relevant
to the problem of the source of the great novel, since Nemours
and Mme de Clèves are in the very same situation apparently as
their creator and La Rochefoucauld. Unless Mme de Lafayette
was a gross hypocrite, it might be argued, she could not have
yielded to La Rochefoucauld, or at least not done so without a
hard struggle, considering the anxious scruples of her heroine
when faced by the same dilemma. Yet on reflection it appears

that the situations are not so similar after all, that the two cases of Mme de Lafayette and La Rochefoucauld, and of the Princesse and Nemours, are in all important respects far too different for the one to have served to any appreciable extent as material for the other. Firstly, as we have seen, what La Rochefoucauld probably inspired in Mme de Lafayette was not the sudden irresistible sensual passion which Mme de Clèves felt for Nemours, but a love which grew up slowly, gathering its strength as it went. Thus, one of the major reasons which prevented the Princesse from giving way to Nemours at the end of the book— her mistrust of the duration of a passion in so charming a young man—can have had no place in Mme de Lafayette's own mind. Secondly, by 1665 Mme de Lafayette had already been living apart from her husband for four years—she cannot have felt so acutely her loyalty to him as the newly married Princesse does to her husband. After all, she was not afraid, in 1666, to admit that they were often teased about their sympathy for each other: "Car, pour ne plus parler de moy, ce n'est pas chose possible à Fr(esnes) et à L'h(ostel) de Ne(vers). J'y suis le souffre-douleurs: on s'mocque de moy incessament",[44] and later on she openly spent all her days with him. After such a feminist disregard for her husband's rights, whether or not she was physically unfaithful to him is really of little significance, for if she did resist him, it cannot have been out of respect for a marriage which by now meant little to her. In her novels and short stories Mme de Lafayette was not drawing on her own experience in marriage or love. She was presenting the problems of her society as a whole without seeking, as do Romantic writers, to express her own feelings and preoccupations. Let us then leave alone those facts in her private life about which we can do no more than endlessly conjecture.

After 1670 or so, Mme de Lafayette's life changed somewhat. She began to attend fewer social occasions, to prefer either to visit the *salons* only of her intimate friends or to remain in her own home whither they came to see her.

With the death of Henriette d'Angleterre in 1670, she had lost her protectress and friend at the Court and thus also much of her prestige. After this, although she never lost touch with those in power—she still attended the big royal celebrations and kept the favour of the king—she naturally visited the Court much less frequently.

At the same time, she was gradually losing touch with her old scholarly friends. Ménage she had neither seen nor heard from for several years now. Their letters had become increasingly curt and irritable: she had less and less time for him now that she found increasing fulfilment in her friendship with La Rochefoucauld and he resented her neglect. At the end of 1665 or the beginning of 1666, she wrote him a brusque, reproachful note:

> Il me semble que le démon qui vous conduisoit l'autre jour ne vous a pas conduit lomtemps, ou du moins, s'il vous conduit encore, ce n'est pas céans. Quand vouléz-vous me conduire à la Bastille? . . .[45]

and that is the last he hears from her unless (which is unlikely) some letters have not survived. Did they have a violent quarrel, or did they simply stop writing and seeing each other, realizing that their friendship had run its course and another taken its place? Nobody knows. All that is certain is that they completely lost touch for the next twenty years. Mme de Lafayette's relations with Huet were also lapsing about this time, although much more gradually. Their correspondence became thinner and in some of the only letters we have of this period Mme de Lafayette is merely acting as intermediary between Huet and La Rochefoucauld on a matter of business. Segrais remained on intimate terms with the Comtesse for some time longer since he lived in her house from 1671, but after his departure in 1676, he lived in the provinces and saw much less of his protectress. It seems as though Mme de Lafayette had no more need of the semi-literary, semi-romantic admiration these men felt for her, now that she had the constant companionship of La Rochefoucauld.

Mme de Lafayette's other intimate friend was of course Mme de Sévigné, who after 1671 began to visit her much more assiduously. The Marquise's daughter whom she adored and to whom she had so far devoted much of her time had married the comte de Grignan in 1669 and in 1671 departed with her husband to live on his estate in the south of France. Thus, the mother was now free to visit Mme de Lafayette, and to entertain her with all the news and all the gossip about Parisian high society. She no longer needed to go out in order to learn what was happening around her, what a certain lady was wearing, with whom a certain gentleman was conducting an affair and so on.

Her health was still deteriorating: there were times when she could neither eat nor sleep for days at a time. She felt faint and sick and her head ached—any movement exhausted her. Yet she rarely complained of her bad health; whenever she mentioned it, it was to laugh about it, to mock herself for being so useless:

Voicy ce que j'ay fait depuis que je vous ay escrit. J'ay eu deux accès de fièvre. . . . Il y a six mois que je n'ay esté purgée: on me purge une fois, on me purge deux; le lendemain de la seconde, je me mets à table. . . . Ah, ah! j'ay mal au cœur; je ne veux point de potage. — Mangéz donc un peu de viande. — Non, je n'en veux point. — Mais vous mangeréz du fruit? — Je croy qu'ouy. — Hé bien, mangéz-en donc. — Je ne sçaurois; je mangeray tantost, que l'on m'ait ce soir un potage et un poulet. Voicy le soir, vite un potage et un poulet. Je n'en veux point, je suis desgoustée; je m'en vais me coucher, j'aime mieux dormir que de manger. Je me couche, je me tourne, je me retourne; je n'ay point de mal, mais je n'ay point de sommeil aussi. J'appelle, je prends un livre, je le referme. Le jour vient, je me lève, je vais à la fenestre: quatre heures sonnent, cinq heures, six heures. Je me recouche, je m'endors jusqu'à sept, je me lève à huit, je me mets à table à douze, inutilement comme la veille; je me remets dans mon lit le soir, inutilement comme l'autre nuit . . .[46]

She suffered such crises at intervals for thirty years. She was rarely completely well; but the less she went out and the more she rested, the better she was likely to feel.

Mme de Sévigné in her letters to her daughter in Provence frequently describes the afternoons she passed at Mme de Lafayette's house, where she and La Rochefoucauld were often the only visitors. Occasionally they would talk of sad and solemn things:

Nous faisons quelquefois des conversations d'une tristesse qu'il semble qu'il n'y ait plus qu'à nous enterrer.[47]

More often, however, they spent hours discussing the latest piece of news, gossiping on their various acquaintances. Mme de Lafayette had moments of gaiety which are often forgotten by critics absorbed in a study of the pessimism of her works. She was keenly interested in other people's behaviour, and loved to hear the latest scandal from Mme de Sévigné. She disliked any form of vanity or hypocrisy and laughed cruelly at anyone of whom she did not approve. She thought the pretentious style of some precious letters absurd and composed two parodies—the *lettre du jaloux*, and the *lettre de l'étourneau*, which are masterpieces of ironic ridicule:

Ce sont de ces sortes de choses qu'on ne pardonne pas en mille ans,
que le trait que vous me fistes hier. Vous estiéz sous les armes, belle
comme un petit ange. Vous scavéz que je suis alerte sur le compère
d'Angeau. Je vous l'avois dit de bonne foy: et cependant vous me
quittastes franc et net pour le galopper. Cela s'appelle rompre de
couronne à couronne.[48]

There was one particular incident which Mme de Sévigné
describes at some length and which shows well the cruelty of
Mme de Lafayette's wit. There was a poor lady, Mme de Marans,
whom the whole group of the rue de Vaugirard had decided to
victimize since they believed she had spread some malicious
rumour about Mme de Grignan, Mme de Sévigné's daughter.
Thus, when next she appeared in their *salon*:

. . . la Marans disoit l'autre jour chez Mme de Lafayette: «Ah, mon
Dieu! il faut que je me fasse couper les cheveux.» — Mme de
Lafayette lui répondit bonnement: «Ah, mon Dieu, Madame, ne le
faîtes point, cela ne sied bien qu'aux jeunes personnes.[49]

On her next appearance in the rue de Vaugirard her short hair
was greeted by another cutting comment, also duly reported to
Mme de Grignan.

Thus Mme de Lafayette inevitably had many enemies, people
whose susceptibilities she had ignored. The self-reliance and
independence of judgment which she had cultivated early on in
life had led her to an absolute, even intolerant lucidity in her
opinion of others and of herself, which she did not bother to
hide. Mme de Sévigné talks of "ces bons tons sincères que vous
connaissez",[50] and here is an extract about her from the Segraisiana, a collection of Segrais's sayings:

Elle n'aurait pas donné le moindre titre à qui que ce fût, si elle n'eût
été persuadée qu'il le méritait; c'est ce qui a fait dire qu'elle était
sèche, quoiqu'elle fût délicate.
Elle était incommodée, néantmoins elle était entrée dans sa
soixantième année quand elle est morte; car elle ne cachait pas son
âge, et elle disait librement en quelle année et en quel temps elle
était née.

She realized that she did not feel affection for others easily. On
the other hand, she affirmed, and her friends corroborate this,
there were a few people whom she really loved.

Quelque peu tendre qu'on me croye, je n'ay guère de négligence
pour mes amis.

She could be kind and generous, to La Rochefoucauld, to Mme de Sévigné, to Segrais, even to Ménage, but refused to simulate any affection for those to whom she was indifferent. As early as 1656, when she asked Ménage to pass on her compliments to Mlle de Scudéry, she said:

> Je vous prie, demandéz à Sapho, quy se (cognoist) si bien en tendresse, si c'est une marque de tendresse de faire des caresses parce que l'on en fait naturellement à tout le monde et si un mot de douceur d'une *ritrosa beltà* ne doit pas toucher davantage et persuader plus son amitié que mille discours obligeants d'une personne quy en fait à tout le monde.[51]

In spite of their more retired life, Mme de Lafayette and her friends kept up their interest in contemporary literary productions. In 1672, at La Rochefoucauld's house, they heard readings of Corneille's *Pulchérie* and Molière's *Les Femmes Savantes,* and in Mme de Lafayette's own *salon* they discussed at length those works they had heard or read. We can believe that although she shared the literary tastes of her contemporaries, Mme de Lafayette never spared a work which she thought mediocre or pretentious.

Occasionally Mme de Lafayette would leave Paris to spend a few days in the country where her mind, spirit and body could recollect themselves in peace, far away from the ceaseless agitation of life in the capital. For she could see beneath the surface of her worldly life and it sometimes seemed empty and wearing: "elle est quelque fois lasse de la même chose", says Mme de Sévigné, and elsewhere: "elle ne veut pas penser, ni parler, ni répondre, ni écouter; elle est fatiguée de dire bonjour et bonsoir; elle a tous les jours la fièvre et le repos la guérit".[52]

Ever since those months in Auvergne, immediately after her marriage, she had found joy and calm in the spectacle of nature, of the flowers, the trees, and the hills, and had pitied her friends living always among the walls of a town. It is as though the need for intervals of peaceful retirement in the country grew in her as she grew older, busier and less healthy. She often went with Mme de Sévigné to visit the abbey of Livry outside Paris where there lived a good friend and relative of the marquise, the abbé de Coulanges. Or she went to stay at the Condé's country property at Saint-Maur in Chantilly, where indeed she more or less took over the administration of the house, and thus made a permanent enemy of Gourville, the resident keeper. She also had a small house at Meudon, where she took walks in the garden, picked the flowers or simply rested and enjoyed the silence, the pure fresh air and the country smells. She returned to Paris refreshed and invigorated.

> Je suis à Saint-Maur; j'ay quitté toutes mes affaires et tous mes amis. J'ay mes enfans et le beau temps: cela me suffit. Je prends des eaux de Forges, je songe à ma santé; je ne vois personne, je ne m'en soucie point du tout.[53]

Mme de Lafayette's most important occupation, at least from our point of view, during these years, was the composition of her masterpiece, *La Princesse de Clèves*. She must have been continually distracted from her work by her numerous engagements— by legal affairs, by her friends, by her duties at Court and so on. Indeed, it is amazing that she should have found time at all to read up the detailed facts about the reigns of Henri II and Charles IX, to work out the perfectly balanced structure of the novel, and to write it in that clear, precise, controlled style which is so moving. She must have done it all in her odd moments of leisure. She kept her work a close secret, as we have seen; even Mme de Sévigné knew nothing about her friend's hobby. Only two other people were in her confidence: Segrais, who lived with her until 1676 and may have looked up some of the basic historical material upon which she worked, and La Rochefoucauld, who probably revised and approved her style. The bulk of the work she did alone. *La Princesse de Clèves* was not published until 1678 and, if one accepts Magne's proof of the validity of Mme de Sévigné's reference to *La Princesse de Clèves* in 1672, Mme de Lafayette took at least six years to write it. She was by this time in full possession of her literary powers and the structure has a tightness and a coherence, the style a unity and distinction that they did not have before and which resemble in no way the writings of her collaborators.

The publication of *La Princesse de Clèves* was given much publicity by Donneau de Visé, editor of the popular newspaper, the *Mercure Galant*. He began an inquiry as to whether Mme de Clèves was right or wrong to confess her love to her husband and letters came flooding in—most of their writers thought she was wrong. For a while the work was all the rage: everyone was reading it, discussing it, criticizing or praising it:

> On est partagé sur ce livre-là, à se manger. Les uns en condamnent ce que les autres admirent.[54]

François, duc de la Rochefoucauld

(*Bibliothèque Nationale, Paris*)

Pierre Mignard

Henriette d'Angleterre

(*Mansell Collectio*

There are letters about it by Fontenelle, Bussy-Rabutin, Mme de Sévigné. A young courtier called Valincour wrote a witty and erudite dialogue discussing it. There is no doubt that the seventeenth-century literary world found the new novel absorbing and original, even if they were not sure that it was not also outrageous and incredible.

We must now come to a consideration of another aspect of Mme de Lafayette's character and activities. We have already noted her practical qualities which equipped her to manage very successfully the material interests of her family and friends. We have seen her fighting her own, her husband's and later La Rochefoucauld's lawsuits, and Mme de Sévigné's letters mention that she helped both Mme de Grignan's husband and Charles Sévigné through her influence at Court. She took great trouble to establish her sons in positions of financial and social security, by shamelessly pestering the king or his ministers. Her elder son being destined to take orders, she obtained a benefice from Louis XIV for him when he was only twelve and he had three by the time he was twenty-one, not so that he might do three times as much work but so that he should receive a triple income. Benefices in the seventeenth century were often a sort of sinecure, giving position and a certain wealth but requiring no duties: both Huet and Ménage were priests solely in name. Then Mme de Lafayette turned her efforts to winning the favour of Louvois, Secretary for War, since her younger son was to enter the army. We have many letters from Louvois to Mme de Lafayette, which are obviously replies to requests for promotion or to justifications of bad behaviour—Armand seems to have been lazy and immoral. Much later his mother was accused of double dealing as she tried to arrange a match for him with the marquis de Lassay's daughter, although it remains uncertain how well-founded the accusation is. She undoubtedly set great store by worldly success for others as well as for herself and her family, and did all she could to achieve it.

It is mainly, however, Mme de Lafayette's diplomatic connection with the Court of Savoy, then separate from but dependent on France, which leads critics to accuse her of materialistic intriguing. This connection had begun years ago in a very natural and trivial way. Mme de Lafayette's stepfather, the Chevalier de Sévigné, had once stayed at the Court of Turin, made friends with the then Regent Duchess of Savoy and corresponded with her after his return; in a sense, Mme de Lafayette was simply continuing in the family tradition. Yet she also had a more personal link with the present Duchess of Savoy, for she had once been the young Jeanne-Baptiste de Nemours who was brought up at the convent of Chaillot with Henriette d'Angleterre. Mme de Lafayette had met and liked her there as she had met and liked her future royal patroness at the Court of France. In 1665, Mlle de Nemours had married Charles-Emmanuel, Duke of Savoy, and it is not unlikely that Mme de Lafayette remained in contact, however intermittently, with her friend all through their married lives.

It is only from the year 1678, however, that any letters between the comtesse and the Chevalier de Lescheraine, the Duchess of Savoy's secretary, and from Louvois about the Court of Savoy have come down to us. The Duke of Savoy had died in 1675 and when Mme Royale, as she was called, became Regent awaiting her son's majority, Mme de Lafayette was her unofficial agent in Paris. In fact her tasks at this time, as we gather from her letters, were trivial enough. Mme Royale used her mainly for two things: firstly Mme de Lafayette did her royal patroness's shopping in the French capital, chose materials, items of clothing and jewels for her:

> Je vous supplie de dire à Mme la Mise. de Saint-Maurice qu'elle me fait griller de ne me jamais mander si elle a receu les hardes de Mme Royale. Elle ne me dit rien de sa robe de chambre. Je luy ay envoyé un second mémoire des autres habits; elle ne me mande point si elle l'a receu. Dites-luy aussi que je n'ay point de nouvelles du velours.[55]

She also received articles—there is much talk of a piece of damask that she is expecting—not as gifts but in lieu of payment of her purchases:

> . . . comme je luy ay envoyé, il y a desjà lomtemps, des hardes pour elle et pour sa fille et qu'elle ne m'a point renvoyé l'argent, apparemment elle songeoit que le damas feroit une partie du payement.[56]

Secondly, and more important, Mme de Lafayette tried to protect her friend's reputation in Paris, and explain her activities to Louvois, representative of the French government. In order to do this, she had to find out the true facts about Mme Royale's behaviour and policy as reigning monarch, and she several times accused Lescheraine of not keeping her fully informed:

Je ne sçay quelle bonne maxime vous avéz de n'instruire jamais les personnes bien intentionnées des changements qui arrivent, afin qu'ils puissent en rendre compte au public et les donner par le costé qui convient qu'on les voie.[57]

Her task cannot have been easy, for Mme Royale chose young favourites, took them as lovers, and then discarded them, regardless either of political expediency or of her reputation. She did, however, succeed in stopping the publication of a libellous pamphlet on *Les Amours du Palais de Turin*.

Mme de Lafayette's work for Mme Royale became more difficult and more important after 1680 and the coming of age and assumption of authority of the young Duke of Savoy, for the policies of mother and son did not agree. The mother wanted a close connection with France, partly perhaps because her son would thus remain more dependent on her, since she had all the contacts in Paris. The son, wanting his own and his country's independence, while superficially currying favour with the French, was secretly working for a break. Mme de Lafayette was thus acting in Louvois' interests by helping the mother against the son. France needed the support of Savoy against her enemies, Spain and the Netherlands, and until the declaration of war in 1688 between the countries of the League of Augsburg and France, when the Duke of Savoy firmly took sides against France, there was great diplomatic activity between the Courts of Turin and Paris. Since Mme de Lafayette was the main French representative of France's supporter in Turin, her rôle could well have been an important one. The Duke of Savoy's ambassadors called her "un furet, qui va guêtant et parlant à toute la France pour soutenir Mme Royale en tout". She informed Mme Royale of the transactions being carried out in the French capital; and she acted as intermediary between Lescheraine and Louvois or Louis XIV. Thus Louvois wrote to her in 1683:

Mais je ne puis croire qu'il soit à propos de proposer au Roy les veues que le Sr. de Lescheraine paroist avoir, lesquelles assurément ne réussiront pas.[58]

In 1686, she passed on letters to Louis XIV from Mme Royale, in which Mme Royale complained of her son's treatment of her.

Yet how important was Mme de Lafayette's rôle between the years 1679 and 1686 or so, and what were her reasons for playing a rôle at all? In fact, she never talks of large political questions, of France's need for Savoy as a base against her enemies; she is much more concerned with personalities, with the behaviour of Mme Royale's protégé, the young comte de Saint-Maurice, or the abbé de Verrue, Turin's ambassador in Paris. Many of her letters are about frivolous topics. One even sometimes wonders whether she was quite aware of France's and Savoy's respective political ambitions. She obviously treated both Mme Royale and Lescheraine as friends, discussing with them, for example, the appearance of *La Princesse de Clèves*, anonymously of course, and once hinting that she disapproved of Mme Royale's behaviour as she could never have done had she been simply her paid agent. She probably had many motives in working so hard for the Duchess of Savoy. Perhaps the most important was the affection she felt for her. It is clear from other sources that she valued friendship highly, that she was consistently honest, loyal and generous to those of whom she was genuinely fond. She had known Mme Royale for about thirty years. This in itself was enough to make her devote herself faithfully to the task of helping her and supporting her when she was in trouble. Moreover, Mme de Lafayette was not above being proud of her political rôle. As we have seen, she loved to be known and respected and her close connection with a royal Court added to her prestige with the government of France. In spite of her ironic and often critical view of contemporary society, she wanted to play a full part in all its activities, political as well as literary.

The last years of Mme de Lafayette's existence were melancholy ones. She was gradually losing her friends. La Rochefoucauld's death in 1680 especially altered her life since in him she lost her most intimate and constant companion; Mme de Sévigné tells us of the depth of her grief:

> . . . la petite santé de Mme de Lafayette soutient mal une telle douleur: elle en a la fièvre; et il ne sera pas au pouvoir du temps de lui ôter l'ennui de cette privation; sa vie est tournée d'une manière qu'elle le trouvera tous les jours à dire.[59]

Then in 1683 Mme de Lafayette's husband died—another death which, although it cannot have caused her such anguish as that of her daily companion, must still have saddened her if only as a reminder of her own mortality. For her health was rapidly deteriorating. Although she had rarely felt completely well, she had still succeeded in continuing her normal life with only occasional interruptions for rest and recuperation, and had only infrequently complained of feeling ill. Now she hardly went out at all and referred more and more in her letters to her ill-health; her will is no longer strong enough to ignore it.

We see a symptom of her loneliness at this time in her turning back to her old friend, Ménage, with whom she had been out of touch since 1666. They picked up their correspondence without at first seeing each other, because Ménage too was old and infirm, and because Mme de Lafayette was frightened that her admirer would be shocked and disappointed at the change in her appearance. She now looked aged and sick. She tried to prepare him: "Vous m'appelez *'ma divine madame'*, mon cher Monsieur: je suis une maigre divinité."[60]

Eventually they paid each other occasional visits as well. Mme de Lafayette's attitude to Ménage had changed much since her youth. She was much gentler, more tolerant; she exploited him less and felt with him more. Now that she had nobody left to admire and love her, she realized the value of the friendship he had once given her and which she had taken too lightly. She needed him now as she never had before:

> Quoyque vous me défendiéz de vous escrire, je veux néanmoins vous dire combien je suis véritablement touchée de vostre amitié. Je la recognois telle que je l'ay veue autrefois; elle m'est chère par son propre prix, elle m'est chère parce qu'elle m'est unique présentement. Le temps et la vieillesse m'ont osté tous mes amis.[61]

She regrets the hardness of her youth:

> Que l'on est sotte quand on est jeune; on n'est obligée de rien, et l'on ne connoist pas le prix d'un ami comme vous. Il couste cher pour devenir raisonnable; il en couste la jeunesse.[62]

Mme de Lafayette's loneliness and bad health in her old age led to frequent bouts of melancholy and depression; it cannot have been easy for someone of her active disposition to accept that her strength was diminished and that she could no longer lead the kind of life she loved and was used to, and she needed to fight all the time:

> Je suis toujours triste, chagrine, inquiète; sçachant très bien que je n'ay aucun sujet de tristesse, de chagrin ny d'inquiétude; je me désapprouve continuellement.[63]
> Il faut aller tout doucement et comme l'on peut; et enfin nous arriverons tous au terme.[64]

In fact, in spite of what she says, Mme de Lafayette remained mentally alert to the end of her life. After the death of her husband, she fought and won a lawsuit to give her full control over the family fortune, with the result that it was now she, old and ill as she was, who administered all the property in Auvergne. Even after 1689, when her younger son married and technically inherited all her wealth, she continued to manage the family's financial affairs, since he was often away at war and his wife, originally a Mademoiselle de Marillac, was apparently impractical, frivolous and anyway quickly became pregnant.

The most compelling proof of Mme de Lafayette's intellectual vitality at this time is contained in the *Mémoires de la Cour de France* for 1688 and 1689, written probably during these years, but not published until 1731. This work is a detailed and entirely factual account of all the activities, great and small, of the king, the Court, his government, and his army for these two years. It is possible that it is a fragment of a longer historical narrative, in which case historians are so much the poorer for what has been lost. For here Mme de Lafayette shows a characteristic far-sightedness and a shrewd wit in observing her contemporaries that is invaluable. She writes always clearly and concisely, offering now and then an ironic comment on an anomaly of the regal system which is rare in a contemporary. Although now physically weak and often in pain, she has lost neither her judgment nor her lucidity.

She herself, however, felt little confidence in her own resources, for it is at about this time that she sought consolation for her suffering in religion. Although she was never an unbeliever, religion had played little part in her life; she very rarely mentions God in either her letters or her literary works. She had perhaps too critical and independent a spirit to be able to submit completely and unquestioningly to the Established Church, or indeed to any authority, and it was only in her old age and at the approach of death that she felt her weakness sufficiently to seek a protector. Her conversion, or more exactly her awakening to religion, was very gradual and was marked throughout by that honesty towards herself and others, which is characteristic of all her life and work. As early as 1686, she began corresponding with the Jansenist priest the abbé de Rancé, whom she had probably first met over twenty years earlier at the Hôtel de Nevers, and confessed to him her doubts and her yearnings towards religion, asking him how he had achieved so certain a faith that she might learn the way. In his answers, however, he talked piously about his own religious experiences or else uttered flattering platitudes, little related to her situation or temperament.

She must have felt that her connection with Rancé was not sufficiently fruitful, for we have also a letter written in 1690 in answer to one of hers from du Guet, another priest with sympathy for Port-Royal, but one more subtle, more worldly and who seems to have understood his correspondent better. Du Guet wrote to Mme de Lafayette as to an intelligent woman, to whom faith could come only through her own efforts; he tries to awaken her soul from its lethargy. He shows her how to direct her thoughts consciously, telling her she must be completely sincere to herself and to God, however difficult this may seem:

> C'est qu'en effet il vous est plus utile de trouver vous-même les sentimens dans votre cœur que d'adopter ceux d'autruy. . . . Jusqu'icy les images dont vous avez essayé de couvrir la religion vous ont cachée à vous-même. . . . Il faut donc commencer par le désir sincère de se voir soi-même comme on est vu par son juge.

Then, at the end of his letter, he apologizes for the unflattering harshness of his language:

> J'ay supposé que c'étoit vous qui vous parliez à vous-même; et j'ai cru que vous auriez moins de ménagement pour vous que je n'en devois avoir.[65]

Such an honest, uncompromising approach was by far the best to adopt with Mme de Lafayette, too sincere and too clear-sighted to be put off with pious clichés, and it seems to have had its effect for she begins now to refer to God more and more in her letters, and to express joy for those of her friends who have found Him. This is how she writes to Ménage in 1691:

> Je me soumets sans peine à la volonté de Dieu. C'est le Tout-Puissant et, de tous côtés, il faut enfin venir à luy. L'on m'a asseurée que vous songiéz fort sérieusement à vostre salut, et j'en ay bien de la joye.[66]

It is difficult to tell how deeply this new faith touched her: it was quite common in the seventeenth century for people, formerly indifferent, to draw nearer to God at the approach of death—La Fontaine is a famous example. Yet one should credit Mme de Lafayette with more than either mere opportunism or even a simple weakening of her defences. Her search was honest and self-critical and she took several years to reach her goal; her faith at the end was probably both sincere and profound.

She died in 1693, having suffered greatly for the last few years: "Ses infirmités depuis deux ans étoient devenues extrêmes; . . . elle avoit une tristesse mortelle."[67]

Several obituaries on her have been preserved; the most moving occurs in this same letter from Mme de Sévigné and in it she praises her friend's honesty, loyalty, generosity and good sense:

> Vous saviez tout le mérite de Mme de Lafayette ou par vous, ou par moi, ou par vos amis; sur cela vous n'en pouviez trop croire; elle étoit digne d'être de vos amies; et je me trouvois trop heureuse d'être aimée d'elle depuis un temps très-considérable; jamais nous n'avions eu le moindre nuage dans notre amitié. . . .
> Ainsi, Madame, elle a eu raison pendant sa vie, elle a eu raison après sa mort, et jamais elle n'a été sans cette divine raison qui étoit sa qualité principale.[67]

We can read too a consecration of her worldly and literary ambitions in the obituary article published by the *Mercure Galant*:

> Elle estoit . . . tellement distinguée par son esprit et par son mérite qu'elle s'étoit acquis l'estime et la considération de tout ce qu'il y avoit de plus grand en France. Lors que sa santé ne luy a plus permis d'aller à la Cour, on peut dire que toute la Cour a esté chez elle. De sorte que sans sortir de sa chambre elle avoit partout un grand crédit dont elle ne faisoit usage que pour rendre service à tout le monde. On tient qu'elle a eu part à quelques ouvrages qui ont esté leus du Public avec plaisir et avec admiration.[68]

But perhaps the most fittingly suggestive summary of her personality is the one written by Anatole France in his preface to the 1889 edition of *La Princesse de Clèves*:

> Prude, dévote et bien en cour, je la soupçonnerais presque d'avoir douté de la vertu, peu cru en Dieu, et, ce qui est plus étonnant pour l'époque, haï le roi.

It only remains now in this introductory section to consider the rôle of Mme de Lafayette's literary works in her life, her motives for writing, and her own view of what she wrote. It is obvious that literary composition was only one among many of her preoccupations, that she thought of it as a pastime to occupy her active mind and perhaps to entertain her circle of friends. She had always been interested in contemporary productions and, with the help of her friends, had developed good judgment and a fine appreciation in artistic matters. She was also fortunate in reaching maturity at a time when public taste was informed and enlightened. The confusion of genres and traditions which reigned in the first part of the seventeenth century had simplified, unified and ripened into a literary system which could take external, formal requirements for granted and afford to emphasize inner excellence. Thus a reaction against the long, loosely composed heroic or gallant novel had already set in when Mme de Lafayette began to write, so that she had only to follow the general trend to produce a work more tightly constructed and more simply written. Had she lived thirty years earlier, she could never have produced a masterpiece of the kind of *La Princesse de Clèves*. As it was, she was attracted by the new potentialities of the *nouvelle* form, its possibilities for brevity and realism, and saw it as a convenient genre for an amateur lady writer.

Mme de Lafayette clearly found difficulty in writing; she had none of the inventiveness of most great novelists. With the exception of her letters to Ménage from Auvergne immediately after her marriage, which at one time with Ménage's help she intended to publish, and some of her business letters to Lescheraine, her correspondence consists largely of shortish, factual notes. Just occasionally, in a flash of wit or emotion, the personality of the writer comes across, but on the whole she wrote letters not to entertain but simply to convey or request information. Her style has none of the elegance nor the vitality of that of Mme de Sévigné. This lack of fluency is probably as much due to Mme de Lafayette's reserved temperament as to the laziness to which she ascribes it herself; she is suspicious of aimless chatter, at least in writing. She brings one of her longer letters to Mme de Sévigné to an abrupt close with the words: "Adieu. Je suis bien en train de jaser."[69] These inhibitions seem still to have functioned when Mme de Lafayette embarked on literary works proper. She needed help and, as we have seen, in her novels she was seconded at different times by Ménage, Huet, La Rochefoucauld and Segrais.

It was not, then, a natural fluency in writing that made Mme de Lafayette become a writer; and neither can it have been an overflowing imagination, since we find the same scenes and situations repeated in all her works. Still less was it a desire for fame, for she published *La Princesse de Montpensier* and *La Princesse de Clèves* anonymously, and *Zaïde* under Segrais' name; the *Histoire d'Henriette d'Angleterre*, the *Mémoires* and another *nouvelle*, *La Comtesse de Tende*, probably written after *La Princesse de Clèves*, were only brought out after her death. It is true that she was excited by the appearance of her novels, made gifts of them to her friends, and did not mind her immediate circle being fully aware of her authorship (as we see from the letters of Mme de Scudéry and Bussy-Rabutin on *La Princesse de Clèves*). The anonymity was directed towards the general public. The Comtesse obviously felt that it was beneath the dignity of a great lady of the nobility to appear as a writer whose words could be read and criticized by mere commoners: "Il y avait une sorte de bienséance à ne pas étaler dans les échoppes du Palais et de la rue St-Jacques, sur le titre d'un livre, le nom d'une dame de la Cour" says Anatole France, in his preface to *La Princesse de Clèves*. Men of letters were still considered social inferiors and the reputation of some of those lady writers who did sign their works, like Mme de Villedieu, was not of the highest.

The feeling which prompted Mme de Lafayette to write her novels was probably a simple desire to set down an attitude to man and his destiny which she had gradually formed as a result of experience and observation. There were certain moral questions which interested her deeply—the nature and consequences of *amour passion*, the importance and difficulty of sincerity between a man and a woman, the too frequent discrepancy between the public and private faces of man. By treating these questions in a fictitious situation, she hoped to find some solution to them. Perhaps she also intended her works as a sort of warning to, as well as comment on, her society. She was not trying to express her personal problems, but rather her detached meditations on issues relevant to everyone. Much of her personality is not in her work; and even within it, we are sometimes not sure of the judgment she means us to make of the incidents she has herself invented.

The complexities and apparent paradoxes of her life and character reappear also in her greatest novel and ensure its continued survival.

NOTES TO PART I

1 *Portraits de Femmes.*

2 Retz, *Mémoires*, t. IV, p. 148, March 1652. Quoted by Ashton in *Madame de Lafayette*, C.U.P., p. 241.

3 *Arsenal*, MS. 4127. Quoted by Ashton, p. 8.

4 Loret, *Muse Historique*, 1st January 1651. Quoted by Ashton, p. 17.

5 *Correspondance de Madame de Lafayette* (ed. by Beaunier, Gallimard), letter 46.

6 *Histoire d'Henriette d'Angleterre* (Flammarion, *Les meilleurs Auteurs classiques*), p. 188.

7 Retz, *Mémoires*, t. IV, p. 148 (see above). Also notes to *Mémoires* by Gui Joly. Passage quoted in full by Ashton.

8 *Op. cit.*, letter 6.

9 *Op. cit.*, letter 9.

10 *Op. cit.*, letter 13.

11 *Op. cit.*, letter 6.

12 *Op. cit.*, letter 3.

13 *Op. cit.*, letter 17.

14 Quoted by Ashton, p. 45.

15 *Op. cit.*, letter 35.

16 *Op. cit.*, letter 56.

17 *Op. cit.*, letter 26.

18 *Op. cit.*, letter 67.

19 *Op. cit.*, letter 140.

20 *Op. cit.*, letter 138.

21 *Op. cit.*, letter 166.

22 *Histoire d'Henriette d'Angleterre*, p. 182.

23 *Op. cit.*, p. 262.

24 *Op. cit.*, p. 189.

25 *Op. cit.*, p. 327.

26 *Correspondance*, letter 102.

27 *Op. cit.*, letter 126.

28 *Op. cit.*, letter 99.

29 *Op. cit.*, letter 136.

30 *Op. cit.*, letter 173.

31 *Op. cit.*, letter 167.

32 *Op. cit.*, letter 143.

33 *Galerie des Portraits de Mlle de Montpensier*, no. XXVI.

34 *Lettres de Mme de Sévigné* (Éd. Pléiade), vol. 2, p. 663.

35 *Correspondance*, letter 37.

36 *Op. cit.*, letter 155.

37 *Op. cit.*, letter 190.

38 *Op. cit.*, letter 191.

39 *Op. cit.*, letter 181.

[40] *Op. cit.*, letter 185.
[41] Bussy-Rabutin, *Correspondance*, III, p. 116.
[42] *Op. cit.*, p. 451.
[43] *Lettres de Mme de Sévigné*, vol. 2, p. 647.
[44] *Correspondance*, letter 195.
[45] *Op. cit.*, letter 194.
[46] *Op. cit.*, letter 212.
[47] *Lettres de Mme de Sévigné*, vol. 1, p. 559.
[48] *Op. cit.*, letter 200.
[49] *Lettres de Mme de Sévigné*, vol. 1, p. 251.
[50] *Lettres de Mme de Sévigné*, vol. 1, p. 669.
[51] *Correspondance*, letter 34.
[52] *Lettres de Mme de Sévigné*, vol. 1, p. 519.
[53] *Correspondance*, letter 213.
[54] *Op. cit.*, letter 221.
[55] *Op. cit.*, letter 232.
[56] *Op. cit.*, letter 248.
[57] *Op. cit.*, letter 245.
[58] *Op. cit.*, letter 280.
[59] *Lettres de Mme de Sévigné*, vol. 2, p. 649.
[60] *Correspondance*, letter 353.
[61] *Op. cit.*, letter 339.
[62] *Op. cit.*, letter 349.
[63] *Op. cit.*, letter 370.
[64] *Op. cit.*, letter 335.
[65] *Op. cit.*, letter 331.
[66] *Op. cit.*, letter 339.
[67] *Lettres de Mme de Sévigné*, vol. 3, p. 829.
[68] Quoted by Ashton, p. 205.
[69] *Correspondance*, letter 212.

PART II

LOVE ROMANCE BEFORE 'LA PRINCESSE DE CLÈVES'

The central situation of *La Princesse de Clèves* is a variation on a universal theme. The novel treats of an adulterous love, a love bound to be unhappy and to end in catastrophe, a love which inevitably brings with it a conflict of loyalties, between its own selfish, primitive urges and the obligations owed to society in general and to the husband in particular. Since literature began, this theme has inspired writers to some of their most passionate and convinced work, but each age and each man within the age has seen the problem differently, has found it easy, difficult or even impossible to solve, and has presented us with works so varied in tone that one hardly sees at first that the basic theme is the same. Before coming to a study of Mme de Lafayette's treatment, it may be useful to trace the development of the theme of love in French literature from the Middle Ages to the middle of the seventeenth century, to see how views of it have altered, how the way in which it develops depends on current attitudes to marriage and duty which in turn evolve with culture and society. We will then be able to place Mme de Lafayette within a tradition by which, consciously or unconsciously, she was formed. *La Princesse de Clèves* is the result not only of its immediate predecessors but of the whole accumulation of love romances since Béroul and Chrétien de Troyes in the twelfth century.

At the beginning of the Middle Ages, serious literature in the vernacular was still very derivative; the various attitudes to love and adultery which we find in the earlier medieval *romans* stem directly from the literary and fabulous traditions which the Middle Ages absorbed from earlier sources. Classical literature was the first formative influence and it reached the centre of medieval culture by means of medieval clerks who read not only Christian writers but also Ovid, and Latin adaptations of Greek and Oriental fables. From Ovid comes the idea of love as all-motivating and all-excusing which we find in the early Latin *contes* and this influence extends into the French *romans antiques,* as they are called—romances based on classical subjects or even on classical works.

A second and probably more important formative influence on medieval romance was the vast body of legend about King Arthur and his knights. This probably reached France from Britain at the beginning of the twelfth century and was added to and remoulded in innumerable romances and tales, most of which have not survived. The legend which is most relevant here is of course the adulterous love of Tristan and Iseut. Here we have the archetype of the loves of the Princesse de Clèves and Nemours, but with all the mysterious and poetic features of a primitive legend. In both stories, love is instantaneous and irrevocable—the magic potion illustrates this in the one as does the fatal meeting at the ball in the other. In both, it exists beyond social law which, however, it cannot disregard: it can, then, bring only suffering and death. But in neither of the French versions by Béroul or by Thomas do the lovers feel any guilt or any duty except to love. All their efforts go towards satisfying their passion, and the tragedy comes because such a satisfaction is impossible. Mme de Clèves suffers not because she cannot satisfy her love—the interpolated stories show well enough that she could, at least temporarily—but because she does not want to, because she feels a duty towards her husband and towards a personal morality, of which there is little hint in any medieval love story. This sense of a duty higher than one's own instinctive desires is the creation of a more sophisticated civilization than the Middle Ages.

We find almost immediately, however, that although in one sense the Tristan story is typical of its time—in that love here admits of no other standards—in another sense it is an isolated phenomenon. For the attitude to love in literature was now to change radically. The Tristan is almost alone in its time in treating a love that is unhappy. All the efforts of medieval poets after it went towards the formation of an ethic of love which could not through its very nature be unhappy. It now took the form of a pure and undemanding devotion, expressing itself through service and eternal loyalty rather than through possession. The woman became an ideal, an untouchable and admirable being, to be admitted to whose service was the supreme achievement of a knight. Both the Ovidian sensuality and the Breton amoral tragedy were submerged or transformed to fit in with the new *amour courtois*. Marriage, unless it were between two *amants courtois* when it was of interest because of its notable spiritual excellence, was of no account in literature, since it provided no obstacle to a relationship as rarefied and respectable as those indulged in by great ladies and their knights. Indeed, *amour courtois* became a social as well as a cultural ideal, since, through the service of a knight to his lady, it preserved and continued the feudal tradition of loyalty from vassal to lord.

We can see the gradual formation of this attitude to love and adultery, which, though a specifically medieval creation, exerted an influence for several centuries, in the works of Chrétien de Troyes. He had begun by assimilating both the classical and Breton traditions: his own list of his works includes translations of Ovid's *Metamorphoses* and of his *Art of Love*, and a version of the Tristan story. The romances of his which survive show his adaptation of these in the light of the new ideal of love and the change in emphasis which this adaptation entailed.[1] For, since all that the true *amant courtois* could ever show was fidelity and respect to his mistress and she on her side must respond on the same spiritual level, little action or dramatic interest could be extracted from the relationship between them. The romances of Chrétien are thus filled with external physical incident, as the knight goes out to seek adventure in order that, through his valour, he may win the favour of his mistress, while little is usually made of the state of their feelings towards each other or of their behaviour when face to face—in any case circumstances often force them to remain apart. What could be a greater contrast to even Thomas' more *courtois* version of the Tristan story?

It is this view of love, remote from human complexity and suffering, which persisted throughout the serious poetry and romance of the fourteenth and fifteenth centuries, becoming more lifeless and stereotyped as time went on. We find this lifelessness, this systematization, which precludes any living tragic conflict, in the first part of the *Roman de la Rose*, where all emotions are represented as allegorical abstractions and so are quite separate from any individual who might originally have felt them. The excellence of love is never questioned nor its power to bring a complete and pure happiness: what are analysed in great detail are the various methods of courting the lady love, of reaching this happiness. Courtship almost becomes an intellectual rather than an emotional pursuit in which the tragic weakness of man beset by an instinctive passion is a possibility not dreamed of. Complete self-domination in the face of the special demands of these chaste and respectable affairs is described without question or hesitation.

The most important contribution of the sixteenth century lies in the new richness and spiritual significance which the old ideal of *amour courtois*, itself become now mere rhetoric, gained through support from other, foreign literatures, being rediscovered at this time. The notion of Platonic love reached France from Italy in the first half of the sixteenth century and was gradually disseminated through French translations of Plato and of the Italian Marsilio Ficino's commentary on the Symposium. It also merged in the work of many poets with the parallel influence of Petrarchan and post-Petrarchan sonnet sequences, which paradoxically enough, had found their original inspiration in the French medieval idea of *amour courtois*, now become Italy's own. Poets still sang in elaborate conceits of the purity of their love and the cruelty of their ladies, but these themes had a further meaning now, as human love was seen in some way as a stage to divine love. The metaphysics of Platonism gave a new sincerity to the worn-out, stereotyped attitudes, already four centuries old.

The *Heptaméron* of Marguerite de Navarre, written halfway through the century, a collection of short stories which follows the formula of Boccaccio's *Decameron*, is perhaps one of the most lively manifestations of this interest in Platonic theories of love. At the same time, however, the author was open to the quite different attitude to love expressed by her other obvious source, Boccaccio himself, who wrote in a similar vein to the authors of the often bawdy, sensual medieval *fabliaux*, but with a wit, a concision and a sense of drama which made him a complete master in his own right. Thus in the *Heptaméron*, within the same work, the two different, literary attitudes to love are directly opposed the one to the other: the one, treated lightly here but which we have seen treated tragically in *Tristan*, holds that love is overwhelming and worth all sacrifices of virtue, modesty, pride; the other, the chivalric and Platonic, believes in the possibility of controlling, indeed eliminating all the unworthy aspects of love, and transforming it into a pure, spiritual experience akin to love of God Himself. There is no doubt which stance Marguerite herself adopts, but she has a regard for the truth of human diversity and a humorous forbearance which permit her to give as much space in this collection to the one attitude as to the other.

Marguerite's purpose in the *Heptaméron* was indeed twofold: she wished to present the behaviour of different pairs of lovers for the psychological truth which it revealed, and she also wished to publicize her own nostalgia for Platonic love by showing it in conflict with other more earthy desires. So she presents a group of lords and ladies, each telling his or her own story almost always about love in some form or other, and then discussing between themselves the implications and possible consequences of what has been told. This very often becomes a discussion between a Platonist and a champion of a less pure passion. On the whole it is the men who are on the side of sensuality and amorality, and the women on the side of purity and Platonic love, often as a way to divine love; and in this distinction, we both look back to the dominating position of the queens in the small medieval courts and forward to the civilizing and refining influence great ladies were to have on society through the cultural gatherings in their *salons*—centres of literary taste as well as of sophisticated badinage in much of the sixteenth and seventeenth centuries. The fact that Marguerite de Navarre was aware of other attitudes to love in contradiction to her own ideal, where her medieval forbears were not, means that she might have reached real tragedy in portraying a living conflict between the two, especially as her tales, all said to be true stories, are placed in convincingly contemporary settings. It is true that, for her, Platonic love was an experience to be lived and not simply to be studied in books. Yet her psychological intuition seems not to have been profound and subtle enough for her to present a clash between the two attitudes within one person, hesitant and suffering like the Princesse de Clèves. Each attitude is always embodied in separate people, indeed often in separate tales—some comic and even crude, others serious and didactic. It was not until the seventeenth century in France that the inner conflict was realized to be of the essence of tragedy. It is possible too that her own bias towards a certain idea of love prevented Marguerite de Navarre from being able to sustain for any length of time any convincing opposition to it in any one of her characters. Thus we find no deeply moving human situation among the tales of the *Heptaméron*.

The best example of Marguerite's failure to make this clash vital and moving is the story of Floride and Amadour, the longest and possibly the most interesting in the collection. It is a story told by Parlamente, obviously spokesman for Marguerite herself, and illustrates the case of a woman who preferred a pure spiritual love to physical submission to her lover. The situation of the main characters is very similar to that of Nemours, the Prince and Princesse de Clèves, for Floride is married to the duc de Cardonne and in love with Amadour; indeed this tale has been seen by at least one critic[2] as a possible source for *La Princesse de Clèves*. Yet the behaviour of the woman, Floride, is very different: she begins by feeling little hesitation in accepting the service and admiration of Amadour, although she knows she can never marry him. His *honnête amour* is seen as in no way incompatible with her love and loyalty to her future husband. Here already, then, one of the main sources of tragedy in the later work is denied, as the Princesse feels with ever greater acuteness the pangs of her guilt towards her husband, even when her love for Nemours is a secret to all but her. Marriage is indeed very summarily dismissed by Marguerite de Navarre as irrelevant to the main issue of the tale, perhaps partly because it would have been so regarded in her time, and partly because the chaste, superior love of Amadour at this stage really did not seem incompatible with the duties of wedlock. Floride's attitude remains the same throughout the rest of the story, through her marriage to the duc de Cardonne and her growing familiarity with Amadour, and she is intensely surprised and shocked when Amadour, able to act on this inhuman level no longer, asks for more from her than Platonic friendship. She maintains her purity at the cost of self-disfigurement, and the situation is resolved only by the opportune death of Amadour in battle, not we may note the husband as in *La Princesse de Clèves*. It seems as though, in order to stress her point about the possibility of such a pure relationship, Marguerite de Navarre must describe her heroine as consistently high-minded, able to conceive of no other mode of behaviour. It is only in the man that she can afford to show any weakness, any crude sensuality, as though this is to be expected from and almost excused in him. Yet even he is not depicted with any of the subtlety with which the Princesse is analysed, nor even Nemours, his exact equivalent. He changes very suddenly: his physical desires are abruptly introduced and thereafter dominate his whole character. He is never shown to us either struggling with himself or lamenting anything but the cruelty of his mistress. The combination in Marguerite of her semididactic aims and her lesser skill at psychological description means that her tale ultimately has little of the profoundly moving effect of its successor, *La Princesse de Clèves*.

Boccaccio was more read in sixteenth than seventeenth-century France, and we have seen how Marguerite de Navarre, while treating her own personal themes, adopted the formal arrangement of the *Decameron* in her *Heptaméron*. For him, love had nothing in common with the pure, chivalric passion of Chrétien; it was often tragic, always physical and violent. There is an interesting novel in French, isolated in its time and apparently without influence, since it was both unfashionable in theme and unpolished in execution, which clearly followed Boccaccio's *Fiammetta* very closely—*les Angoisses douloureuses qui procèdent d'amour* (1538) by Hélisenne de Crenne. The book is written in the form of a confession by a married woman of her love for a young man, who is apparently unfaithful to her. Hélisenne de Crenne owes nothing to the spiritual idealism of treatments of love in French literature since the Middle Ages, but, through Boccaccio and presumably through her own experience, she reached those eternally tragic accents of adulterous love which we first found in the Tristan legend. The heroine's love is immediate and irrevocable: she hardly tries to hold out against it, and the novel consists of her efforts to deceive her husband and see her lover, interspersed with lamentations on her lot. Like Iseut in Béroul's Tristan, she feels no struggle, no duty towards her marriage, no guilt about her frequent dissimulations. Complex hesitations of that kind had as little place in this more primitive love tradition as among the unnatural purities of the other—we are in fact no nearer to the inevitably moving effect an inner conflict must produce. What we do find here, however, and rarely elsewhere in pre-seventeenth-century love literature, is a tragically passionate narrative, made even more convincing by a realistic touch which looks forward to the sometimes cynical pessimism of *La Princesse de Clèves*: the young lover here too is unworthy of his lady's admiration; he is shallow, conceited, and quite incapable of the self-abandonment which she demands of him.

Towards the end of the sixteenth century, Italian pastoral, the *Arcadia* of Sannazar and Tasso's *Aminta*, supplanted Boccaccio in the affections of the French reading public, since it could more easily be adapted to fit in with their own abstract idealism. Thus they took over from Tasso little of his bucolic tenderness, his delicate acceptance of physical as well as spiritual passion, but adopted his pastoral settings—either directly or indirectly through Spanish imitations—and his preference for descriptions of young, innocent love. Spanish novels they found easier to absorb whole-sale and their influence was more lasting and profound. Spain preserved more faithfully medieval chivalric ideals, and a novel like the *Amadis de Gaule*, whose plot depends on the service through adventure of the knight to his lady, sustained the interest of the French public in this kind of love relationship while entertaining them with exciting narrative. Yet, although the direct descendants of this mingling of sentiment and adventure are the French epic romances of La Calprenède and Gomberville, for the moment the French were more interested in sentiment than adventure. From Spain too, from the romances of Diego de San Pedro and Juan de Flores for example, came the emphasis on honour and especially on the honour of a young girl. We find a close imitation of the *Arnalte e Lucende* of San Pedro, in a French novel—*Histoire de l'amant ressuscité de la mort d'amour* (1555) by Valentinian. This still owes much to medieval chivalry in the man's attitude of respectful adoration towards his lady, but she herself is made more interesting as her love gradually overcomes her modesty and as in the end she nevertheless breaks faith with her lover.

Thus, by the beginning of the seventeenth century, certain formulae seem to be fixed in the writing of romantic literature. The primitive idea of the tragic weakness of man, enslaved by physical passion, is with a very few exceptions still right out of fashion. Love is pure and deliberate—a purity nourished by the relics of medieval chivalric romance, handed down directly and through Spain, (there is another edition of *Lancelot* at the end of the sixteenth century), by a new interest in Platonism, and also by the popularity at this time of the late Greek romances of Heliodorus. The hero and heroine are more often young and unmarried—again both Spain and Heliodorus can account for this, and to a lesser extent Italian pastoral literature. These formulae, based on a sentimental idealism rather than on reality, allowed for little tragedy and indeed little psychological variety of any kind. Between 1600 and 1630, innumerable romances were written on similar kinds of situation by amateurs or by professional hack writers like Des Escuteaux and Nervèze. The obstacles to a pure love between young people could only be external or rather unconvincing—the parents' objections or the girl's modesty.

It is obvious that this sudden vast production of sentimental novels must have answered to a need as well as creating it. It is now that the first real *salons* were formed as centres of refinement in literature and language, whose tone was set by the great ladies of the time. There had been similar social gatherings in the court around Marguerite de Navarre in the middle of the sixteenth century, but they had been disrupted by the religious wars and did not institute a general movement. Now, when the State was reaching relative stability under the strong rule of Henri IV and then of Richelieu, social standards and ideals had an opportunity to grow. The most famous *salon* was the *chambre bleue* of Madame de Rambouillet although hers was not the first: great lords and ladies gathered here with men of letters to discuss new literary works, hold endless conversations on the psychology of love, and play little games which were often based on how a lover ought or ought not to behave in given circumstances. The ladies, nourished on Platonism and chivalric romances, always saw themselves as the stronger partner and decided which qualities the ideal lover should possess—chastity, respectfulness and eternal fidelity. The gentlemen could not but agree since in the *salon* they were on the ladies' own territory. The new society which attached less and less importance to military valour and more and more to social elegance and charm left them dispossessed and unemployed. They could only now write poems, romances or letters in admiration of their mistresses. The exaltation of an innocent, chaste love in which the woman would keep her position of strength over her lover by never giving herself to him was the preoccupation of all the novel-reading public, following the lead given by the great ladies, and in their hands lay the success or failure of aspiring authors. It was thus natural that an instinctive physical desire which could humiliate the woman and lead to tragedy was hardly ever portrayed—although people still knew it could exist. Literature had to expose, not the unhappy truth, but the delightful dream, and we only see glimpses of any anti-social threat in secondary characters and situations.

Probably the best place in which to study this body of literature is in D'Urfé's *l'Astrée* (1607–27), which contains at its most subtle and original the greater part of what could be found elsewhere. The central theme of the novel is the love of the shepherd, Céladon, for the shepherdess, Astrée: it is a love which remains constant through long separation and apparent infidelity, and which entails unquestioning obedience and absolute respect towards its object. The action comes not from the nature of the love itself which demands nothing and so cannot but be satisfied, nor from the characters who are strong in their bond to each other, but from an initial external misunderstanding which has effects disproportionate to its importance. Indeed, the interest of the work for us does not lie in the characters of Céladon and Astrée at all, for excessive humility in one case and pride in the other make them lifeless models. It lies much more, firstly in the endless discussions on the origin and nature of love and on the appropriate behaviour of lovers, in which various shepherds, shepherdesses and priests indulge on the slightest pretext. These discussions are used mainly as vehicles for the propagation of D'Urfé's ideas on Platonic love as a stage towards divine love, but the author presents another point of view—in Hylas, fickle but charming, who treats love lightly as a delightful sensuous pleasure. Thus the disputes gain substance and vitality. Secondly, within the story of Céladon and Astrée appear innumerable shorter stories, dealing with other minor characters and all centred on a love affair. These usually present variations on the theme of Platonic love, and describe lovers in different situations behaving in the appropriate way—such is Célidée who deliberately disfigures herself (like Floride) to end the rivalry between her two lovers by proving whose love depends least on her physical attractions. But some of these minor stories are written in a much lighter vein, usually those in which Hylas figures: love becomes an excuse for exciting and amusing intrigue and is neither pure nor eternal.

Like Marguerite de Navarre, D'Urfé is conscious of attitudes to love which contradict his own, yet like her he can only present this contradiction theoretically, as Hylas and the Platonist Silvandre talk together, or in separate incidents. He does not make us feel the tragic complexity of a living reality, as the egoism of a Nemours clashes directly with the purity and integrity of a Princesse de Clèves. He can only go a certain distance in expressing his ideas in living terms, making his secondary characters especially, where he was bound less by convention, sometimes interesting and convincing: his moral idealism still prevents him like his contemporaries from placing at the centre of his work the sad confusion of life.

The one obstacle that can make a pure relationship like that between Astrée and Céladon an unhappy one—and even here the unhappiness is not emphasized, except as an excuse for rhetorical lamentation, since the lover must be an ideal lover and must accept his suffering gladly—is the strange resistance of the lady to admitting her love or rewarding her lover by her hand in marriage. For this resistance, although usually supported by the will of fate or of the lady's parents, also comes from the heroine herself. It has its roots in many feelings: at its lowest in a concern for her reputation, but more often in a sense of a duty to herself, in a desire to keep her individuality whole and free, in an attempt to preserve her power over her lover; and at its highest in an ideal of pure love which would only be sullied by physical possession. Antoine Adam, calls it "pure chimère, exigence d'impossible pureté, refus d'accepter les conditions normales de la vie"[3] and truly it reflects an idealism which cannot entirely have been borne out by the daily lives of those who professed it. And yet this exaggerated modesty recurs so often and with so strong a ring of truth that it must have been based on a deeply felt desire on the part of a lady to preserve her superior moral position, whatever the cost. We may still find relics of it in the Princesse's refusal to behave as behave all those around her, in her desperate clinging to a purity in which nobody any longer believes.

There is little point in considering in detail the characters of the innumerable long novels produced in French between the 1620s and the 1640s, by Gomberville, La Calprenède, Georges de Scudéry. They all follow the same pattern. There are kings, queens, princes and princesses, usually now historical figures taken from antiquity, who are separated by Fate and who only meet again after innumerable vicissitudes throughout which their love has remained pure and constant though unacknowledged and unrewarded. Occasionally secondary characters in these long novels do display a violence of physical passion not compatible with the precious ideal, but they can hardly be said to embody a conscious attitude to love as the main characters do. Their behaviour is often the result of the author's historical source and is only included for the sake of exciting intrigue. Their psychology is never developed and they are usually portrayed as the villains of the piece, yet they show how different traditions of love continued latent throughout all this period, apparently exclusively concerned with a spiritual purity. The sentimental aspect is altogether now much less important than between 1600 and 1620. Perhaps writers felt there was no more to be said on this after D'Urfé had written *l'Astrée*. The fashion now was for exciting episode—battles, shipwrecks, disguises, all of which recur regularly in the romances of this kind. This type of incident was probably largely taken from Heliodorus' *Theagenes and Chariclea* and other similar works, to whose original readers it obviously had more immediate relevance, considering the sort of society in which they lived. They had now become literary devices and satisfied the longing for adventure of aggressive noblemen who could feel their ambitions for power being gradually stifled by the growing authority of the king and his advisor.

The theatre presents a much more varied and interesting field of analysis. Dramatic authors had to please a rather different public from novel writers, for especially in the early part of the century, it was as much the lower classes who went to the theatre as the nobility and men of letters. Thus writers for the theatre had not the same obligation to please their aristocratic patronesses and did not need to depict only unnaturally chaste relationships as their novelist colleagues did. Any situation which was capable of exciting dramatic development was grist to their mill. They borrowed haphazardly from Italy and Spain and probably remained closer to their originals than did D'Urfé and his like, showing little of the bias of the novelists towards sentimental purity. They retained the exciting adventure of Spanish theatre and romance, and the complicated intrigues of Italian pastoral, without continually subordinating them to depiction of a static, unreal relationship. We find in Hardy, probably the most prolific dramatic writer of this period, many kinds of characters and situations, by no means all of which deal primarily with love. Even when he is treating the relationship between a lover and his mistress he does not always do it in the same way. *Lucrèce ou L'Adultère puni*, for example, presents the unhesitating infidelity of both a husband and a wife; *La Belle Égyptienne*, the immediate, physical desire of a nobleman for a Bohemian girl. Both these plays are set in Spain and it may be from the Spanish *comedia* that comes this dark violence of passion that leads to murder and abduction. Hardy was attracted by it because of the melodramatic intrigue that went with it—such as would delight the rowdy audiences which attended performances of his plays.

From Italy, more than from Spain, came the vogue for pastoral plays which in France had little of the philosophical pretentions of a pastoral novel such as *l'Astrée*. They were however important in always having love as their main preoccupation, and they thus trained writers to analyse human emotion, to see into the subtleties of love relationships, and to present these in living and dramatic terms. In this way, as we shall see, the pastoral acted as a sort of technical training ground in psychology for later, dramatic authors. The kinship is obvious in the sentimental plays of Thomas Corneille and in an early play of Racine, *Alexandre*, but we can also find traces of it in the plays of Corneille, particularly his early comedies. We even see a direct evolution within the work of one man, the dramatist, Mairet, if we compare his earlier, pastoral play, *Sylvie*, with his later tragic drama, *Sophonisbe*. The intrigue of Sylvie (1626 or 7) is typical of its time and very slight: Thelane, Prince of Sicily, disguises himself as a shepherd in order to court Sylvie, a shepherdess. He is betrayed to his father who would like him to marry someone else and who places both lovers under a spell. This is eventually broken by Florestan, Prince of Cardia, for love of Meliphile, Thelane's sister, and all ends happily for everyone. In *Sophonisbe* (1634) Mairet's talent has developed from the depiction of a lighthearted love imbroglio among shepherds and shepherdesses to presenting the tragic conflict of a great queen, as she wavers between her passion for her former lover and her duty to her husband and her country.

In this play for the first time the author has consciously inspired his heroine with a different kind of love, a passion irresistible and overwhelming, not abstract and controlled, and against which her only recourse can be death. This change in approach is due to the renewed influence of classical drama, Roman here rather than Greek. Latin literature was beginning again to influence literary fashions and ideals, and the conception of love that the new French dramatists, such as Mairet and Corneille, found here had nothing in common with the spiritual purity of the relationship between Astrée and Céladon, nourished on the medieval, chivalric code and Platonic metaphysics. The French were rediscovering a love physical and irresistible in its nature, violent and fatal in its effects, the love of Paris for Helen, of Camille for Curiace, of Sophonisbe for Massinisse, and later of Hermione for Pyrrhus or Phèdre for Hippolyte. Indeed it is at this time that the ideal of *amour courtois* really began to lose its dominant position, attacked from all directions, at first by these new literary models, and soon, as we shall see, by social and political as well as literary changes. Sophonisbe, one of the first of the new heroines, shows little of the strength of Pauline in resisting her love and although she finally accepts her death with some of the high-mindedness of a Rodrigue or a Polyeucte, she has none of their joyful conviction. She sees herself throughout as a victim of a destiny against which she can only make a vain attempt to fight. Her situation is a truly tragic one, as tragic as Iseut's, Hermione's or the Princesse de Clèves', since she is weak in the face of her love and yet fulfilment of it can only lead to disaster. The play has little of the truth and power of Racine's plays or Madame de Lafayette's novel, since Mairet had not their genius and perhaps since he came too early in this century to be able to use the still undeveloped language of psychological analysis with real subtlety and richness. Yet he was the first, since writers of the Tristan story, to see the full tragic potentialities of the weakness of man in the face of an overwhelming, irrational passion.

Corneille's plays present us with a rich variety of attitudes to love, as he was more or less influenced by his Spanish or Roman sources, and as he experimented with the problems arising from different kinds of relationship. He sometimes sees love as a pure and valuable emotion, based on a rational as well as an instinctive esteem, which will inspire the hero to great deeds performed in the service of his lady—very much as his contemporary novelists do, although he illustrates it with a much greater vitality and awareness of its implications in reality. This is the form love eventually assumes for Rodrigue, but only after an agonizing sacrifice has had to be made and only at the cost of happiness and perhaps, were it not for the intervention of the king, of life itself. Considering the importance Corneille always attached to splendid acts of heroism in the service of a cause greater than any individual, one can say this kind of passion remained always his ideal, but one which he was aware could only rarely be achieved.

He also presents us with characters of the opposite kind, all of whose loyalties are to a love, present and immediate, and whose sufferings are the result of this love alone and not of the difficulty they find in reconciling it with some other principle for which they feel as deeply; then his heroines (for they are women: unlike Marguerite de Navarre, Corneille seems to regard them as the weaker, impure sex) have much of Hermione or Phèdre in them. Such especially is Camille, the violence of whose passion for Curiace, antisocial and even anarchic, is equalled only by the violence of Horace's patriotism. Both are uncompromising, intolerant and irrational, the one in springing to his country's aid and the other in her mourning for her lover. To complete the picture of possible reactions to a choice between love and patriotism, Corneille has placed two characters, Sabine and Curiace, who suffer, hesitate and only reluctantly decide, realizing that neither decision can be completely right.

Then too love may be considered an enslavement, resented because it cannot be reconciled with a noble idealism. For Marguerite de Navarre, D'Urfé or La Calprenède, love acted as a spur to great deeds: it was through love that both the lover and the lady found and affirmed their own personalities before any legal tie bound them. For Alidor of *La Place Royale,* love will only prevent him from fulfilling his individual potentialities. It has come on him without his rational consent and will continue all his life to dispose of him as it will. It is only Alidor's yearning for freedom which prevents him from marrying Angélique, since they love each other and their respective parents are happy to consent to the marriage. This play presents a strange mixture of the two traditions of which we have been speaking: on the one hand, Corneille is following the primitive, classical idea of love as irresistible and all-powerful; on the other, he is clinging to the sophisticated idealism, the search for self-discipline and self-affirmation, implicit in *l'Astrée* or the *précieuses'* cult of refinement. The first tradition had long lain unused with the popularity of *amour courtois* and then Platonic love, which taught that passion, so long as it remained pure, became the very means for a deliberate self-affirmation. Now the primitive idea was being revived, and Corneille was perhaps the first to place the two traditions in direct conflict with each other, to portray a passion as it exists in reality, incompatible with a noble idealism now dissociated from love of any kind. As we have seen, Marguerite de Navarre and D'Urfé, although conscious of both traditions, always kept them separate in practice, confronting them only in theory, where it was easy to show the one as spiritually and intellectually superior to the other. It may be that *La Place Royale* is *La Princesse de Clèves'* first direct ancestor, for the Princesse's tragedy also arises from a clash between these two traditions, between a conscious ideal of behaviour on the one hand and on the other a passion which prevents the ideal's fulfilment.

La Place Royale is a disconcerting play because Alidor is such a difficult person to understand: his resistance to his love seems so obscurely motivated, so unjustifiable that we find him rather unconvincing beside his more attractive mistress, Angélique. Corneille may have realized both that Alidor's ideals were too elusive and that the problem he was posing was too profound for comedy. When he later began to write tragedies and tragicomedies, some more specific principle was set against the bondage of physical love.

The most relevant of Corneille's plays to our purpose is *Polyeucte*, since the situation of its heroine, Pauline, is very similar to that of the Princesse de Clèves—indeed Mme de Lafayette herself through the abbé de Charnes cites Pauline as a possible source for her own work.[4] Both ladies have to choose between duty to a husband for whom they feel only respect, and submission to the man they really love, and each makes the same, difficult decision. Pauline is indeed perhaps the first heroine in French literature to feel any such inner conflict, to recognize that love can be guilty and selfish and that it must be subordinated to some higher, more valid ideal, that fulfilment of individual passion should not be the principal aim of life. Neither Iseut nor Marguerite de Navarre's Floride wavered one moment from the love that possessed them; whether it remained pure or involved physical possession made no difference to its ultimate supremacy in their code of values. Corneille presents us with a rich and moving internal action, as Pauline struggles throughout the play against the decision to be made.

Basically, then, her conflict resembles that of the Princesse de Clèves as she has to choose between a deliberately imposed conception of duty and a love which exists in spite of her conscience and her reason. There are, however, two main factors that make her behaviour significantly different from that of the Princesse. Firstly, Corneille belonged to his time in believing in the ultimate power of man's will, although unlike his contemporaries he realized what struggles and suffering must come before. So his heroine has a strength of resistance of which she is conscious from the beginning and which enables her to forecast and be ready to counter the dangers of a meeting with her lover. Mme de Clèves, belonging to a later more pessimistic age, shows her weakness in her very inability to foresee what will happen when she meets Nemours: at least, at the beginning, she is taken completely by surprise, and even when she can no longer underestimate the tremendous power her love has over her, she is incapable of facing it squarely but continually runs away from it —only to abandon herself to it in her solitary retreat. Secondly, Pauline's loyalty to her husband is gradually transformed into a sort of love, a conscious devotion that Pauline wishes to feel and which is founded on admiration and respect. Here Corneille is again, as in the character of Rodrigue, trying to formulate an ideal, semi-Platonic relationship between a man and a woman, which will lead them on to higher duties and a higher love; and here he is more successful even than in *Le Cid,* for both partners are involved and both eventually triumph as their human love progresses towards divine love. The Princesse de Clèves' feeling for her husband is never more than friendship: it does not give her the spiritual strength necessary to overcome the fatal passion she feels for Nemour.

Yet something in common remains in the two heroines' attempts at resistance. Thus the Princesse continues to resist Nemours, partly out of a hankering after a guiltless, spiritual relationship with her husband, such as Pauline achieves. Madame de Lafayette still half belonged to this former Cornelian age, still half believed in such a love or rather would have liked to believe in it, if reality had allowed her, so she emphasized the depth of the affectionate respect the Princesse feels for her husband, and the value of the relationship she might have had with him, had it not been for the irruption of an irresistible, primitive passion. We can now begin to understand in what way some of the peculiarities of Madame de Lafayette's treatment of adulterous love can be ascribed to her historical situation. Her life bestrides two epochs of French literature. As we shall see, she was writing at a time of disillusionment in human values, of a belief in snatching the pleasure of the present moment, which put a debased form of love above everything else; and yet she still kept a hold on the idealism of the previous age in which she had been brought up, become now an empty morality which had lost or forgotten its *raison d'être.* Ultimately Astrée, Rodrigue and Pauline all sought a pure, superior kind of relationship, not so much because they believed in its intrinsic value as because through it they could feel more intensely their own strength, their own freedom, their very identities as individuals. The Princesse has no such high idea of her potentialities: all she wants is a life in which she is not lost and enslaved. Her desire for purity is negative: she needs it not to fulfil herself but simply to save herself from complete destruction.

The sources of Mme de Clèves' situation and behaviour are to be found then more in the early seventeenth-century theatre than in the early seventeenth-century novel. The novel was too specifically *salon* literature, too tied to a particular moral code to attract the greatest writers. It was in the thematic freedom of the theatre that the Platonic attitude to love was first attacked by the primitive and classical idea of the fatality of physical passion. For Corneille and his contemporaries at least a conciliation was still possible between sensual enslavement and spiritual nobility, which preserved the integral dignity of man even if it ultimately led to his death, since they still believed in man's strength when faced with a crisis. The study of literature after 1645 shows a gradual disillusionment in man's capacity for purity and heroism, a growing awareness of his miserable wretchedness, such as we find later expressed in Pascal's *Pensées* and the *Maximes* of La Rochefoucauld. In romantic literature, in both novels and plays, this took the form of a more indulgent attitude to love, the tender passion which overwhelms man's being and yet is welcomed and enjoyed. The austere purity of the relationship between Astrée and Céladon or the gravity of Pauline's eventual love for Polyeucte were forgotten—all that remained of them was a preoccupation with love as the most important thing on earth. Men depicted it as necessarily unhappy but preferred this unhappiness to the happiness of a life without love. Such an attitude led in lesser writers to a facile sentimentality since, while recognizing the tragedy to which passion might lead in practice by overcoming all other ties and duties, they refused to see it as tragedy and persisted in the unconvincing notion that such suffering and death were pleasant and enviable. We see here in fact the victory of the primitive love tradition over the sophisticated ideal of chivalric or Platonic love, but it is a victory which sometimes can hardly be recognized as such: writers such as Segrais or Mme de Villedieu turned this violent and tragic idea of passion into a frivolous entertainment for refined gatherings of great lords and ladies, preserving its basic nature but removing all that made it seem dangerous and antisocial. The result is that in their works the relationships between a lover and his mistress are as shallow and unconvincing as in those of their more idealistic predecessors: their idea of passion differs but they are no more successful at placing it in that context of reality which would be bound to expose its falsity. Madame de Lafayette was the only novelist to realize the terrible consequences of an irresistible passion in action.

It may be worth making a few remarks on the kind of society which produced such a romantic code before it is shown how these attitudes were embodied in literary forms. The Frondes of 1648 and 1652 were the final abortive attempt of the nobility to act for themselves, to fulfil their ambitions and seize power. After this, the rule of Mazarin was tightened and Louis XIV inherited a country already well-controlled. The relevant features of his repressive policy are well known: how he increased the costly splendour and prestige of the Court so that all the nobility would be drawn towards it away from their provincial castles right within his sphere of authority and thus be rendered both powerless and poverty-stricken; how he occupied them in trivial but time-consuming duties such as attending him unceasingly from the moment he woke up to the moment he went to sleep; how he drew his chief ministers from among the *bourgeoisie* who would never dare defy him since they could be nothing without him. In these circumstances, it is no wonder that the great lords and ladies engaged in endless love intrigues, analysing their emotions in every detail in order to give interest to their empty lives. Corneille's contemporaries had also of course had affairs which did not necessarily remain on the austerely pure level about which we read in their novels, but they had also had other ambitions which they nurtured on their provincial estates and came to Paris to pursue. The love between La Rochefoucauld and Madame de Longueville for example served to stimulate their strength and increase their confidence in carrying out their treasonable plans; as in the novels they read, each must through his actions prove himself worthy of the other. Love now could have no ulterior aim since it could not be surpassed by glory or honour—it must find its purpose and all its interest in itself.

The influence of the *salons* as centres of culture and fashion continued to be strong: problems of love casuistry, the formation of a kind of art of loving, were more and more the subject of conversations. We are given a clear picture of this atmosphere in the immensely popular *Clélie* (1656) by Mlle de Scudéry. Here, the author in a sense goes back to the formula adopted by D'Urfé, by using incidents as excuses for discussions on love and as illustrations of some of its problems. In the novels by La Calprenède and Gomberville and in Mlle de Scudéry's earlier works, much more emphasis had been placed on exciting adventure for its own sake. Yet Mlle de Scudéry has none of the intellectual austerity nor the spiritual idealism of D'Urfé: she is very much a feminist writer and affirms the right of women to passion (by which she does not mean a purely Platonic relationship), and pleads for their freedom in satisfying this passion if they so desire. In fact, her claim becomes an attack on marriage, since she cannot conceive of the sincerity of a love which is thus imposed upon one by a legal tie. There is real emotion and originality here but in practice it is largely destroyed by the unconvincing setting of ancient Rome which the novel adopts and the looseness of its form. It is in *Clélie* too that we find the famous *Carte du Tendre*, in effect a pictorial illustration of the kind of conversations held in Mlle de Scudéry's *salon*. Again the satisfaction of his love seems to be the *raison d'être* of every man; and we are given the various techniques he must adopt, the various rituals he must perform before winning his lady. The courtship is seen entirely from the man's point of view: the lady represents a prize, whose love is to be won only after great efforts, and in this sense her position in the *Carte du Tendre* is very like the one she holds in *l'Astrée* or indeed in medieval romances. The work bears some similarities to the *Roman de la Rose*, except that what was before a profoundly serious cult has become now just a form of superficial flattery. There are several kinds of love that the patient lover can win— Tendre sur Estime, Tendre sur Reconnaissance, and Tendre sur Inclination. This last, significantly enough, is hardly examined at all—no efforts are required to attain it and it is represented darkly as leading only to "mer dangereuse, terres inconnues".

In the theatre we can see the change to this new attitude well illustrated in the later plays of Corneille. Like *Le Cid* and *Horace*, *Suréna* depicts a conflict between love and a higher glory, but now the emphasis falls much more strongly on love, seen as a tender, overwhelming passion, to which any opposition can only be difficult and painful. Corneille has not altered his themes: he has simply altered his attitude to them, as he has lost his youthful idealism and is following the changing literary fashion. His younger brother, Thomas Corneille, also a popular playwright in the 1660s and 70s, expresses the same sort of attitude: he too takes as his stock situation a clash between a galant and tender love and an inhuman, unattractive glory and he works it out with every possible cliché on the exquisite wounds of love, and countless lengthy banal lamentations by the hero. There is no real conflict here, no genuine pain. Love wins from the beginning and its victory is never once sincerely regretted nor seen as a disaster. After Racine's successes with *Andromaque*, *Bérénice* etc. Thomas Corneille produced plays in which all the emotions are born of love alone, where love is the motivating force of all the characters in all their actions. Indeed the play *Ariane* strikes the reader as little more than a toned-down, more awkward Racine, which misses all the great playwright's realism and subtlety.

It is by Racine himself of course that this idea of the weakness of man in the face of love is most powerfully worked out, since unlike the others he took it to its logically disastrous conclusion. He, almost alone, with the exception of Mme de Lafayette in another genre, realized the anguish that must be suffered by a man or woman who knows that satisfaction of his love is impossible, and yet in whom this knowledge can do nothing to extirpate a passion which both tortures him now and will ultimately be fatal to his very existence. He palliates nothing, transforms nothing out of a frivolous desire to entertain, judging that the most valuable kind of entertainment is that which comes from the audience's experience of reality, not of an escapist's dream. Here, in the monologues of Hermione or Phèdre, we find again the eternally tragic accents of the Greeks and Romans, or of the primitive Celt as he sung the story of the ill-fated lovers, Tristan and Iseut, not overlaid now by a sophisticated casualness, a superficial conventionality, but the very voice of truth.

There is the same emphasis on romantic intrigue and the fatality of love in the shorter *nouvelles* that were being written in the 1650s and 60s, by Segrais, Mme de Villedieu, Boursault and others. The unconvincing plots of the earlier heroic novels were no longer acceptable, for their readers had no more sympathy with a moral code which rested on a lengthy and unrewarded constancy. They were bored by descriptions of daring deeds, of battles, of shipwrecks, since their own existences were led entirely within closed walls and found their interest only in men's minds and hearts. So they preferred to read shorter narratives, filled entirely with love intrigue and concerning people whose lives were more like their own. The historical settings they adopted, anyway closer to their own time than the Rome or the Middle East of their predecessors, were a thin cover for descriptions of life as it was lived in the Court and *salons* of their own time. Eventually, Boursault and Duplaisir among others abandoned this artifice completely in some of their stories and wrote directly of contemporary life.

Love is of course of paramount importance in all these works and it is usually a love which has come easily and been accepted immediately, with all its implications. We are far here from the pure, high-minded conversations of Floride and Amadour. The obstacles which prevent its fulfilment and thus provide the action vary in importance: they may, as in Segrais' *Honorine*, simply be hesitation on the part of the lady as to which of her lovers to accept, or else they may be connected with political expediency, in more historical tales like Saint Reál's *Don Carlos*. Very commonly too now we find the situation, treated three times by Mme de Lafayette, where a married woman is in love with a man other than her husband. With the discarding of the sixteenth and seventeenth-century ideal of a pure, Platonic relationship between a man and a woman, to which marriage with all it implied of carnal intimacy was irrelevant, literary fashion had returned to this more primitive theme, exploiting every opportunity for drama and excitement. Indeed, such a subject provided obvious sentimental complications to which all could respond, besides being a very real problem in the daily life of the period. Mme de Lafayette was one of the first to use it in *La Princesse de Montpensier* (1662), but by the time she produced *La Princesse de Clèves* in 1678 the fashion was well established. How do her contemporaries treat this situation of the married woman in love? What are the relative emphases they place on love and duty? Has Madame de Lafayette any immediate predecessors from which she has drawn for her own personal treatment of the theme?

Segrais' *Eugénie* (1656), one of the *Divertissements de la Princesse Aurélie*, is the first of this sudden spate of *nouvelles*, with a near contemporary setting and dealing entirely with a problem of love; and here the problem is the very one that we have been discussing, that of the married woman in love with another man, although the story is seen indirectly from the point of view of a second lover of whose love the woman does not know. Madame de Lafayette would obviously have been familiar with this tale since she knew Segrais well, and it is very likely that it is to him that she owes the idea of writing a *nouvelle* at all. In the story of *Eugénie*, however, in contrast to *La Princesse de Montpensier*, published a few years later, the character of the married woman, torn between duty to her husband and yearning for her absent lover, is sparsely treated: since her lover is absent, she is under no great immediate temptation and all we hear of her struggle is one single lament to her maid. This is not enough to make her a moving figure. Segrais is much more interested in describing firstly the complex emotional position into which the second lover, who is disguised as the maid, is plunged as a result of this confession, and secondly the misunderstandings which arise because of his disguise. Segrais has hit on the tragedy of the married woman as if by accident, while merely seeking the excitement of an original and surprising plot.

Mme de Lafayette's *La Princesse de Clèves* has a more immediate source in the work of Mme de Villedieu. Mme de Villedieu was an extremely prolific writer, as well as an adventuress and an eccentric, who wrote by profession and in 1669 was granted a pension by the king. Although none of her work is either original or profound it was immensely popular and provides us with a valuable indication of the sort of books people liked to read in the 1660s and 70s. After producing a heroic novel, derivative of Gomberville and La Calprenède, she turned to the semi-historical, semi-sentimental *nouvelle*, already now established by Segrais' work and by *La Princesse de Montpensier*. Her plots were based on some kind of amorous intrigue, whose appeal lay in the attractiveness of love, the sweetness of its satisfaction and the charm of the gallant lover. Innumerable obstacles of a purely external nature arose, and all were surmounted with an undiscerning ease. Quite often we find at the centre of a tale a married woman in love, and the lover is then given a complication to deal with right from the beginning—and yet how exceptional was Madame de Lafayette's tragic realism in this genre, and how exceptional too the note of heroic idealism in La Princesse de Clèves' behaviour!

The action of the first *Annales galantes*, for example, a collection of these *nouvelles* published in 1670, depends on the immediate acceptance by the Comtesse de Castille, said to be exceptionally virtuous, of the love of an unknown pilgrim; he soon turns out to be a wealthy French nobleman and she unhesitatingly leaves her home to flee to Paris with him. This is how she excuses her weakness: "notre crédule dame déplorait dans son âme la fatalité de son étoile mais elle ne croyait pas qu'on pust éviter de s'y soumettre".[5] Passion is satisfied immediately and without a struggle, because it is considered *a priori* to have a fatal strength that cannot be resisted. The consequences of the heroine's action —the search for her by her husband, his eventual discovery of her and murder of her lover—are told us because they are dramatic and exciting, not because they move us to pity for the woman's fate. Her reactions throughout the story are too simplified and stylized for us to feel with her at all. There is no psychological development, little analysis of emotion after the hero and heroine have first fallen in love.

The stories of the *Désordres de l'amour* (1675) have perhaps more substance to them and the second one is often cited as a possible source for *La Princesse de Clèves*. It is true that the two plots have some rather surprising similarities, and it is very likely that Mme de Lafayette had read this tale and that it had suggested to her certain episodes of her great work. (It is very improbable, owing to the dates of publication of the two works, that the borrowing should have been the other way.) Yet a study of the story by Mme de Villedieu shows that this admission does nothing to diminish our estimate of Mme de Lafayette's greatness as a novelist, since her treatment of these episodes has a depth and a significance far beyond anything in Mme de Villedieu's tale. In both works the wife resists her love for another man out of loyalty to her husband and even confesses this love to him. But the two characters of the wife and husband in Mme de Villedieu's story remain lifeless and flat: we are shown almost nothing of their inner conflicts; the wife's disclosure comes two pages after the beginning of the work and the love to which she is confessing is news to the reader as much as to her husband. We are shown neither the gradual awakening of love in her nor the increasing guilty shock as she becomes aware of it—she is said to have been in love with this man since her childhood. The fact that she confesses to her husband at all is of course evidence of the conflict that must be raging within her, and Mme de Villedieu should be given credit for having invented this potentially inter-esting situation. Yet, since she develops it so little, one cannot

help feeling that she invented it not because of the emotional
struggle it would imply, but as a new turn for the intrigue to take.
She does not make her heroine act in this remarkably virtuous
way from any consistent ideal of purity and honour (as both
Corneille and Mme de Lafayette did), since she then immediately
removes any occasion for virtue in the heroine by the extraordinary
and unconvincing generosity of her husband. He does not blame
her at all and soon conveniently dies, telling her on his deathbed
to marry her lover. This she immediately does, unlike the Princesse
de Clèves, and the bulk of the story is filled with the subsequent
infidelities of her second husband, a rake like Nemours, as they
are related in the historical source. After the initial hitch, all the
characters act in the way fashionable at the time: they give in to
love immediately, absolving themselves and each other from any
guilt by shifting the responsibility for their actions onto the
stars. Mme de Lafayette took up the opening part of the story,
the part invented by Mme de Villedieu, but gave it a force and
reality of its own by describing in detail the guilty conflict of the
heroine and by ascribing to the husband a much more real and
more tragic reaction when he hears her confession; the resulting
novel has very little in common with Mme de Villedieu's story.

There is another *nouvelle* of this period whose plot is even more
strikingly similar to that of *La Princesse de Clèves* and whose
existence is rather puzzling. It is called *La Vertu Malheureuse* and
was published anonymously as a *fait divers* by the *Mercure Galant*
in January 1678. *La Princesse de Clèves* came out in May of the
same year. We read again the confession by a wife to her husband
of her love for another man and here too, as in *La Princesse de
Clèves* but not in Mme de Villedieu's story, the confession is
overheard by the lover. The virtue of the wife is emphasized
more than it was by Mme de Villedieu; her conflict is described
in some detail and like the Princesse she refuses to marry her lover
after the death of her husband. It is most probable, considering
the closeness of the details of this tale to those of *La Princesse de
Clèves*, and the short interval that was to elapse before the publication of the latter, that *La Vertu Malheureuse* was the result of a
manuscript leakage of *La Princesse de Clèves*—somebody was
perhaps deliberately forestalling Mme de Lafayette. It has been
suggested indeed[6] that she actually arranged this leakage, so that
the confession scene in *La Princesse de Clèves* should not appear so
extraordinary, but this seems highly unlikely considering that

there had already been at least two confessions (in *Les Désordres de L'Amour* and *Polyeucte*).

There is little point in studying in detail other tales dealing wholly or partly with the situation of the married woman in love with another man—Saint Réal's *Don Carlos* (1674) or Boursault's *Le Prince de Condé* (1675) for example. In both we find a certain complaisance to love, a lack of restraint in the lovers when they meet, and a series of lamentations on the cruelty of destiny; in neither have we the original combination of tragic realism with moral idealism that we have in *La Princesse de Clèves*. It is only in a *nouvelle* written after *La Princesse de Clèves* in 1683—*La Duchesse d'Estramène* by Duplaisir—that there is any of Madame de Lafayette's subtle intuition into human behaviour and here it is obviously only because the author is using *La Princesse de Clèves* as a model. He portrays at some length and with some success the relationship between a husband and wife who feel only esteem for each other, the inner struggles of the one, guilty of an adulterous love, and of the other who must learn to accept this love in his wife. Still, Duplaisir's ending has none of the stark tragedy of that invented by Mme de Lafayette: it is the lover who dies and we witness a reconciliation between husband and wife which suggests a sort of happiness in the future.

Let us now summarize what has been said in this chapter and try to place Mme de Lafayette within the long French tradition of love romance begun in the Middle Ages. We can distinguish throughout this tradition two different currents of thought, two attitudes to the problem of love in relation to the individual and society. First comes the basic, primitive conception of love as an overwhelming desire for physical as well as spiritual intimacy; this desire cannot be fought and it automatically rejects all other claims, of individual dignity or social honour. This is the conception which, apart from its appearance in some early medieval romances, lay in abeyance in French literature for several centuries, reappearing in works of the sixteenth and early seventeenth centuries as the result of Italian, Spanish and classical influences, largely in secondary characters and theoretical discussions. It is the second, more specifically French attitude, which dominated the serious romance and poetry of the twelfth to fifteenth centuries—the idealistic belief in an individual's power to master his love, to use it as he wills, to mould its nature, purifying it and controlling it often as a means to another, higher end. All these works are chaste and optimistic; they describe man's aggressive strength as he surmounts every peril, physical or moral, not his weakness in the face of a power stronger than he.

It was not until classical literature had acquired the popular prestige to enable it to penetrate right into the field of serious writing in French, until the 1630s and the time of Corneille, that the first, the primitive attitude, again made itself clearly felt; then conflicts between the two conceptions became an important source of drama and tragedy, in the moving figures of Sophonisbe, Alidor and Pauline. After this, idealism quickly lost its sway in the world of literature, and romance and the theatre concentrated on a superficial, watered down version of the first, the primitive conception of love as a violent, irresistible force. It is to this period that Mme de Lafayette chronologically belongs, but at the same time she both remained behind it and progressed beyond it. For in *La Princesse de Clèves* she combines an anachronistic yearning for the old idealism, the now out-grown belief in the possibility of a deliberately willed, honourable relationship between a man and a woman, with an acutely realistic awareness of the tragic implications of what her contemporaries were offering as light entertainment.

NOTES TO PART II, CHAPTER 1

[1] see Pauphilet's *Legs du Moyen Âge*, in which the author postulates that the heroine of *Cligès* is a *courtois* adaptation of Iseut. Such is the divine purity of her adulterous love that she acknowledges no rights for her husband and he is eventually disposed of as an obstacle unworthy of interest.

[2] Alexis François, *De l'Heptaméron à La Princesse de Clèves*. R.H.L.F. 1949.

[3] see *Histoire de la Littérature française au XVIIe siècle* (Éd. mondiales), vol. 1, p. 415.

[4] l'abbé de Charnes, *Conversations sur la Critique de La Princesse de Clèves*, 1697.

[5] Madame de Villedieu, *Annales galantes*.

[6] see H. Ashton's *Madame de Lafayette, sa vie et ses oeuvres*, p. 164.

2. THE MORAL THEME

Having described the literary tradition to which the themes of Mme de Lafayette's novels belong, and having suggested how much she owes to contemporary attitudes, we must now study in more detail the complex originality of her treatment of them. As we have seen, the greatness of her work can be ascribed to the combination in it of two qualities: first to the disillusioned and lucid realism with which she regards the world of her contemporaries, and second to the relics of the idealism of a former age which still subsist for her as pale and empty shadows. These two attitudes can be traced in most of Mme de Lafayette's works, but it is in *La Princesse de Clèves* that they are the most evenly balanced and the work owes much of its power to the mysterious ambiguity that this balance provides.

Mme de Lafayette belonged to a period which delighted in narratives of love intrigues, which thought of love as a supreme and exquisite if anti-social force. She shared this attitude to love but without falsification, seeing all its tragic consequences in an individual case. She was not ready to accept that in practice man would always yield immediately and joyfully to a guilty passion, rejecting or forgetting all his other duties. Where Segrais and Mme de Villedieu had given very little space to descriptions of any inner conflict and had relied only on brief, conventional epigrams as psychological explanations, Mme de Lafayette bent all her energies to the depiction of the mental distress of her characters which the external action served only to bring into relief. If a guilty passion overrides all other values, what suffering must precede and accompany their final abandonment! What disintegration of the individual personality must ensue! Her contemporaries barely mentioned the existence of any standards other than those of love and then only (as in *Les Désordres de l'amour*) in order to give a new twist to the intrigue before it proceeded on its inevitable course. Mme de Lafayette realized the power that these values had for such people as Chabannes, Alphonse or the Princesse de Clèves, and so brought out the more starkly the tragedy of their defeat.

For these characters find the strength, at least for a while, to resist their subjection to the mysterious and uncontrollable force of love, or if, as in the case of Chabannes and Alphonse, they do not resist, they try to dominate and mould it as they will. This attempt at a deliberate self-assertion against sensual enslavement obviously has its roots in the Platonic love of Marguerite de Navarre or D'Urfé, and in the moral heroism of Corneille's characters, all of whom draw strength for decisive action from their own, newly found self-consciousness; but in Mme de Lafayette's novels it seems to take on a particular form, which recurs so often in her work that we cannot but see it as intimately linked with her own temperament and personal experience. Her works bear witness to her belief not in the power of a desire for freedom or for glory to keep the individuality strong and whole, but rather in that of a complete honesty within relationships—if it can be attained—to mould them and to make them what the characters themselves want them to be, not what by nature they are. Only if each feels a complete confidence in the other's sincerity, only if they can, as it were, work together to preserve their relationship from forces stronger than either of them alone, can a man and woman even attempt to avoid the humiliation in store for all who yield to the servitude of love. Mme de Lafayette believes or would like to believe (for nature is always ultimately too strong), that man can form his own destiny—not by any extraordinary heroism, but simply by preserving his own identity against the powers of chaos and confusion. Only by being absolutely sincere, not just to himself, but also to his or her partner in a relationship, to the Princesse de Montpensier, to Alphonse or to the Prince de Clèves, can either Chabannes, Bélasire or the Princesse de Clèves save themselves from complete loss of control.

Not that Mme de Lafayette adopts a wholly idealistic view of human ability to withstand the ravages of love. In the end all her heroes and heroines are broken down by their passions and their resistance is finally only an act of despair. Mme de Lafayette's greatness also lies then in the lucidity and realism of her analysis of this eventual breakdown. By localizing her characters in a definite milieu, by describing that milieu at length and by thus suggesting in detail its effect on them, she gives her works a living, concrete force which those of her contemporaries have not. Segrais and Mme de Villedieu are content to ascribe the tragic situations of their lovers to a mysterious, unspecified, universal fatality, the same, in fact, which in the Tristan story takes the form of a magic potion and in Racine's Greek plays that of the goddess, Aphrodite. In this way, the message of all these works is from the beginning a general one telling us of man and love everywhere. *La Princesse de Clèves*, as perhaps all novels should, plays itself out first on the level of a particular, individual case set in a localized milieu, and only afterwards and by implication as a general statement on eternal, human problems. Thus it is that while adopting a similar attitude to love as Racine, for example, Mme de Lafayette concentrates on illustrating this attitude in one specific case in the particular world that she knew rather than on its general validity for everyone. The instruments which the fatality of love uses to work out its destructive purpose form part of the daily life of the Court which Mme de Lafayette's heroes and heroines are bound to lead—its conventions which first bring the lovers together and then prevent them escaping each other, its moral atmosphere in which love is taken lightly and yet is every-one's obsession—and whose dangers for a sensitive young person are specifically pointed out again and again. The way in which the characters grow weaker in the face of passion, indeed the birth of the passion itself depends on the Court society in which they move, rather than on any universal system of the way love develops in any individual at any time. Indeed, it is doubtful how far in *La Princesse de Clèves*, the least directly moral of all Mme de Lafayette's fictional work, the author was making a general statement at all.

As well as specifying the external reasons for the destructive effect of love on her characters, Mme de Lafayette also describes with great subtlety and lucidity the inner progression of that love, distinguishing each individual from the other. Probably from her observation of the Court in which she lived—(the sources of her themes will be discussed as each novel is treated)—she had learnt to understand the various, almost imperceptible stages by which a person gradually becomes aware of his love, the alternations of blindness and lucidity through which he passes, of submission and resistance, of doubt and triumph; she describes the agonies of jealousy, the vanities of self-deception and the final tragically complete self-knowledge, when it is too late for anything to be remedied. And in each of her characters, in the Princesse de Montpensier, Alphonse, Nugna Bella, Henriette d'Angleterre, the Princesse de Clèves, the Comtesse de Tende, love develops differently, the lover reacts in his own special way—more blindly, more violently or with a greater strength of resistance. In this individualization of passion as well as in the realistic description of its moral environment lie the reasons for the tragic immediacy of Mme de Lafayette's work.

As has already been suggested, Mme de Lafayette's idealism and realism are given a different relative importance in each of her works. The central character of her first *nouvelle*, *La Princesse de Montpensier* (1662), is treated entirely in a pessimistic realistic tone, and it is only in a secondary character, the Comte de Chabannes, that we can see hints of that peculiar, twisted idealism which makes for the strength of *La Princesse de Clèves*. Mme de Lafayette takes in this tale a young French princess whose family has a leading position at the Court, ascribes to her a kind of life which must have been very common both in the sixteenth century, in which the story is set, and in the seventeenth century, and shows us how tragically such a life in such a milieu could easily end. The heroine is married to the Prince de Montpensier, having already fallen in love with the Duc de Guise, whom she had met frequently during her previous engagement to his younger brother. She thinks she has forgotten him but a chance meeting reunites them; their love immediately revives; they evolve various deceptions which will allow them to meet and only escape being discovered because a devoted friend of both husband and wife rapidly takes the Duc de Guise's place as the husband enters his wife's room. This causes the end of this friendship and the friend is killed shortly afterwards; Guise is frightened away and soon forgets the Princesse, and she herself dies of grief.

Is Mme de Lafayette here simply telling the true story of someone she knew? It has for example been suggested that this *nouvelle* was inspired by the affair between Henriette d'Angleterre and the Comte de Guiche, who also just missed being surprised by Henriette's husband. Although this could be true the *nouvelle* carries to a very different conclusion what was in reality nipped early in the bud by the king. More probably only the general atmosphere of the story is directly inspired by the lives of the people of the Court, and of Henriette d'Angleterre in particular. Mme de Lafayette moreover deliberately disclaims any historical source in her opening *avertissement* and no trace of a similar incident can be found in sixteenth-century memoirs.

La Princesse de Montpensier shows in germ many of the qualities of *La Princesse de Clèves*. We find for example a striking realism and a relevance in the contrasting descriptions of life at the Court and in the country. After the heroine's marriage she first meets the hero again in the country and Mme de Lafayette contrives a set of circumstances which makes it more or less inevitable that this meeting will revive their love—the Princesse sails in a boat on the lake, her husband is absent and the Duc d'Anjou, whom Guise accompanies, is a rival for her favour. In the country, however, they cannot show each other their love since here there are not those conventions of social visiting which lovers at the Court can use as a mask for their private meetings. So the action is switched to the Court. (Thus it is only when they return again to the country that the lovers come near to being discovered by the husband—a secret love affair cannot be carried on in the solitude of a country estate.) The scenes in Paris are mostly taken up with a complicated exposition of the hidden intrigues of love and ambition carried on underground and in which the lovers become involved in spite of themselves. Guise takes advantage of these intrigues, of the rumours which associate his name with that of Madame, sister of the King (just as Nemours does in a similar situation), and of the contact into which the lovers are bound to come as they both perform their duties as courtiers, to reveal and press his love on the Princesse. He uses social appearances as a cover for his real wishes, deliberately seeking out Mme de Montpensier in order to speak privately to her. The code of the Court demands that the necessary distances be preserved, but they only hide the ceaseless agitation of true emotion and desire underneath.

The Princesse herself is weak almost from the beginning and quickly fits into this code of hypocrisy, masking reality beneath social appearances as the Princesse de Clèves never does— although she has not the experience to avoid mistakes entirely; at the masked ball, for example, her emotions outrun her prudence and she herself is taken in by appearances. She is a woman initially virtuous but also inevitably weak as soon as her virtue is attacked, and Mme de Lafayette analyses much less fully than in *La Princesse de Clèves,* but already with some lucidity, the agonies the heroine feels as she slowly weakens. We watch her growing guilt as she tries first to combat the irresistible force of love through a regard for her reputation or through fear of her husband, as she deceives herself on the true motives of her actions, as the pain of jealousy finally brings her openly to admit her love and as she then submits completely. Those people whom she frequents are, with one exception, as weak as she is and can do nothing to help her: her lover is indiscreet and demanding, and finally faithless, and she feels only dislike for her husband, who appears violent and brutish. Neither of these men has that moral integrity of the Princesse de Clèves' husband which gives support to the dictates of her conscience. Mme de Lafayette is here portraying common seventeenth-century humanity as her disillusioned eye sees it and her moral condemnation of it is absolute and unconditional:

> Elle (the Princesse) mourut en peu de jours, dans la fleur de son âge, une des plus belles princesses du monde, et qui aurait été sans doute la plus heureuse, si la vertu et la prudence eussent conduit toutes ses actions.[1]

Yet there are also hints of a more idealistic view of man in *La Princesse de Montpensier*, in the character of the devoted friend of husband and wife, the Comte de Chabannes. He is in love with the Princesse, declares this love to her at the beginning and then preserves towards her an unflinching loyalty in spite of her growing weakness for another and his disapproval of her behaviour. It could be that Mme de Lafayette had two models in mind when creating this character: she was in part recalling the attitude of a lover to his mistress, approved by an earlier age, and illustrated for example by D'Urfé's Céladon. The lover must be strong in controlling his selfish desires and think always and unquestioningly of his mistress's interests. Only thus, in the end, will he win her affection. Yet Chabannes has a more convincing reality than his prototype, and this he may rather owe to his other model, the real-life Ménage, friend and admirer of Mme de Lafayette. Like Chabannes, and unlike Céladon, he was considerably older than the lady whom he courted, and took some interest in her education. His feelings for her were probably more akin to a protective, relatively undemanding friendship, which in Mme de Lafayette's eyes was worth more than the physical passion of a younger man.

Mme de Lafayette's idealism demands of Chabannes that he should both remain loyal to his mistress, who cares for him less in proportion as she cares for another more, and that at the same time he should preserve his own integrity by advising her on her behaviour according to his own conscience:

Le comte, avec une sincérité aussi exacte que s'il n'eût point été amoureux, dit au prince tout ce qu'il connaissait en cette princesse capable de la lui faire aimer; et il avertit aussi Mme de Montpensier de toutes les choses qu'elle devait faire pour achever de gagner le cœur et l'estime de son mari.[2]

He must follow only the highest principles of honour and trust and not the baser urges of self-interest. His is an endless conflict between advising his mistress to act as she should and does not wish to, and helping her to act as she wishes but should not. By following the first line of conduct, although he satisfies his conscience he incurs her dislike and causes her suffering; by following the second he selfishly hopes for some reply to his devotion, which of course he never receives. His love drags him lower and lower until in the end he reluctantly agrees, for purely egoistical reasons, to carry messages and arrange a meeting between the two lovers whose behaviour he detests. His last noble act, his ultimate attempt to save his lady from dishonour and even death, as he quickly takes the place of her lover when the Prince is about to discover them together, is a gesture not of triumph but of despair. Because of his love, he has failed in his duty as a friend, not only of the Princesse but also of her husband: "Je suis criminel à votre égard . . . et indigne de l'amitié que vous avez eue pour moi; mais ce n'est pas de la manière que vous pouvez vous l'imaginer. Je suis plus malheureux que vous et plus désespéré,"[3] he says to the Prince, as he is discovered. So Mme de Lafayette's tragic realism kills the idealism she had inherited from the authors she admired most—her observation of real life can give her no hope. She can only portray it as the losing side in a conflict which leads to suffering and death.

The complex and original character of Chabannes seems to us at least as interesting as that of the Princesse, but his rôle is almost incidental to the plot. Except at the end it would develop in the same way without him. Is it perhaps a sign of Mme de Lafayette's inexperience at this stage, that her themes are not balanced as perfectly here as they are in *La Princesse de Clèves*, that our attention is diverted from the central protagonist to a secondary character, that the interest is thus divided and that the impact of the plot suffers in consequence? The author is as yet too conditioned by the literary tradition to which she belonged. She still sees the husband as an unsympathetic brute, and conventionally places all the nobility and fidelity in the character of a 'over; her pessimistic realism demands that her heroine should be ultimately disappointed in the principal lover, the man for whom she has sacrificed everything, so the author has created a second, nobler lover whose importance is surprising in the context. In *La Princesse de Montpensier,* Mme de Lafayette's idealism and realism have not yet achieved that harmonious balance of tones that makes for the subtlety and formal perfection of *La Princesse de Clèves.*

The work which follows chronologically *La Princesse de Montpensier* is the *Histoire d'Henriette d'Angleterre,* begun in 1665 and finished in 1670. Mme de Lafayette makes it clear in her preface to the work that she is relating the true story of Henriette's love affairs and of the Court intrigues in which she was involved between 1661 and 1665, exactly as the Princesse told them to her.

> Un jour qu'elle me faisoit le récit de quelques circonstances assez extraordinaires de sa passion pour elle: «Ne trouvez-vous pas, me dit-elle, que si tout ce qui m'est arrivé, et les choses qui y ont relation, étoit écrit, cela composeroit une jolie histoire! Vous écrivez bien ajouta-t-elle; écrivez, je vous fournirai de bons mémoires».[4]

Thus what we have here is not a moral statement by Mme de Lafayette on the life of the society in which she lived, embodied in a plot and characters, but the day to day reality of this life as it was actually lived by one of the most eminent members of the society. We will, then, find very little indication of Mme de Lafayette's own views, but will see at length the raw material on which she drew to form these views and to illustrate them in works of fiction. The *Histoire* will be studied in this chapter to see what themes, recurring in Mme de Lafayette's novels, were suggested to her by her direct observation of life around her. The difference in atmosphere between this and her other works—the matter-of-fact, almost gay tone of Henriette's recital beneath which the possibility of tragedy can only vaguely be sensed, the concentration of both author and characters on each present moment—mean that these themes are given none of the consistency and seriousness they have in the fictional works; even so, it is profitable to compare them with the more careful treatment they receive in the author's true works of art.

Primarily, it is clear how closely descriptions of Court life in *La Princesse de Montpensier, Zaïde* and *La Princesse de Clèves* resemble the seventeenth-century reality. Here, as there, every courtier becomes involved through love, ambition or spite, in some intrigue conducted secretly as the daily round of social duties proceeds smoothly and inevitably on its way. The two champions of intrigue in the *Histoire* are Mlle de Montalais, one of Henriette's attendants, and the Comte de Vardes, who plot variously for and against the king's love for Louise de la Vallière and Guiche's love for Henriette, but there are many others too, plotting for a major or minor cause. All these intrigues are presented in every detail but with great clarity by Mme de Lafayette, just as the schemings of the Vidame de Chartres or of the Duc d'Anjou are given concisely but fully for their relevance to the main plot. Confirming her condemnation of this atmosphere of secrecy and plotting in Court life is Mme de Lafayette's description of the effect it may have on a sensitive and inexperienced girl, who is suddenly introduced into it. Like the Princesse de Montpensier, Henriette, gay and popular, enters quickly into the spirit of the Court and offers little resistance to the Comte de Guiche's protestations of love; the various social pressures of her daily life are doing their work on her:

> Enfin la jeunesse de Madame, l'agrément du comte de Guiche, mais surtout les soins de Montalais, engagèrent cette princesse dans une galanterie qui ne lui a donné que des chagrins considérables.[5]

Mme de Lafayette describes tactfully and realistically the attractiveness of love, but hardly suggests here the tragedy to which it can lead. Henriette is really only playing at courtship, like a character out of a conventional romance. Indeed, the light-hearted manner of Henriette as she tells her story precludes the emergence of any very strong impression of suffering. The most she feels is a certain grief at the first banishment of Guiche and at their final parting. The dangers into which she runs are not mortal; unlike Mme de Lafayette's fictional characters she risks losing through her love not her very identity and even her life, but simply the favour of the king. Mme de Lafayette in her novels has taken to extreme and terrifying conclusions situations which in reality usually remained almost harmless, because through a process of selection and exaggeration she has uncovered their true qualities—their futility and their menace.

The third theme which runs through both the *Histoire* and the novels is that almost defensive belief in honesty and integrity which is all that remains of the idealism of a former age. Henriette is only saved from disgrace by finally rejecting the lying counsels of her corrupter, Vardes, and persisting in telling the truth about the intrigues in which she has been involved. Thus she wins back both the love of the Comte de Guiche and the favour of the king. A comparison can be made between the value of sincerity as it is suggested here, probably by Henriette herself as she told the story to her confidant: "Madame se tira de ce labyrinthe en disant toujours la vérité, et sa sincérité la maintint auprès du roi."[6]— and the Princesse de Clèves' confession to her husband.

Zaïde, published in 1669 and again in 1670, is usually recognized to be partly by Mme de Lafayette and partly by Segrais, under whose name it was published and who claimed responsibility for the structure of the plot: "Zaïde, qui a paru sous mon nom est aussi d'elle. Il est vrai que j'y ai eu quelque part, mais seulement pour la disposition du roman, où les règles de l'art sont observées avec grande exactitude."[7] Perhaps because of this, it is a much more conventional novel than Mme de Lafayette's other works: it is set in Spain and consists of several stories linked together often by the slightest of narrative threads. The love affair between Consalve, a Spanish nobleman, and Zaïde, a Moroccan princess, which is the core of the plot, is stylized in the extreme and derivative of the whole tradition of pastoral and lyrical love romance going back to *l'Astrée*. It contains little realistic psychology or original morality and most of the action depends on external tricks of fortune rather than on character. It is in the shorter episodes and flashbacks, which form little *nouvelles* on their own, that we feel the personal hand of Mme de Lafayette.

The story of Consalve's previous love affair with Nugna Bella, a great lady at the Court of Alphonse, King of Léon, and of that disillusionment with his friends and his mistress which causes him to leave the Court for ever, gives us what we may now recognize to be a description of Court life characteristic of Mme de Lafayette. We find again the same atmosphere of intriguing, of petty self-interest, as in *La Princesse de Montpensier* and the *Histoire d'Henriette* and we are struck by the author's emphasis on the hypocrisy of a sophisticated life, on the gulf between social appearances and emotional reality: "Je sais que, comme il est dangereux de cacher quelque-chose à nos amis il l'est aussi beaucoup de ne leur cacher jamais rien,"[8] says one of the characters. Thus Consalve becomes disgusted with Court life because he discovers the hypocritical duplicity of his friend and his mistress, both of whom professed to be working for him and were really only working for themselves and each other. Consalve's friends are obsessed by a sense of their own advancement which here seems even stronger than love, itself now only an instrument for mere material gain. Their emotions are superficial and their existences futile and vain. These attitudes are repeated even more markedly in the final episode of *Zaïde*, which centres on two Moroccans, Alamir and Félime. In both stories we watch the effect of such an atmosphere on those characters who exceptionally do have profound and sincere feelings: one, Consalve, is forced by his disgust to flee the Court; the other, Félime, a minor character, can only resign herself and suffer. These episodes show clearly that mistrust of love as it is commonly felt, which is also one of the determining factors in the Princesse de Clèves' decision not to marry Nemours. In Nugna Bella love is used to serve her ambition; in Alamir (as later in Nemours himself) it is kept alive only by the resistance of the loved one.

By far the most powerful and original of these secondary episodes is the story of Alphonse and Bélasire, which, taking into consideration its brevity, is perhaps as great a psychological masterpiece as *La Princesse de Clèves*. Initially, Alphonse and Bélasire, like the Princesse de Clèves and her husband in a different way, want to make of love something noble and sure, not a force to which they are enslaved but a mutual intimacy which they can mould and preserve as they will. They begin by being suspicious of love because of their fear of the suffering it will bring them and try to resist it until they discover how alike their wishes are. Then they want to safeguard their relationship by placing it on a basis of complete sincerity and trust one in the other. Love however cannot be so reasoned. It is, Mme de Lafayette implies, by nature a selfish and suspicious emotion which can never be content for long. Indeed it would seem that contentment means its death. Bélasire, to show she trusts him, tells Alphonse of all her former suitors, but Alphonse immediately suspects that she has not told him everything. His confidence in her is shaken and from now on he is more and more tormented by his mistaken jealousy, first of her supposed past lovers, and then of his friend whom he suspects quite wrongly of courting her. In the end, Bélasire can bear his morbid temperament no longer and retires to a convent. The similarities between the behaviour of Alphonse and of the Prince de Clèves in the second half of *La Princesse de Clèves* are obvious. On one occasion they use almost the same words:

> . . . après avoir tant souffert par la jalousie, je ne voulais pas me mettre au hasard d'avoir tout ensemble celle d'un amant et celle d'un mari.[9]
>
> J'ai tout ensemble la jalousie d'un mari et celle d'un amant.[10]

Both suffer because they can no longer trust the person they love, and both paradoxically go on to seek more and more reasons for their mistrust. The Prince's jealousy is partly justified; Alphonse's torment is completely self-fabricated. Love is a mysterious force, says Mme de Lafayette, which once it has penetrated a man's heart dominates him completely, ruins his happiness in spite of his rational efforts to discipline it and finally destroys his existence. The only escape lies in flight; Bélasire, Alphonse and the Princesse de Clèves all retire into solitude. This tale succeeds for one of the same reasons that *La Princesse de Clèves* succeeds, because of the perfect balance between Mme de Lafayette's idealism and her realism; the characters make a conscious effort towards an ideal which they can never reach, and so we feel a sympathy with them which makes their failure all the more tragic.

It is unlikely that any of Mme de Lafayette's work would be read today, were it not for the publication in 1678 of *La Princesse de Clèves*. Here we find the most balanced and complex expression of those personal themes with which she had been experimenting for sixteen years, and which it now took her six years to perfect —her dislike for the superficiality and duplicity of Court life, her faith in honesty and individual integrity and her tragic view of the irresistible force of love. Although *La Princesse de Clèves* absorbs us especially by its subtle and original analysis of the two main characters, in a letter of 1678, in which Mme de Lafayette talks of *La Princesse de Clèves* as though it were by someone else, she picks out as the most important feature of the novel its realistic description of Court life:

> Et surtout, ce que j'y trouve, c'est une parfaite imitation du monde de la cour et de la manière dont on y vit. Il n'y a rien de romanesque et de grimpé; aussi n'est-ce pas un roman: c'est proprement des mémoires et c'estoit, à ce que l'on m'a dit, le titre du livre, mais on l'a changé.[11]

Yet she is here not falsifying the message of the novel which is a moral one, but emphasizing how closely the background narrative of events, including the four interpolated stories, is linked to the main psychological action—indeed how far the latter is determined by and inherent in the former.

The introductory description of the Court, which leads up to the appearance of the young Mlle de Chartres, suggests throughout how great are its dangers for so innocent a person. Mme de Lafayette sums up with these words:

> L'ambition et la galanterie étaient l'âme de cette cour, et occupaient également les hommes et les femmes. Il y avait tant d'intérêts et tant de cabales différentes, et les dames y avaient tant de part que l'amour était toujours mêlé aux affaires et les affaires à l'amour. Personne n'était tranquille, ni indifférent; on songeait à s'élever, à plaire, à servir ou à nuire; on ne connaissait ni l'ennui, ni l'oisiveté, et on était toujours occupé des plaisirs ou des intrigues. Ainsi il y avait une sorte d'agitation sans désordre dans cette cour, qui la rendait très agréable, mais aussi très dangereuse pour une jeune personne.[12]

These dangers can indeed be defined in the words "agitation sans désordre", which imply that same gulf between appearance and reality that we have already noted. The appearances of order are maintained, hiding but not suppressing the confused reality of emotion and ambition underneath. The sincere idealism which inspired the efforts of the earlier seventeenth-century *précieuses* towards refinement and purity has disappeared and all that is left is the stiffened mask of what had originally been a reality. Man's aim is not now self-realization at his highest potential, but simply the preservation of that mask of himself which this high potential had once created—hence the static hyperboles with which Mme de Lafayette opens the description, "grandeur, magnificence, galanterie, majestueux, belles personnes, hommes admirablement bien faits, parfaite pour l'esprit et le corps . . .", beneath which lie the chaotic weaknesses of emotion, manifest first in the complicated intrigues with which the description proceeds and later within the protagonists' own hearts. Men no longer believe in the hyperboles except as a protective veneer; all that seems real to them is the force of their own desires, which are necessarily self-destructive since they are irrational and uncontrollable. Thus, Diane de Poitiers can depend only on the lust of the king for the dignity of her status, and the king himself depends entirely for his happiness on her fidelity of which he is never sure. Not even the highest in the land can control his own fate. No wonder the young princess will find here no moral values strong enough to protect her from the violence of real emotion—only an empty social code.

This distinction between the nobility of appearances and the wretchedness of reality is clearly illustrated in the two most important of the interpolated stories (which are also the two invented ones), whose place in the story is deliberately chosen for their relevance to the Princesse's feelings at the time. The first one (like Consalve's story in *Zaïde*) deals with the terrible suffering which comes upon a man when he suddenly realizes the treachery of his loved one, when he sees the difference between the mask in which he believed and the truth as it is now revealed. Sancerre thinks that his love for Madame de Tournon is returned and only discovers at her death that she had secretly promised to marry another. His anguish at her loss is ten times greater because he has also lost his respect for her love, the purity of his memories. Love must be accompanied by admiration and esteem; it demands a mutual confidence which brings with it the surety of respect. In *La Princesse de Clèves*, as in Alphonse's story, Mme de Lafayette suggests the impossibility of such a relationship because man is too weak to make of his mask a reality; this incapacity is inherent in him but it is rendered more dangerous by a society which provides no moral code to give life to the mask. By its general atmosphere of intrigue and by its frivolous, pleasure-seeking routine, it only offers temptation and excuses for self-indulgence.

The story of the Vidame de Chartres and Mme de Thémines has a similar message, except that it is told from the viewpoint of the deserter, not of the deserted one. Here, each party in the triangle, Catherine de Médicis, who demands Chartres' complete loyalty to her, Chartres himself and his mistress, Mme de Thémines, play an elaborate game of subterfuge with one another until nobody is sure what is the disguise and what the truth. For the queen this ends in fury, as Chartres' infidelity comes home to her, for Mme de Thémines in the pain of thinking she has lost her lover and for Chartres in the humiliation of losing both his mistresses. Our sympathy however goes only to Mme de Thémines since she is the only one who is really hurt by this circle of intrigue. Both the queen and Chartres are entirely selfish products of this kind of society, who recognize and take advantage of the general atmosphere of duplicity—the queen by having Chartres spied on, and Chartres through his treachery and the facility with which he shifts his affections as prudence demands.

Mme de Lafayette sees those people who are profoundly and tragically affected by this cynical immorality as exceptional. Most men can adapt themselves to any kind of life, however futile and degrading—indeed it is they who in the first place created the routines of this life and through whom its dangers will be felt. Nemours is not just the symbolic lover, the instrument through which the tragic fatality of love will work itself out within the Princesse's heart, as Hippolyte is for Phèdre. Mme de Lafayette conceived of this fatality in practical, localized terms as it affected two individuals through the agency of another. For her as for her heroine, Nemours is the supreme product of seventeenth-century Court life. Beneath his perfect good looks and charming manners, beneath his wit and his popularity, he gradually emerges by small touches as conceited and superficial. And at the same time as he slowly reveals himself to us, the Princesse too becomes more aware of his true nature. At first, during the letter episode, she sees him only as unfortunately influenced by the immoral atmosphere in which he lives and not in any way tainted himself, but then as his indiscretions pile up, as he retells the story of her confession which he accidentally overheard, as he finally tries one night to enter her chamber, she cannot but admit that the fault lies also in his own character. Ironically, the Princesse's lucidity does not prevent her love from growing in intensity, although it is partly this lucidity as to the unworthiness of the object of her passion which eventually helps her to save herself, or so she thinks, before it is too late. The Princesse's final flight from her lover is as much a comment on seventeenth-century Court life, as characterized by Nemours, as a general statement on the strength or weakness of men everywhere.

Let us now study in more detail the tragic working out of the fatality of love in the Princesse de Clèves and her husband, their dignity and idealism, their attempts, however humble and futile, to resist their destiny and their inevitable collapse under the physical reality of emotion. The Princesse arrives at the Court, inexperienced and protected only by the careful education given her by her mother. She soon marries the Prince de Clèves, who adores her and for whom she feels nothing. Mme de Lafayette, by some chronological juggling, has engineered Nemours' absence when the Princesse first arrived and was married, and now makes all the Court ring with praises of his charm and wit. The Princesse's curiosity is fatally aroused by the time of the ball at which she first meets him and where they dance together without knowing each other's identities. The scene is full of foreboding; all feel the hand of a preordained fate which must work itself out:

> Quand ils commencèrent à danser, il s'éleva dans la salle un murmure de louanges. Le roi et les reines se souvinrent qu'ils ne s'étaient jamais vus, et trouvèrent quelque chose de singulier de les voir danser ensemble sans se connaître.[13]

And again

> il (the duc de Guise) ne put s'empêcher de lui dire que M. de Nemours était bien heureux de commencer à être connu d'elle par une aventure qui avait quelque chose de galant et d'extraordinaire.[14]

Is it going too far to see in this dance the seventeenth century's equivalent to the *Tristan's* magic potion? Their love is thus born at a royal social occasion, and all its manifestations will similarly adapt themselves to the routine of Court life—or rather Nemours and even once the Princesse will deliberately use this routine, so that for others the appearances of distance are maintained and the truth of their passion is revealed only to the other. For the Princesse, the occasion of the ball given by the Maréchal de Saint André serves to make her and perhaps Nemours too aware of her love by her disinclination to go in Nemours' absence; he several times takes advantage of a customary social call, or of his meetings with the Princesse as they attend on the dauphin's queen, of whom they are both favourites, to hint at his love for her. In this central psychological action we find the same gulf between the mask and the reality as we found in the subordinate stories. The difference here however lies in the Princesse's near-incapacity to preserve the mask except by fleeing from danger, and in her distress at the very necessity for a mask. Her need to keep a constant identity is great, but her emotions are too strong for her: the primitive fatality of love is gradually gaining complete power over her.

Why is it that she cannot like all the rest, like Nemours himself, like the Princesse de Montpensier, give in to it and allow it to work itself out unimpeded by her? Why is it that at every crisis, on every occasion when the Princesse has offered, even in spite of herself, a grain of hope to the man she loves, she is immediately horrified by her action? It is not because of the tainting of any hypothetical purity, but rather because of the dreadful feeling of insecurity that it gives her. Through it, she is not only losing control of her behaviour and her emotions, but is also estranging herself from her one protector, from the one man who can help her to maintain her integrity amid the chaos of egoism and weakness in which she lives. What strikes her most powerfully each time is that if the Prince de Clèves knew all the truth about her actions he would inevitably lose confidence in her and what she suffers from as much as anything is the need to lie to him, however pure her motives may be. Although she does not love him, she knows that without his esteem and his trust she in her weakness is lost. These are her thoughts immediately after her mother's death:

> Elle se trouvait malheureuse d'être abandonnée à elle-même, dans un temps où elle était si peu maîtresse de ses sentiments et où elle eût tant souhaité d'avoir quelqu'un qui pût la plaindre et lui donner de la force. La manière dont M. de Clèves en usait pour elle lui faisait souhaiter plus fortement que jamais de ne manquer à rien de ce qu'elle lui devait. Elle lui témoignait aussi plus d'amitié et plus de tendresse qu'elle n'avait encore fait; elle ne voulait point qu'il la quittât, et il lui semblait qu'à force de s'attacher à lui, il la défendait contre M. de Nemours.[15]

Similarly, the Prince seeks frankness and loyalty in his relationship with his wife and it is only when he feels this confidence in her, when his ideal of her is not tarnished, that he too is relatively strong and happy. The confession scene, then, when the husband and wife are closest together, when their trust in each other is at its strongest, is bound to be the climax of the novel. Let us trace the stages by which the Princesse gradually brings herself to the act of confession, and then the downward path to destruction which they both take after it, like Alphonse and Bélasire in similar circumstances. In spite of all their efforts, they cannot escape the basic selfishness of love.

The resistance of the Princesse has its seeds in the education her mother gave her during her youth, spent secluded in the country. Besides warning her daughter of the dangers of Court society, Mme de Chartres instils into her more positive ideals which will haunt the Princesse throughout her life: she wants "tranquillité" for her daughter, the opposite of the "agitation" of the Court, and tells her that the only way to achieve it is through domestic happiness, and she speaks also of the content-ment that comes of a good reputation.

> et elle lui faisait voir, d'un autre côté, quelle tranquillité suivait la vie
> d'une honnête femme, et combien la vertu donnait d'éclat et d'éléva-
> tion à une personne qui avait de la beauté et de la naissance; mais
> elle lui faisait voir aussi combien il était difficile de conserver cette
> vertu, que par une extrême défiance de soi-même et par un grand
> soin de s'attacher à ce qui seul peut faire le bonheur d'une femme,
> qui est d'aimer son mari et d'en être aimée.[16]

The Princesse is already conditioned to think of her husband as
her main source of strength. Yet just as Mme de Chartres' advice
contains the seeds of one half of the novel's action, so her
behaviour when they arrive at the Court makes the other half
inevitable, for, in spite of her principles, she is not afraid to marry
her daughter to a man she does not love. How full of foreboding
is the short sentence describing this:

> elle (Mme de Chartres) reçut la proposition qu'on lui faisait et elle
> ne craignit point de donner à sa fille un mari qu'elle ne pût aimer en
> lui donnant le Prince de Clèves.[17]

Moreover, Mme de Chartres has trained her daughter to have
complete confidence in her, to depend on her utterly—hence the
Princesse's initial blindness and naïveté, which allow her at first
to welcome her love without recognizing its dangers or even its
name (the Princesse de Montpensier who had already been in love
had no such excuse), hence too that feeling of utter abandonment
when her mother dies, which leads to her gradual turning towards
her husband as a second protector.

The section of the novel between the death of Mme de Chartres
after she has made her daughter admit that she is in love with
Nemours, and the Princesse's confession to her husband contains
a powerful description of the growth of the heroine's passion.
The psychological truth and complexity of these passages account
for much of Mme de Lafayette's greatness; in a parallel and yet
contradictory progression, the Princesse gains a growing lucidity
and despair about her love and yet submits more and more
completely to it. She alternates between moments of rational
strength and moments of blind weakness which themselves contain their own kind of suffering, but, as the moments of strength
invariably only come after the moments of weakness, she cannot
help herself and her tortured monologues lead only to a desire
for flight. Not one of them ends in a solution or even in a positive
conclusion; like Phèdre and Hermione and unlike Pauline, the
Princesse acts instinctively under the stress of emotion (as in the

letter scene with Nemours), or allows her desires to delude her
into thinking that she is acting for the best (as when she lets her
lover take her portrait), and only later recoils in horror at her
weakness. So it is that she becomes increasingly helpless in the
face of her passion; however great the efforts she makes to control
her actions, all her plans break down in the presence of Nemours.

Gradually, however, after her mother's death, the thought of
her husband and guilt at his blind esteem of her, preoccupy her
more and more. She is much struck by his words on sincerity
when he tells her of Mme de Tournon's game of duplicity and
describes the qualities he would demand of the woman he loved:

> car la sincérité me touche d'une telle sorte que je crois que si ma
> maîtresse, et même ma femme, m'avouait que quelqu'un lui plût,
> j'en serais affligé sans en être aigri.[18]

The Princesse is shamed by his trust in her, and after this it is her
knowledge of this trust which helps her to resist her love for
Nemours, as much as the more positive ideal of her own dignity:

> Ce que M. de Clèves lui avait dit sur la sincérité, en parlant de Mme
> de Tournon, lui revint dans l'esprit; il lui sembla qu'elle lui devait
> avouer l'inclination qu'elle avait pour M. de Nemours. Cette pensée
> l'occupa longtemps; ensuite elle fut étonnée de l'avoir eue.[19]

Her greatest weakness, the scene spent with Nemours composing
the letter, she countenances because her husband is also present,
although of course he knows nothing of the special relationship
between them.

> La présence de son mari et les intérêts du vidame de Chartres la
> rassuraient en quelque sorte sur ses scrupules. Elle ne sentait que le
> plaisir de voir M. de Nemours, elle en avait une joie pure et sans
> mélange qu'elle n'avait jamais sentie.[20]

The confession is the climax of the Princesse's heroic resistance.
She herself sees it as the highest mark of trust that a wife can give
her husband:

> Songez que, pour faire ce que je fais, il faut avoir plus d'amitié et
> plus d'estime pour un mari que l'on n'en a jamais eu.[21]

Her husband agrees, at least at first, and the two are closely and
movingly united in their suffering. For both there is something
higher than alternatives of joy or pain—there is that nobility of
performing one's duty to which only exceptional people can

attain. Neither thinks of suffering, for each is impressed only by the ideal image the other has of him.

In the Princesse's conscious thoughts then, the ideal of sincerity to her husband does more than anything to keep her away from Nemours. And yet, we may wonder sometimes if Mme de Lafayette is not even more pessimistic about human nature than we thought, if she does not regard even this positive force of conscience in her heroine as really her final weakness. Is her heroine not shifting a responsibility that has become too big for her? The thought of confessing to her husband had come to her before as the only relief when she was desperate in her isolation:

> Quels retours ne fit-elle point sur elle-même! quelles réflexions sur les conseils que sa mère lui avait donnés! Combien se repentit-elle de ne s'être pas opiniâtrée à se séparer du commerce du monde, malgré M. de Clèves, ou de n'avoir pas suivi la pensée qu'elle avait eue de lui avouer l'inclination qu'elle avait pour M. de Nemours.[22]

Now she actually admits her love, not as the result of a deliberate decision—indeed afterwards she is horrified at her action—but because her husband has placed her in a situation where she no longer knows what to say:

> Mme de Clèves ne répondit point; et son silence achevant de confirmer son mari dans ce qu'il avait pensé:
> «Vous ne me dites rien, reprit-il, et c'est me dire que je ne me trompe pas.»[23]

Only now, when she can evade him no more, does she at last tell the truth. Man is so tainted, says Mme de Lafayette, that even in those rare moments when he appears to be acting most nobly, who knows what unconscious selfish urges are behind his behaviour?

Be it the Princesse's greatest strength or her greatest weakness, the confession is anyway the climax of the work, the moment when the couple come closest together, and after it the centre of interest seems to shift slightly from the Princesse to her husband. Before, the drama was hers alone; now he is involved, and she feels herself to some extent less responsible. He is now almost as interesting a character as his wife. All the second half of the novel until the Prince's death shows us the utter failure of the Princesse's idealism, of her efforts to combat the fatality of love through the mutual support of a noble, honest relationship, for in the end neither husband nor wife has the strength to give this support.

Both gradually succumb to their respective obsessions, which drive them to think only of themselves. For the Princesse, after her initial horror at what she has done, the fact that her husband knows of her guilty love gives her a momentary calmness that she has not felt before, a calmness due probably, although again Mme de Lafayette does not make it clear, to a feeling of having transferred her responsibility, and to a sense of a duty performed. She leaves the direction of her conduct entirely to her husband and her trust in him makes her feel strong. Then Mme de Lafayette shows how this temporary calmness is gradually destroyed: firstly, as we shall see, through the failure of her husband to continue his confidence in her, which leaves her again with nothing to give her support; and secondly perhaps, although again Mme de Lafayette only implies the Princesse's motives, through her false sense of virtue at having confessed, as she becomes yet more absorbed by her passion. The confession has in the end only marked a stage on her downward path. She is now most preoccupied by emotions born exclusively of her love, by jealousy or disappointment at Nemours' conduct.

Underlying her main conflict is a second one, in which the bulwark against her love is not now her purity in her own eyes and those of her husband, but a growing disillusionment in Nemours' quality as a lover, and this conflict gains more and more in importance up to the end of the novel:

> . . . mais quelque douleur dont elle se trouvât accablée, elle sentait bien qu'elle aurait eu la force de les supporter si elle avait été satisfaite de M. de Nemours.[24]

At this point we are still not clear as to which feeling has priority. Mme de Lafayette describes only the Princesse's mental state at one moment, without accounting for its inconsistency with her behaviour at another moment. She still has the strength for her usual flight back to the country, but it is in the country that her greatest, final weakness occurs—the weakness which will precipitate the whole catastrophe. As she looks at the picture of Nemours in the solitude of her chamber, she consciously allows herself to dwell on her love for him and on his virtues; she is softened and absorbed, as she would never have let herself be in the earlier part of the book:

> . . . elle s'assit et se mit à regarder ce portrait avec une attention et une rêverie que la passion seule peut donner.[25]

She even subconsciously wants to go out and look for him when she thinks she recognizes him at the door:

> Peut-être souhaitait-elle, autant qu'elle le craignait, d'y trouver M. de Nemours. . . . Elle fut longtemps à se résoudre à sortir d'un lieu dont elle pensait que ce prince était peut-être si proche.[26]

The growing speed with which, in spite of occasional moments of strength, the Princesse weakens after the apparent heroism of her confession, is paralleled by the Prince's growing mistrust and then jealousy. It is indeed in the beginning the fault of the Princesse that suspicion should enter his mind at all, since no sooner has she made her confession than she diminishes its force by half, by refusing to reveal the name of the man she loves. The admission that she loves someone else is the pinnacle of her achievement which she cannot attain a second time. The Prince is of course obsessed by the identity of his wife's lover and his curiosity causes an immediate retraction of his trust in the Princesse, although at that time he also immediately regrets it. Then it is this obsession which causes his first deliberate lie to his wife as he tricks her into revealing that it is Nemours she loves. After this there can no longer be complete confidence between them. Their estrangement grows and grows, nourished especially by the lack of explanation either can find, except in suspicion of the other, for the fact that the story of the confession has been spread abroad. This scene shows the gulf between this husband and wife, who tried so hard to remain loyal against the forces which separated them. Here the tragic failure of the confession as a solution is most apparent and in this failure is included the failure of all efforts to combat the irresistible power of love. Neither has anything to live by since neither believes in the other any more:

> Il ne savait plus que penser de sa femme; il ne voyait plus quelle conduite il lui devait faire prendre, ni comment il se devait conduire lui-même; et il ne trouvait de tous côtés que des précipices et des abîmes.[27]

and later the Prince blames his wife for having expected so much of him as to have revealed to him her passion for another. Like Alphonse, beneath the force of jealousy, he has become as weak and selfish as a Guise or a Nemours. Events now move fast to their conclusion as the Prince, blinded, has Nemours followed and immediately reads into his spy's words more than was intended.

François Clouet

Henri II, roi de France

(Photographie Giraudon)

François Clouet

Jacques de Savoie, duc de Nemours

The shock of the certain knowledge of his wife's infidelity kills him and, tragically, he can only half believe her when she earnestly affirms her innocence at his deathbed. "Je ne sais, lui dit-il, si je me dois laisser aller à vous croire".[28]

It is clear from what has preceded that the figure of the husband is at times as important as that of his unfaithful wife, and that he is as attractive a character. His conflict in the second half even often supplants hers, as he tries to remain reasonable and loyal, to find strength against his tragic destiny. In this detailed and sympathetic portrayal of the husband, usually the figure of fun, lies much of Mme de Lafayette's originality. No one had previously depicted such a character with her humanity and realism, and the fact that his tragedy balances that of the Princesse makes the novel doubly moving.

The last scenes, in which the Princesse makes her final decision not to marry Nemours, are perhaps the most powerful of the novel, as Mme de Lafayette's idealism and her pessimism join in a conclusion about which critics will always argue. A more normal and probably credible ending would have been for the Princesse eventually to marry Nemours, since it is to this that her emotions have been leading her since her confession to her husband: Racine's characters, completely dominated by the fatality of their passion, would not have hesitated, once all obstacles, even moral obstacles, had been removed. Their belief in love never wavers. The Princesse's behaviour on the other hand now exhibits an almost Cornelian heroism. A careful study of the evolution of her motives will however show how guarded Mme de Lafayette still remains in her affirmations, how all is done to make the final renunciation appear a negative, empty and futile act, reflecting man's weakness as much as his strength.

Immediately after her husband's death, the Princesse is calm and strong in her respect for his memory. She feels she has come through to a full and final lucidity about her desires and her duty, although even now Mme de Lafayette hints at her self-deception as she believes that she is mourning exclusively for her husband:

Elle sentait néanmoins une douleur vive de s'imaginer qu'il était cause de la mort de son mari, et elle se souvenait avec peine de la crainte que M. de Clèves lui avait témoignée en mourant qu'elle ne l'épousât; mais toutes ces douleurs se confondaient dans celle de la perte de son mari, et elle croyait n'en avoir point d'autre.[29]

Then her first sight of Nemours plunges her into a more acute conflict than she has ever experienced before. At this point it is still the memory of her husband which helps her most to resist her passion, as though now that he is no more than a name he provides a firm rock to which she may cling. Insensibly, however, her memory of him fades and is succeeded by a disillusionment in love, which makes her fear any involvement in life. She no longer believes Nemours' love to be either lasting or profound and she realizes that a passion such as she felt for him and her husband for her is exceptional. She knows now that the only place where she can find that "tranquillité" (now called "repos", since it comes only after all the torment of living) which she has always been seeking is in solitary retirement. We are left robbed of a belief even in that fatal power which has been the centre of the whole novel; we feel again that cynicism we felt when reading those early background descriptions of the Court, of which Nemours in the end is a typical product.

It seems to be during the vital scene with Nemours that the Princesse begins to think more of her "repos" than of her "devoir" in her fight to resist her love. The sight of Nemours has dimmed the brightness of her ideal image of her husband. She is now preoccupied much more by the character of Nemours himself as she has come fully to comprehend it. Now too the Princesse for the first and last time gives way to her love in the presence of her lover and the description of these moments is most moving. She herself ascribes this softening to the fact that she has already resolved never to see Nemours again, a decision which allows her thus to yield to her desires, be it ever so little. Yet a close study of the scene shows a complex, living alternation of the Princesse's emotions as, while reciting to Nemours all her reasons against their marriage, she weakens and looks at him with eyes full of love, asking him with the natural curiosity of a woman in love to tell her of all the circumstances of his passion for her, and even breaking out with invocations against her destiny. We can follow this alternation within a single speech, as Mme de Clèves takes pleasure in admitting her love to Nemours and then immediately removes any hope this might give him:

«Il est vrai,» lui dit-elle, «que je veux bien que vous le sachiez et que je trouve de la douceur à vous le dire. Je ne sais même si je ne vous le dis point plus pour l'amour de moi que pour l'amour de vous. Car enfin cet aveu n'aura point de suite et je suivrai les règles austères que mon devoir m'impose.»[30]

Is she not at this and various other moments on the point of yielding to him? Is she being sincere with herself and him when she gives as a reason for allowing herself to declare her love her conviction that the admission will lead to nothing further? Is she not really succumbing to her passion and trying desperately to convince herself that she is not? Even at the end of the scene she has not the strength finally to dismiss Nemours but says he must trust to time to effect a change in his favour:

Enfin, pour se donner quelque calme, elle pensa qu'il n'était point encore nécessaire qu'elle se fît la violence de prendre des résolutions; la bienséance lui donnait un temps considérable à se déterminer.[31]

In the end it is never really she who makes the decision. It is made for her by force of circumstances, as she falls seriously ill and is thus gradually detached from the realities of the present by the passage of time and by her prolonged absence alone. All her efforts at sincerity with herself in these last scenes lead only to confusion as the reasons for and against her marriage seem to balance each other perfectly, leaving her as helpless as at the beginning of the novel. The outcome can only be provided by a sort of *deus ex machina*. Complete disillusionment in the validity of Court life is thus coupled with an equal disillusionment in the strength of any individual man to form his destiny; nothing is left except an empty retreat from life. No other seventeenth-century work is as pessimistic as this: the action is conducted on a purely human plane and man fails utterly on all counts.

We have talked much of Mme de Lafayette's reticence in making quite clear the Princesse's motives on various occasions, since the Princesse herself is not clear about them, and she is reticent too in making any final moral judgment on her heroine —as she has done explicitly for the Princesse de Montpensier and implicitly for Alphonse. It is possible that, with her training in the casuistry of love, she was here deliberately posing a knotty moral problem, intending it to be discussed, as indeed it was, in the *salons* of her friends. Was the Princesse right or not to resist her love? Her course seems to be the virtuous one but the sterility of her sacrifice at the end makes it doubtful. Was she right to confess to her husband? Was she morally responsible for her actions or is she the victim of a mysterious fatality? On none of these questions does Mme de Lafayette give us any answers; the ambiguity of the work, the variety of possible interpretations, is proven by some critics' condemnation of it as an immoral painting of the attractiveness of love.[32] Although Mme de Lafayette certainly did not intend it as this, it is again possible that she was unconsciously satisfying her own frustrations in the sympathetic portrayal of the violent passion between Nemours and the Princesse. Is it not indeed part of *La Princesse de Clèves'* greatness that it will haunt us for ever with its questions unsolved?

La Comtesse de Tende was found among Mme de Lafayette's papers and only published after her death in 1724. The date of its composition thus remains in doubt. Some critics see in it an early sketch of *La Princesse de Clèves*;[33] others a late reply by Mme de Lafayette to criticisms of her major work. The second hypothesis seems the more likely one, largely because of the differences in style between this brief *nouvelle* and Mme de Lafayette's other fictional works, and its similarities with her *Mémoires de la Cour de France*, of 1688–90. Both these later works are written in brief, cynical statements of fact unlike the long subtle periods of *La Princesse de Clèves*. By this time, Mme de Lafayette seems to have lost all her idealism: *La Comtesse de Tende* shows us her disillusionment in man at its most terse and unqualified. None of the characters have any of the pretentions to virtue of even a Chabannes, an Alphonse or a Consalve: they are ordinarily weak men and women, acting as is natural to them in the circumstances in which they are placed. Perhaps the author is here writing for those people who had criticized as unconvincing the heroism of the Princesse's behaviour. Yet no one, not even the husband who acts with generosity when his wife's infidelity is finally revealed to him, is presented antipathetically. Mme de Lafayette describes her characters' actions simply as facts and refrains from those moral comments which do occasionally appear in *La Princesse de Montpensier* or in *La Princesse de Clèves*. Here too the background of Court life is much less important than it has been in the other works: the brevity of the tale forces the author to concentrate on her main figures and especially on the Comtesse herself, and so to give us a less localized statement than we find in her great masterpiece. The fatality to which man's wretchedness inevitably makes him succumb, works less through the particular conventions of seventeenth-century Court life and more through universal human traits—through the characters' innate selfishness and vanity.

The plot of the tale is very similar to that of *La Princesse de Montpensier, La Princesse de Clèves* and the *Histoire d'Henriette d'Angleterre*: it again deals with a married woman in love with another man. Mme de Lafayette is obviously preoccupied with this one theme and interested in the different ways in which it may be treated. Here, the heroine falls in love immediately and is from then on, like Racine's characters, tortured almost entirely by those emotions which are born of love alone—by her remorse on behalf of the friend whom her lover has married, by her jealousy of this same friend, by her fear of her husband and by the shame of her position. The quick switches in her state of mind are described with an extreme and unadorned terseness:

> La Princesse de Navarre (the Comtesse's friend) lui faisait tous les jours confidence d'une jalousie dont elle était la cause; cette jalousie la pénétrait de remords et quand la Princesse de Navarre était contente de son mari, elle-même était pénétrée de jalousie à son tour.[34]

Mme de Lafayette takes pains to explain the Comtesse's immediate weakness by giving a brief, realistic sketch of her temperament at the beginning of the tale; she is very young, impetuous, half Italian and flattered by her lover's attentions. She is thus very unlike the Princesse de Clèves, the product of so austere an upbringing, and even unlike the Princesse de Montpensier, whose early unsatisfied love for Guise had given her some lucidity and a certain maturity. Everything is against her, for, besides her superficial temperament, her husband at least at first is indifferent, fickle and selfish.

The conduct of the love-affair rests on the same basis of deceit and subterfuge as we have seen described in Mme de Lafayette's other works, although the setting is always private rather than public—there are no social gatherings except off-stage. Since the reality of her emotions is beyond her control, the Comtesse can only aim to keep up appearances in the eyes of her husband. Several scenes are built up entirely on the contrast between the truth and the disguise with which the lovers attempt to hide it— as on the occasion when the husband discovers his wife's lover at her feet, or in the various confidences which the Princesse de Navarre imparts to her friend not knowing that she is her successful rival. Such duality however cannot last: the tension will break, just as it did for the Princesse de Clèves when she confessed to her husband, and the Comtesse de Tende too will be forced to confess. Mme de Lafayette's intention in writing a second confession must have been to point out by contrast the exceptional heroism of the first confession by the Princesse de Clèves, not, as a few critics have suggested, to make the first one seem more credible by describing a second. For everything combines here to force the heroine to admit her love to her husband; the emotional reality has finally broken through the disguise when the Comtesse becomes pregnant, and it is clear that she can hide the truth no longer. Her lover dies, so that no help will come to her from him; her confession is presented not as a voluntary appeal to her husband as to a protector, but rather as a kind of deal with God, that she may escape hell by admitting her sins before dying: "n'ayant plus que de l'horreur pour sa vie, elle se résolut de la perdre d'une manière qui ne lui ôtât pas l'espérance de l'autre".[35] We are indeed far from the gratuitous idealism of the Princesse de Clèves.

La Comtesse de Tende seems then to be less attached to Mme de Lafayette's environment and to her own views on man's behaviour in it. Its factual concision and emphasis on realistic psychology give it perhaps a modernity that Mme de Lafayette's other works have not, although they deprive it of the originality which gives *La Princesse de Clèves* and parts of *Zaïde* their strength.

NOTES TO PART II, CHAPTER 2

[1] *La Princesse de Montpensier* (ed. *Romans et Nouvelles de Madame de Lafayette* by Émile Magne, Classiques Garnier), p. 33.

[2] *Op. cit.*, p. 9.

[3] *Op. cit.*, p. 30.

[4] *Histoire d'Henriette d'Angleterre* (in *Mémoires de Madame de Lafayette, les meilleurs Auteurs classiques*, Flammarion), p. 183.

[5] *Op. cit.*, p. 217.

[6] *Op. cit.*, p. 247.

[7] in *Segraisiana*: a collection of Segrais' sayings, the accuracy of which cannot be proved.

[8] *Zaïde* (ed. *Romans et Nouvelles de Madame de Lafayette* by Émile Magne, Classiques Garnier), p. 65.

[9] *Op. cit.*, p. 106.

[10] *La Princesse de Clèves* (Harrap, 1970), p. 87.

[11] *Correspondance* (ed. by André Beaunier), Vol. II, letter 221.

[12] *La Princesse de Clèves*, pp. 11, 12.

[13] *Op. cit.*, p. 20.

[14] *Op. cit.*, p. 21.

[15] *Op. cit.*, pp. 35–36.

[16] *Op. cit.*, p. 7.

[17] *Op. cit.*, p. 16.

[18] *Op. cit.*, p. 41.

[19] *Op. cit.*, p. 59.

[20] *Op. cit.*, p. 81.

[21] *Op. cit.*, p. 87.

[22] *Op. cit.*, p. 66.

[23] *Op. cit.*, p. 86.

[24] *Op. cit.*, p. 104.

[25] *Op. cit.*, p. 118.

[26] *Op. cit.*, p. 119.

[27] *Op. cit.*, p. 102.

[28] *Op. cit.*, p. 127.

[29] *Op. cit.*, p. 129.

[30] *Op. cit.*, p. 135.

[31] *Op. cit.*, p. 141.

[32] see *Madame de Lafayette par elle-même* by Bernard Pingaud (*Les Écrivains de Toujours*), p. 106.

[33] notably André Beaunier in *L'amie de La Rochefoucauld*, p. 44.

[34] *La Comtesse de Tende* (ed. *Romans et Nouvelles de Madame de Lafayette* by Émile Magne, Classiques Garnier), p. 406.

[35] *Op. cit.*, p. 409.

3. TECHNIQUE OF PSYCHOLOGICAL ANALYSIS

Character in medieval romance was conceived from two different points of view. On the one hand, it was used as a consistent illustration of an ideal way of life, even a philosophy—thus Lancelot and Guinevere in Chrétien de Troyes' *Lancelot* and Tristan in Thomas' version of the story. Or else, often within the same work, characters were only interesting for what they did, not for what they thought and felt. Thus readers of romance sought either a hyperbolical poetic utopia or exciting, romantic adventure, but never life as they knew it.

The literary discoveries and new ways of thinking introduced by the Renaissance altered the nature of the novel, by imparting to people a consciousness of themselves as individuals, and giving them a curiosity for different kinds of behaviour. These new interests sometimes produced generalizations on human nature, spiritual meditation such as we find in the Platonic poems of Scève or Héroët, but they led also to attempts at psychological realism, as writers studied the history and fiction of Greece, Rome and Italy rather than their philosophers. We find Brantôme, for example, preoccupied by people as individuals and training himself to discover their basic nature from details of appearance and behaviour. Then Montaigne was the first to become absorbed by a study of his own personality as distinct from anyone else's. Even when, in the third book of the *Essais*, he affirms that he is describing himself only as an example of humanity, this interest in the general is given rather as an excuse for and justification of his fascination by the particular than as the *raison d'être* of his whole work.

There are too, occasional examples of a concern for individual psychology in the sixteenth-century novel, especially in the work of Hélisenne de Crenne, of which mention was made in another chapter. Indeed, no work could be more personal and particular than the *Angoisses Douloureuses*, which is nothing other than the lyrical and dramatic expression of one soul's lived experience. Because of its confessional nature, however, its psychological explorations are necessarily limited and we only really get to know the author herself as she recounts her conflicts and her despair: her lover's fickleness remains unmotivated and her husband's behaviour is brutish and shallow. We have not yet here the complexity of viewpoints of *La Princesse de Clèves*, with its dynamic interplay of several natures one with another.

Certain stories of the *Heptaméron* of Marguerite de Navarre are in fact more interesting from our point of view because of their central position in the tradition of novel-writing, and because of the double aim the author is pursuing, illustrative of two aspects of Renaissance humanism. Firstly, the conversations before and after the tales make it clear that they are meant to exemplify certain general attitudes to life, especially of course a Platonic view of love, and in this they simply give more serious philosophical pretentions to the medieval, poetic notion of *amour courtois*. The story of Floride and Amadour illustrates the case of a woman in love who nevertheless remains virtuous and Floride stays true to type all the way through. She is described in the conventional clichés of pure love with only rare realistic touches, and her final self-disfigurement in the interests of this love is given as the logical if heroic conclusion of her Platonism. Secondly, however, Marguerite de Navarre insists much in her Prologue on the truth of her tales as records of living cases (some have seen in *Floride et Amadour* the story of Marguerite herself and Bonnivet), in which she is interested for the variety of individual psychology they present. Amadour, the less ideal of the two lovers, comes across in the author's descriptions as a more convincing human person, with the sly cunning and physical desires of any sixteenth-century French courtier. Dramatic play is made, as in *La Princesse de Clèves*, of the contrast between the mask of purity he must put on before his mistress, and the physical reality underneath. Some of his speeches express effectively a kind of crafty subterfuge in which the conventional clichés and ordered rhetoric are given a dramatic point by their falsity and are not simply vague generalizations on what is going on:

> Madame, j'ay toute ma vie désiré d'aymer une femme de bien; et pour ce que j'en ay trouvé si peu, j'ay bien voulu vous expérimenter, pour veoir si vous estiez, par vostre vertu, digne d'estre autant estimée qu'aymée. Ce que maintenant je sçay certainement, dont je loue Dieu, qui addresse mon cueur à aymer tant de perfection; vous suppliant me pardonner ceste folye et audatieuse entreprise, puis que vous voyez que la fin en tourne à vostre honneur et à mon grand contentement.[1]

This realistic psychology, which itself propels the action forward, is potentially very close to that of *La Princesse de Clèves*. Unfortunately it appears only in occasional passages and alternates with the vague, static, exaggerated descriptions which are intended to illustrate the author's philosophical theories. Marguerite de Navarre has not succeeded in fusing meaningfully the general and the particular; and as a result even her analysis of Amadour is superficial and summary compared with Mme de Lafayette's analysis of the Princesse de Clèves. The technique of the psychological novel is only just being born.

In *l'Astrée* there are passages which continue sixteenth-century individual realism, especially in the description of secondary characters, but the author has been influenced much more by the philosophical pretentions of his predecessors—thus unfortunately determining the kind of novel which will be fashionable for the next forty years. Here we see most clearly how at that time psychology was treated as a branch of philosophy, whose study was based on abstract reasoning, rather than, as later, as a kind of science, based on empirical observation. Most of the psychological interest is contained in the general discussions on the origins and nature of love, and many of the incidents are only excuses for these discussions, as the characters come for judgment before the courts of love. The language is abstract and stylized in the extreme:

> Il ne faut pas, belle Bergère, beaucoup de paroles pour maintenant résoudre vostre doute, mais de nécessité conclure que puisque les hommes se portent avec tant de violence au désir de leur contentement et la volonté n'ayant jamais que le bon pour son objet, ou pour le moins ce qui est estimé tel, il s'ensuit que puisque l'Amour n'est autre chose que ce désir, ainsi que vous mesme l'avez dit, celuy-là aime plus qui a plus ces objets de bonté devant les yeux . . .[2]

Yet the subtle refinement and genuine profundity of the debates show a great advance on the preceding century in theoretical psychological analysis. Unfortunately the same vocabulary is used to describe individuals and particular happenings, and here all it can do is to deaden the action and make the characters into types. People speak in conventional formulae; the monologues and dialogues are static and explanatory instead of being dramatically pointed; everyone seems unnaturally capable of detaching himself from his own predicament and generalizing individual experience:

«Et de qui parlez-vous,» dit Daphnide. «De vous, Madame,» luy répondis-je, «qui vous plaisez à faire mourir tout le monde d'Amour, adjoustant tant de beauté à celle que la Nature vous a donnée, qu'il ne faut point que personne espère de vous voir sans donner sa liberté pour rançon.»[3]

This stylized psychology inevitably brings with it an abundance of irrelevant, banal detail as the author tries to give substance to a stock type, and also pages of unconvincing lamentation on the strokes of destiny. It is all too easy to miss the basic drama of the situation, and although the action of some of the scenes is purely psychological, action and analysis remain separate in the narrative. These faults are indeed natural when we consider D'Urfé's aim in *l'Astrée*: like most other novelists of his time, he does not try to give a realistic record of certain happenings but to provide a philosophical dissertation, a manual of *savoir vivre* and a description of an ideal way of life.

There is little point in stopping long over the series of novels written after this until we reach Madeleine de Scudéry's *Clélie* (1656), and especially the short stories of Segrais (1657). *Cassandre* and *Le Grand Cyrus* simply adopt wholesale the conception of character and morality embodied in *l'Astrée* but give much more emphasis to exciting action. The conception is always the same, involving a pure, constant lover and a chaste and determined mistress, and the individual illustrations vary little; all the interest lies in the extraordinary exploits which these characters incidentally perform. There is little analysis of motives: emotions are revealed in brief, abstract or metaphorical clichés (which only had a meaningful substance in the genuinely philosophical discussions of *l'Astrée*), or in long rhetorical lamentations in which the characters often talk of themselves in the third person: "le plus infortuné des hommes".

Madeleine de Scudéry's *Clélie*, however, marks a return to that interest in psychological analysis which we found in *l'Astrée*, showing at the same time some advance on its forerunner, no doubt attributable to the training in sentimental observation and casuistry the author had acquired in her own and other *salons*. The analysis of *Clélie* is more specific and more alive than that of *l'Astrée*:

Et pour les Dames, s'il n'y avait point de passions au Monde, je ne sçay ce qu'elles feroient . . . car outre qu'elles seroient assurément esclaves, il est encore vray qu'elles seroient dans une oisiveté fort ennuyeuse, puisqu'elles ne sçauraient que faire de tout le temps qu'elles employent à se parer.[4]

We see this especially in the numerous portraits of contemporary personalities and even in the famous *Carte du Tendre*, which, though it could not be more systematized and more abstract, is the result of the author's study of seventeenth-century French society and not of the theoretical philosophy of Platonism. Psychology is becoming an art in its own right and one of the faults of the romance before *La Princesse de Clèves* is gradually disappearing as a result of a change in social habits and fashionable taste. *Clélie* still however contains a superfluity of static, uninteresting detail to describe each motive, each action. The author has not learnt the art of selection, cannot weld together psychology and plot, in fact has not yet realized that a novel is not an encyclopedia of sentimental description but the embodiment of sentiment in action.

Indeed it was only by the discarding of the very form of these long novels and by giving a new prestige to the *nouvelle* or short story that this change was brought about at all. So far in the seventeenth century, the *nouvelle* had had little importance as an art form, aiming in the work of Sorel and Scarron solely to entertain through exciting action—either romanesque or realistic. These tales have none of the psychological seriousness of the *Heptaméron*: the characters are summary types who remain the same all the way through, and their emotional reactions are banal in the extreme. The plots, however, did have the virtue of being fast-moving, and when Segrais gave back to the *nouvelle* a place in the literary field beside the novel, he was in fact creating a new genre which would combine the virtues of romance and short story but have none of their faults. Their subject, he said, should be serious and their plots psychological, but the aim of the *nouvelles* must remain the representation of reality in action, as in the lighter works of Sorel:

> Il me semble que c'est la différence qu'il y a entre le roman et la nouvelle que le roman écrit les choses comme la bienséance le veut et à la manière du poète; mais que la nouvelle doit un peu d'avantage tenir de l'histoire et s'attacher plutôt à donner les images des choses comme d'ordinaire nous les voyons arriver que comme notre imagination se les figure.[5]

Thus the modern novel, as we now know it, was born at least in theory; character must be dynamic and individual instead of general and systematized; the novel must depict primary reality, daily events as they affect a certain group of individuals, not illustrate philosophical truths.

Unfortunately none of the *nouvelles* which now began to appear with increasing rapidity—those by Segrais himself first, then those by Madame de Villedieu, Saint Réal, Préchac—fulfil the expectations aroused in us by the theories of the *Divertissements de La Princesse Aurélie*. It is true that the characters are varied, active and individual, that they are based increasingly on observation of contemporary behaviour and not on an ideal system of purity and constancy, and that psychology and action are more closely related. But we have only to compare Segrais' *Eugénie* (an obvious source of *La Princesse de Montpensier*) or Mme de Villedieu's *Les Désordres de L'Amour* (a possible source of *La Princesse de Clèves*) with Mme de Lafayette's masterpieces to see how miserably they fall below their potentialities. Even if the conception of character is original, as is certainly that of Eugénie, it is described in the vague, conventional clichés of preciosity, and the dialogue is rhetorical and long-winded:

> Tu vois sa bonne grâce, sa bonne mine et son adresse. Mais si je t'avais raconté le cours de sa passion et la suite de son amour, tu avouerais sans doute qu'il est encore sans comparaison plus aimable pour une maîtresse que pour tout le reste du monde dont il a si généralement acquis l'estime. Tu condamnerais mes rigueurs. Tu admirerais sa constance. Et tu conclurais sans doute, comme j'ai souvent fait moi-même, que je ne méritais point d'être servie par un si parfait chevalier ou qu'il méritait lui-même un plus heureux destin que celui qu'il a rencontré en passant inutilement sa jeunesse à m'aimer sans fruit et à se voir réduit au désespoir pour récompense.[6]

The characters may act in an interesting way but their motives are insufficiently analysed. Just as Astrée and Céladon had to fit into a certain Platonic pattern and their struggles be described in terms of general principles (often given a capital letter, Amour, Volonté etc.) so these less ideal personages conduct their conflicts in ordered antitheses which, while resembling those of *La Princesse de Clèves*, have not their concision and relevance. Ultimately, indeed, the characters' alternations and struggles are only intended to provide a varied and exciting intrigue, for although the plot is largely sentimental, the emphasis is always much more on action than on emotion.

This then, in brief, is the background against which Mme de Lafayette's art of psychological analysis should be seen. The theoretical discussions of the *Divertissements de la Princesse Aurélie* have made a great step forward in the conceptions and aims of the novel, but the actual works of Segrais and his contemporaries remain trite and superficial. It will be the task of Mme de Lafayette to combine the sentimental profundity of *l'Astrée* and *Clélie* with the dynamic realism of Mme de Villedieu and thus to exploit to their full dramatic potential the various techniques of psychological analysis of which so far writers had hardly been aware.

La Princesse de Montpensier was published in 1662, only five years after Segrais' *Divertissements*. The author obviously owes much to the theories of her friend, especially in her conception of the new genre, the *nouvelle*, with its interest in emotion and its near contemporary, realistic setting. In these spheres she carried out Segrais' precepts better than Segrais did himself. Yet in comparison with *La Princesse de Clèves*, Mme de Lafayette's technique of psychological analysis in *La Princesse de Montpensier* remains still too close to that of her lesser contemporaries. She has not yet learnt the art of relating in every detail the central psychological crisis to the action. The main plot is simple enough, involving only three characters, similar to those of *La Princesse de Clèves*— husband, wife and lover—but it is complicated firstly by a secondary character, Chabannes, whose prominence, as we have seen, is out of proportion to his rôle in the action, and secondly by an abundance of somewhat irrelevant detail on the loves of Anjou, Madame and so on. Mme de Lafayette here, like Segrais and Mme de Villedieu, wants to entertain her readers by the surprises of an intrigue describing not only the inner conflict of one or two individuals, but also the external interplay of interests and ambitions. The secondary plots of *La Princesse de Clèves* are relatively much briefer and more relevant, and the importance of the central action is hardly ever obscured. Thus too the tragic dénouement of *La Princesse de Montpensier* is the result of an external chance and not of psychological development, as the Princesse's husband happens to hear a noise on the night her lover comes to visit her. The dénouement of *La Princesse de Clèves* appears as the final and unavoidable consequence of the Prince's growing jealousy and his wife's growing weakness.

This disproportional emphasis on odd tricks of plot often implies a neglect of inner psychological analysis. Too often in this tale Mme de Lafayette is content with brief, conventional notations of motive which make Guise and the Prince especially uninteresting types. Chabannes, too, although potentially a very striking character, is occasionally described in trite, generalizing

clichés—this, for example, is how we are told of his love for
the Princesse:

> . . . il devint passionnément amoureux de cette princesse; et, quelque
> honte qu'il trouvât à se laisser surmonter, il fallut céder et l'aimer
> de la plus violente et de la plus sincère passion qui fût jamais.[7]

La Princesse de Montpensier has however in spite of its faults some
very good passages which, though different in kind from the
felicities of *La Princesse de Clèves,* nevertheless give us glimpses of
Mme de Lafayette's talent in psychological revelation. The main
method of analysis of conflict in *La Princesse de Clèves,* the inner
monologue, cannot be used here since the main character soon
loses control over her destiny and so ceases to question herself
on her emotions and duties. Mme de Lafayette reveals her
heroine's nature with telling truth in this tale through small,
objective details of behaviour which in spite of the abstract
rhetoric used to describe her feelings make of her a convincing
individual:

> . . . la princesse, qui n'avait dans la tête que le Duc de Guise et qui
> ne trouvait que lui seul digne de l'adorer, trouva si mauvais qu'un
> autre que lui osât penser à elle qu'elle maltraita bien plus le Comte
> de Chabannes à cette occasion qu'elle n'avait fait la première fois
> qu'il lui avait parlé de son amour.[8]

Mme de Lafayette shows in this tale too her gift for a dialogue
whose very restraint makes the characters' words more moving.
Chabannes comes much more alive in his speeches, where his
passion is disciplined by his hopelessness, than in the author's
objective descriptions. Mme de Lafayette has left behind her the
high-flown, expository monologues of her predecessors, whose
very prolixity made them both unconvincing and dull. Chabannes'
speeches are not of course realistic as is the dialogue in a modern
novel; they are deliberately arranged for a certain artistic as well
as dramatic purpose but this arrangement serves to make us feel
all the more intensely the passion beneath: it is a discipline
imposed not only by the author but by the character himself:

> Si après tout ce que je viens de vous représenter, Madame, votre
> passion est la plus forte et que vous désiriez voir le duc de Guise,
> que ma considération ne vous en empêche point, si celle de votre
> intérêt ne le fait pas. Je ne veux point priver d'une si grande satis-
> faction une personne que j'adore . . .[9]

La Princesse de Montpensier then is a mixed work, which in its methods of psychological analysis does not fundamentally differ from the mass of *nouvelles* written by minor authors after it. Yet it is worth study if only for the occasional moments of truth and poetry which it contains and which reveal the latent genius of its author.

The faults of *La Princesse de Montpensier* do not reappear in *La Comtesse de Tende*, written most probably at the end of Mme de Lafayette's literary career, and a comparison between the two *nouvelles*, which because of their brevity are more alike in technique than either is like the longer *Princesse de Clèves*, shows the progress made by Mme de Lafayette in telling a story with the utmost effect in the minimum of space. *La Comtesse de Tende* contains very little description of external intrigue: the reader's interest is concentrated almost entirely on the Comtesse, her husband and her lover, with the lover's wife remaining within the limits of her minor rôle as Chabannes does not. The action is psychologically determined throughout and the final catastrophe is the logical outcome of the weakness of the heroine. Mme de Lafayette's analysis of character, although as brief or even briefer than in *La Princesse de Montpensier*, is always relevant and dramatic; indeed it is often its very concision that makes it so, as in this description of the Princesse's fall:

> . . . elle vit l'abîme où elle se précipitait et elle résolut de l'éviter. Elle tint mal ses résolutions.[10]

Gone are the vague, monotonous abstractions that still occur in *La Princesse de Montpensier* and in their place come these precise, steely thrusts which by their complete detachment bring out all the more the pathetic destiny of these wretched human beings.

The brevity of *La Comtesse de Tende* however as well as making the analysis more pointed, necessarily limits it too. The characters are more passive and simpler than those of *La Princesse de Clèves* and thus a plot which depends on their moral conflicts is bound to be less varied and interesting. *La Comtesse de Tende* is a very good short story but must necessarily lack the complexity of a longer, work.

We can ignore most of *Zaïde* from the point of view of this chapter, since it does not aim to present us with dramatically convincing individuals but with poetically touching idealizations in the central plot concerning Zaïde and Consalve, with a general

cole des Clouet, vers 1540

François de Clèves, duc de Nevers

(Photographie Giraudon)

École des Clouet, vers *1549*

Catherine de Médicis, reine de France

picture of the Court in Consalve's story, or with complicated intrigue in the story of Alamir. Psychological description is static and rhetorical, not sufficiently closely linked to the action which progresses on its own by the twists and jerks of coincidence and fatality. It is only in the story of Alphonse that we see Mme de Lafayette's personal skill at analysis of character at work. Here as nowhere else, not even in *La Princesse de Clèves,* the action depends solely on the mental conflict of its hero. We watch Alphonse pass from a reluctant attraction to passion, and then from trust in his mistress to so violent and unmotivated a jealousy that she is forced to turn him away. We follow all the tortuous motives for the hero's actions, the struggle between his reason and his morbid suspicions, the contradictions between his conscious thoughts and his unconscious fears. Each stage is clearly and minutely described:

> Je ne lui donnais plus de repos; je ne pouvais plus lui témoigner ni passion ni tendresse: j'étais incapable de lui parler que du Comte de Lare; j'étais pourtant au désespoir de l'en faire souvenir et de remettre dans sa mémoire tout ce qu'il avait fait pour elle. Je résolvais de ne lui en plus parler, mais je trouvais toujours que j'avais oublié de me faire expliquer quelque circonstance et sitôt que j'avais commencé ce discours, c'était pour moi un labyrinthe; je n'en sortais plus et j'étais également désespéré de lui parler du Comte de Lare ou de ne lui en parler pas.[11]

One can go little further in the description of the moral agonies of an individual soul. Since the tale is told by the main character who tries little to read into the minds of those around him, its scope is necessarily more limited than that of *La Princesse de Clèves*. Bélasire, the mistress, however emerges convincingly, through her speeches and behaviour; she is a distinct individual reacting in a personal way to her lover's eccentricities, and not the puppet and foil she could so easily have become.

The tale is told almost entirely in the form of a long soliloquy, interspersed with snatches of direct and indirect dialogue. These occur especially at the beginning and consist largely of such witticisms on love as one might have heard in any seventeenth-century *salon* or seen reproduced with little dramatic relevance in a work like *Clélie*. Here, however, beneath the smooth surface, we are given hints of the catastrophe to come, just as the sophisticated conversations of *La Princesse de Clèves* have a double meaning for certain of the characters taking part:

J

Je lui dis que j'avais de la honte de ne la connaître pas encore; que néanmoins je serais bien aise de ne la pas connaître davantage; que je n'ignorais pas combien il était inutile de songer à lui plaire et combien il était difficile de se garantir de la désirer.[12]

In the second part of the tale the generalities disappear and their place is taken by Alphonse's soliloquies and Bélasire's reproaches to him. The hero and heroine are now fully involved in their personal destiny, but in spite of their involvement they are controlled enough to be able to express themselves in an ordered, rational way:

«Mais, Alphonse,» me dit-elle encore, «si je l'avais aimé, pourquoi ne l'aurais-je pas épousé?» «Parce que vous ne l'avez pas assez aimé, Madame,» lui répliquai-je, «et que la répugnance que vous aviez au mariage ne pouvait être surmontée par une inclination médiocre. Je sais bien que vous m'aimez davantage que vous n'avez aimé le Comte de Lare; mais pour peu que vous l'ayez aimé, tout mon bonheur est détruit . . .»[13]

Here again, as in the speeches of Chabannes, the philosophical classifications of earlier writers have left their mark: the philosophy itself has disappeared but the classifications remain: the method is disciplined, but not the whole.

In *La Princesse de Clèves*, Mme de Lafayette was at the height of her narrative powers; she had discarded much of what was meaningless or irrelevant in the works of her contemporaries and in her own earlier productions and the genre in which she chose to write limited her neither in length nor in range. She herself is the narrator of the tale, and it is long enough to give a profound, complex picture of several characters reacting one to another.

Whereas the novels and short stories of her predecessors were full of general epigrams on love and man, which are illustrated by the characters and plot, Mme de Lafayette, in spite of her undoubtedly close association with La Rochefoucauld, uses them here very sparingly. We find them occasionally in connection with secondary characters, the Vidame de Chartres, for example, the reine dauphine or Nemours, for the behaviour of these three is meant to be representative of seventeenth-century social life, and so it can be described in moral generalizations, sometimes ironic, sometimes not:

Les personnes galantes sont toujours bien aises qu'un prétexte leur donne lieu de parler à ceux qui les aiment.[14]

They are rarely employed to describe either the Prince or the Princesse de Clèves, for their behaviour is too exceptional to be able to be thus classified. When they do appear in reference to these two main characters, they describe only their weaknesses. Thus, with reference to the Princesse, Mme de Lafayette says:

> Les paroles les plus obscures d'un homme qui plaît donnent plus d'agitation que des déclarations ouvertes d'un homme qui ne plaît pas.[15]

The hero and heroine can illustrate almost nothing, since the effects of their behaviour contradict their motives and their motives themselves contradict each other. It is as though Mme de Lafayette, almost alone among seventeenth-century writers, is suspicious of any sort of universalization of the particular and trusts herself, at least in her masterpiece, to do no more than record the facts of primary reality. She avoids all the abstract generalizing of D'Urfé or Mlle de Scudéry and presents us with exactly what we now demand of a novel—the wretched ambiguity of reality.

Since Mme de Lafayette has taken as her heroes not typical examples of a certain view of life, but solidly located and subtly distinguished individuals, she can draw interest enough to fill a book from their immediate, inward struggles; nobody has met them in literature before, as they have met an Eugénie or even a Princesse de Montpensier. There is no need to supplement the action with irrelevant, static and detailed description of a banal state of mind or with complicated intrigue. Even the apparently digressive portraits of Court personalities at the beginning of the novel or the interpolated stories, although the space they occupy may be excessive, have a direct relevance to the heroine's moral condition. The central psychological theme itself is presented with the utmost bareness: all details of emotion, thought or behaviour are rigidly determined by it and have an effect on it. Each marks a stage in the characters' emotional development and we know no fact about them which has not a dramatic rôle to play. Thus we are told very little of the external appearance of the hero or heroine or of the rooms in which they live (except, as we shall see in another chapter, on ceremonial occasions); we can gather of their daily lives only what is relevant to their love and jealousy. What does the Princesse do at Coulommiers when she is not confessing to her husband, talking of love with Mme de Mercœur or looking with tender eyes at a portrait of Nemours? This selectiveness, this concentration is of course typical of all great seventeenth-century works of art, of the plays of Racine and Molière, of the polemic of Pascal or the *Fables* of La Fontaine, but we have not yet found it in the novel. So far this genre had been regarded as an inferior one and the author was allowed all the freedom he was denied in the higher genres. Even the fashion for brevity introduced by Segrais had not necessarily brought selectiveness with it: witness the overblown monologues of *Eugénie* or the romanesque complications of Mme de Villedieu's plots.

The central plot of *La Princesse de Clèves* is almost entirely psychological. The action in which we are interested and for which all the secondary episodes exist is produced by the changes and sufferings in the hearts of the Prince and Princesse de Clèves —even Nemours is important mainly in so far as he affects them and their relationship. We watch the heroine pass from utter ignorance of the ways of the world and of her own heart, through a gradual self-knowledge with which come growing pain and growing agitation, to reach in the end not a lucid serenity but rather a hopeless admission of defeat and a desire to abandon the world. Interwoven with this is the inner development of Mme de Clèves' husband, his passage from an overwhelming love to resignation, and then from a sad admiration of his wife to morbid jealousy and finally to death. From these emotional conflicts comes all the dramatic impact of the work. Yet they do not happen unprovoked: they are not completely self-fabricated as are those of Alphonse. It is the trivial events of Court life—and trivial they must be, so that interest in them for their own sakes may not decrease the effect of the main psychological action—which cause the swings from instinctive hope to lucid despair in the heroine, for it is they which cause the characters first to act and then to reflect on their actions. The Princesse's love is revealed to her on the occasion of the ball given by the Maréchal de Saint André; she unwittingly discloses it to Nemours during the scene of the *jeu de paume*, and at the painting of her portrait; her husband learns of the identity of her lover through his supposed selection to accompany Madame on her journey to Spain. Although *La Princesse de Clèves* is a purely psychological novel in a way that even *La Princesse de Montpensier* is not, yet the plot does include external action. In this way, indeed, we are given a more realistic and complete view of an inner conflict than we would otherwise have. For are not most inner conflicts, at least of normal people, brought on in the first place by external circumstances? Are not the Prince and Princesse de Clèves thus more typical than Alphonse or Constant's Adolphe? By including non-psychological action, and by making it at the same time as unimportant as possible for its own sake, Mme de Lafayette has written a more credible as well as a more complex novel.

We must now turn to Mme de Lafayette's art of narrative. How does she make a story interesting even though its localized realism does not demand our attention through its relevance to any philosophical or psychological system, and even though its concentration on a moral tragedy does not evoke the facile suspense of exciting, external incident? On some occasions, as we shall see, Mme de Lafayette employs devices similar to those used in the theatre—dialogue and spoken or unspoken soliloquy—and then we can see parallels between her narrative technique and the dramatic technique of Corneille or Racine. This is of course natural, since all three authors in order to sustain their public's interest depend solely on the exploration of the inner motives and reactions of individual characters. But the theatre, especially seventeenth-century classical theatre, is necessarily restricted in its methods of psychological analysis: character can only be revealed from two points of view, from that of the character himself and from that of other characters whose number must be limited; we can only be given a picture of the hero's past by a recapitulatory speech which must be brief and comprehensive. The novel on the other hand by the looseness of its form can show in detail the slow beginnings of a passion and can describe successively each stage leading up to the crisis. The novel also embraces every kind of analysis and can look on a moral dilemma from many different angles. It can show us the author's view as well as the views of the characters; it can, without artifice contrast the hero's conscious thoughts with his unconscious motives, what he reveals to others with what he hides within himself, and all this at many different times and places. The theatre could not do this without bursting its framework. So it is that we now accept that analysis of inner conflict can best be done in a novel, and use the term *psychological novel* but not *psychological play*. It is from this point of view, more than from any other, that Mme de Lafayette has written the first modern novel. She exploited as no other seventeenth-century novelist came near to exploiting all the rich dramatic potential of the many methods of psychological analysis which a novelist by definition can use.

The book opens with a series of static portraits, in which everyone is described in the most abstract and hyperbolical terms:

> . . . le chevalier de Guise . . . était un prince aimé de tout le monde, bien fait, plein d'esprit, plein d'adresse et d'une valeur célèbre par toute l'Europe . . .[16]

Such portraits have little to distinguish them from many found in other contemporary romances and short stories, and probably from those composed in a seventeenth century *salon*. Their meaningless exaggerations and their vagueness would never be to the taste of a modern public. Yet, while apparently following this convention, Mme de Lafayette discreetly slips into her portraits traits of an original realism, which show both her desire to locate her tale convincingly in its historical period and also her talent for picking out distinctive characteristics in people: "le Prince de Condé, dans un petit corps peu favorisé de la nature",[17] or of Nemours: "Il avait tant de douceur at tant de disposition à la galanterie qu'il ne pouvait refuser quelques soins à celles qui tâchaient de lui plaire".[18] We are next shown these portraits in action, when all the agitation and dissimulation beneath these too perfect, polished masks is uncovered. Right at the end of this section appears the portrait of Mlle de Chartres herself, as she then was, significantly different from the other portraits that have preceded it, for in it we learn nothing of her character at all. We are only told of her youthful beauty in the most conventional of terms:

> La blancheur de son teint et ses cheveux blonds lui donnaient un éclat que l'on n'a jamais vu qu'à elle; tous ses traits étaient réguliers, et son visage et sa personne étaient pleins de grâce et de charmes.[19]

and then of the education she has received from her mother. By this gap, Mme de Lafayette implies the emptiness of her as yet unformed mind, nourished only on the precepts of the person on whom she depends, and contrasts it with the sophisticated maturity of the others. No definitive portrait of the heroine can yet be given, since it is her moral formation that is to be the subject of the book.

In the first half of the work, character is revealed much more by external details of behaviour than it is later on, for Mme de Lafayette is here most concerned to build up the atmosphere of the Court into which the ignorant Princesse is plunged and which, through its representative, Nemours, is to have such a fatal effect on her. Thus, the secret intrigues of the great personalities are described in succinct but intricate detail, either directly by the author or else by one of the characters, Mme de Chartres or the *reine dauphine*, as they take it upon themselves to enlighten the heroine or as they become involved in the plot. Besides revealing the true nature of the king, Diane de Poitiers or the Vidame de Chartres, all this background description indirectly helps us to understand the changes in the state of mind of the innocent Princesse, whose curiosity is acutely aroused and who has at this point too little experience to guard herself against the dangers of knowledge. Then the characters of the people who are closest to the Princesse are more fully described, these too for the effect their opinions and actions will have on her. The *reine dauphine* and Nemours are particularly important in this respect and Mme de Lafayette reveals them, after the initial conventional portrait, almost entirely through their worldly, witty conversation and sophisticated reactions, just as they would have been revealed to the heroine herself.

«Comment!» reprit Mme la dauphine, «M. de Nemours ne veut pas que sa maîtresse aille au bal? J'avais bien cru que les maris pouvaient souhaiter que leurs femmes n'y allassent pas; mais, pour les amants, je n'avais jamais pensé qu'ils pussent être de ce sentiment.»

«M. de Nemours trouve,» répliqua le prince de Condé, «que le bal est ce qu'il y a de plus insupportable pour les amants, soit qu'ils soient aimés ou qu'ils ne le soient pas.»[20]

We hardly see them from the inside, for the author is not interested in their moral problems—the secret melancholy of the *reine dauphine* is only hinted at as she talks in confidence with Mme de Clèves.

The various emotions of the heroine too, at this point of the novel, are revealed as much by details of behaviour, as she reacts instinctively to some word or event, as by abstract description. For she herself is not yet at all aware of her states of mind and is quite incapable of controlling the immediate expression of her feelings. Shortly after her appearance at Court, she cannot help blushing modestly when she notices how hard her future husband is looking at her in the jeweller's shop; when he taxes her with her coldness she can only speak in the conventional clichés which her mother has taught her:

> . . . je ne sais ce que vous pouvez souhaiter au-delà de ce que je fais, et il me semble que la bienséance ne permet pas que j'en fasse davantage.[21]

After her marriage, her actions reveal her growing curiosity about Nemours and a powerful inclination to please him; she refuses instinctively to appear at the ball of the Maréchal de Saint André because Nemours will not be there, then cannot control her disappointment that he will not realize why she is not there. After this, the balance changes and these details of involuntary reaction become more important for the tortured self-analysis they provoke afterwards in the Princesse than for what they themselves reveal of her character. Indeed, all they ever show is her overwhelming love for Nemours, as it manifests itself differently on different occasions, and after the first quarter of the novel both she and the reader are fully aware of the strength of this love. When her face expresses all her apprehension as Nemours falls from his horse, when she cannot prevent bitterness from entering into her words and looks because she believes she has several successful rivals to his love, and when she becomes all gentleness as he clears himself of suspicion, on all these occasions her actions are followed by lengthy inner monologues. After the confession, the emphasis shifts again as the Princesse is forced repeatedly by her jealous husband to think and talk of her love, so gradually losing all the power to control it that she had so painfully acquired. Her ordeal lasts too long and she is beginning to yield. She flees again to Coulommiers, where the continuous solitude encourages her to let herself go and look with tender eyes on Nemours' portrait, play with ribbons of the colours that he wore at the tournament. Gone again are the tortured inner monologues and the Princesse, unable to master her passion, reveals herself to us spontaneously as she did at the birth of her love. Then her husband's death again changes the direction of her thoughts and only during her final interview with Nemours, in the isolation which two lovers feel when they are alone together, does she for the first time reveal her thoughts to him in her looks and words:

Madame de Clèves céda pour la première fois au penchant qu'elle avait pour M. de Nemours et, le regardant avec des yeux pleins de douceur et de charmes . . .[22]

and again

Il (Nemours) lui fit voir . . . la plus vive et la plus tendre passion dont un cœur ait jamais été touché. Celui de Mme de Clèves n'était pas insensible et, regardant ce prince avec des yeux un peu grossis par les larmes:
«Pourquoi faut-il,» s'écria-t-elle, «que je vous puisse accuser de la mort de M. de Clèves . . .»[23]

Most often in order to tell her story of mental conflict Mme de Lafayette gives her own straight description of the state of her characters' hearts, and these descriptions have a concision, a dramatic relevance and a profound truth that make them different in kind from their equivalent in *Zaïde* or any work by a contemporary novelist. As we have already seen in *La Comtesse de Tende*, Mme de Lafayette has a gift for the brief, exploratory remark. Here is how she describes two friends who are rivals for the Princesse's love:

Ils louèrent d'abord Mlle de Chartres sans se contraindre. Ils trouvèrent enfin qu'ils la louaient trop, et ils cessèrent l'un et l'autre de dire ce qu'ils en pensaient.[24]

We find many such concise, shrewd statements in connection with secondary characters especially, and so each one is made a convincing individual as well as part of a whole.

Nemours however although he is analysed at much greater length than anyone apart from the Prince and Princesse de Clèves, is described in rather banal terms, particularly in his rôle as the Princesse's lover. Here alone does the author employ those trite, lengthy, hyperbolic phrases which add so little in substance to *Zaïde* and so much in weight. She has obviously found it difficult to make his love interesting: for the purposes of the plot it must be deep, constant and respectful, and thus will have little to distinguish it from the love of a Céladon or a Consalve. In painting this aspect of Nemours' character Mme de Lafayette does not succeed in breaking through the veil of conventional, sentimental rhetoric, which has evolved through the centuries:

. . . il s'abandonna aux transports de son amour et son cœur en fut tellement pressé, qu'il fut contraint de laisser couler quelques larmes.[25]

Nemours also talks in grandiloquent yet colourless terms in his various lyrical soliloquies on his love for the Princesse and in his galant conversations with the *reine dauphine*. On these latter occasions, however, the artificial language of love is given a dramatic point and does not jar on the generally subtle, concise narrative as do the straight descriptive passages. For through his apparently exaggerated compliments and his wit Nemours is attacking his mistress's heart and she is reacting exactly as he intends she should:

> Pour moi, dit tout haut M. de Nemours, je suis l'homme du monde qui dois le moins y en avoir, . . . on m'a prédit . . . que je serais heureux par les bontés de la personne du monde pour qui j'aurais la plus violente et la plus respectueuse passion. Vous pouvez juger, Madame, si je dois croire aux prédictions.[26]

These conversations always have a relevance to the moral drama of the Princesse which makes their artificiality acceptable.

There are a few other occasions on which Mme de Lafayette fails to transcend her training in the romance tradition: in the letter written by Mme de Thémines, a typical though excellent piece of sentimental casuistry, or in Sancerre's expressions of anguish at the death of his mistress:

> Je n'ai jamais vu une douleur si profonde et si tendre; dès le moment qu'il me vit, il m'embrassa, fondant en larmes: «Je ne la verrai plus,» me dit-il, «je ne la verrai plus, elle est morte! Je n'en étais pas digne; mais je la suivrai bientôt.»[27]

Never however are either the Prince or the Princesse described in these banal terms, and it matters little to the impact of the work that the background against which they move should sometimes lack life and originality, since it is deliberately concerned with characters who can feel only superficially.

With the two main characters the author's analysis is always concrete and specific. The emotions of the Princesse are described in direct relation to a particular event and to a particular person, so that she always emerges clearly as an individual. Indeed, Mme de Lafayette takes the detailed precision of her analysis so far that we find it difficult to gain a general, consistent picture of the heroine at all. Her emotions and motives are noted according to their importance at any given moment and they may easily contradict what she was feeling a few pages before. In this way, Mme de Lafayette, without departing from her rôle as objective narrator of facts, suggests the chaos and indecision of the Princesse's mind as she favours first one course of action and then another—now desiring above all that Nemours should be a worthy object of her love and now thinking only of her duty to her husband regardless of whether Nemours is worthy or not. The author's narrative is simultaneous with the heroine's psychological waverings and Mme de Lafayette herself allows us no hint as to her own judgment of her heroine's dilemma and character. Moreover, the Princesse's feelings reveal inconsistencies not only between two different occasions but at one and the same time, and again the author does not always indicate which motive has priority. She is described on the one hand in terms of lucid self-criticism, and on the other in terms of subconscious, unacknowledged desires. This sort of self-deception is especially noticeable in the final part of the novel after the Prince's death, when her two levels of consciousness are shown to change places: Mme de Clèves begins by refusing to acknowledge the survival of her love for Nemours, then acknowledges it with no intention of giving in to it, and finally gives in to it completely and refuses to satisfy it precisely because she cares too much to risk changing it in any way. Nowhere does Mme de Lafayette pinpoint this switch in her heroine's motives; she states each priority as she comes to it and leaves the Princesse's indecisiveness to emerge on its own. So we have the impression of really living the Princesse's final days in the world with her and not of observing them from some remote, omniscient viewpoint. In describing her heroine in this way, in thus identifying with her, Mme de Lafayette is departing far from the seventeenth-century practice of classification and generalization, and even perhaps points forward to the modern technique of the subjective narrative.

Since the novel is mainly concerned with the Princesse's struggles and discoveries about herself, the author makes less use of the brief concise remark which is so revealing when used in connection with minor characters. At every turning-point of the action, Mme de Lafayette devotes one or two paragraphs to a concentrated, ordered summary of her heroine's psychological state as it has been affected by the crisis. And so the novel consists of a series of external incidents, each of which is followed by a passage of psychological analysis. The analysis must be most powerfully done, since on it depends all the interest of the work as a moral tragedy. In the first part of the novel, Mme de Lafayette describes her heroine as she, the narrator, sees her. She analyses her emotions, traces the thread linking one thought to another, ordering in this way the chaos of the Princesse's heart so that the reader obtains a balanced, clear-cut picture of all that she is feeling. Each phrase summarizes one of the numerous contradictory elements which make up the Princesse's dilemma:

> L'on ne peut exprimer la douleur qu'elle sentit de connaître, par ce que lui venait de dire sa mère, l'intérêt qu'elle prenait à M. de Nemours: elle n'avait encore osé se l'avouer à elle-même. Elle vit alors que les sentiments qu'elle avait pour lui étaient ceux que M. de Clèves lui avait tant demandés, . . . elle trouva combien il était honteux de les avoir pour un autre que pour un mari qui les méritait. Elle se sentit blessée et embarrassée de la crainte que M. de Nemours ne la voulût faire servir de prétexte à Mme la Dauphine, et cette pensée la détermina à conter à Mme de Chartres ce qu'elle ne lui avait point encore dit.[28]

Or sometimes two emotions are shown by their juxtaposition within one balanced, antithetical statement to contradict one another, again revealing the Princesse's helpless indecisiveness:

> Elle croyait devoir parler et croyait ne devoir rien dire. Le discours de M. de Nemours lui plaisait et l'offensait quasi également; elle y voyait la confirmation de tout ce que lui avait fait penser Mme la Dauphine; elle y trouvait quelque chose de galant et de respectueux, mais aussi quelque chose de hardi et de trop intelligible.[29]

These passages of analysis rarely if ever arrive at a solution or even at a conclusion since the Princesse herself can never decide on a definite course of action. Her conflicting desires, her love for Nemours and her wish to resist him, are equal in strength, with the result that she remains always in a state of deadlock. The antithesis is never resolved; no answer to the dilemma is ever reached:

> Cette pensée l'occupa longtemps; ensuite elle fut étonnée de l'avoir eue, elle y trouva de la folie, et retomba dans l'embarras de ne savoir quel parti prendre.[30]

As the action reaches its climax and as the Princesse's lucidity and powers of self-analysis grow, these summaries by the author of her psychological state become summaries by the character herself, which the author only introduces by the words: "elle se disait", or "elle pensait", or "elle se demandait". They become indirect inner monologues, more immediate and more dramatic. At moments of great stress, the Princesse even breaks out into

direct speech, but this happens rarely, probably because a spoken
soliloquy is always rather unconvincing. Even though the author
is now reproducing the actual words in which the character
frames her thoughts, we find the same clear organization that we
noticed before. Here indeed it is more significant as it has a
dramatic rôle to play. It is no longer a mere narrative technique,
imposed on her material by the author, but expresses the intense
effort made by the Princesse herself to discipline her emotion, and
this effort is a basic premise of the plot. The author's narrative
style becomes the language of the characters' thoughts. Here is
an example of an inner monologue by the Princesse, in which the
attempt at a symmetrical ordering of the parts makes all the more
tragic the impression of helplessness that emerges from the whole,
and from which the heroine can only escape in flight. She is
meditating on the intensity of the jealousy she felt for the woman
whom she supposed to have written to Nemours:

> Quoique les soupçons que lui avait donné cette lettre fussent effacés,
> ils ne laissèrent pas de lui ouvrir les yeux sur le hasard d'être trompée
> et de lui donner des impressions de défiance et de jalousie qu'elle
> n'avait jamais eues. Elle fut étonnée de n'avoir point encore pensé
> combien il était peu vraisemblable qu'un homme comme M. de
> Nemours, qui avait toujours fait paraître tant de légèreté parmi les
> femmes, fût capable d'un attachement sincère et durable. Elle trouva
> qu'il était presque impossible qu'elle pût être contente de sa passion:
> «Mais quand je le pourrais être,» disait-elle, «qu'en veux-je faire?
> Veux-je la souffrir? Veux-je y répondre? Veux-je m'engager dans
> une galanterie? Veux-je manquer à M. de Clèves? Veux-je me
> manquer à moi-même? Et veux-je enfin m'exposer aux cruels
> repentirs et aux mortelles douleurs que donne l'amour? Je suis
> vaincue et surmontée par une inclination qui m'entraîne malgré moi.
> Toutes mes résolutions sont inutiles; je pensai hier tout ce que je
> pense aujourd'hui et je fais aujourd'hui tout le contraire de ce que
> je résolus hier. Il faut m'arracher de la présence de M. de Nemours;
> il faut m'en aller à la campagne, quelque bizarre que puisse paraître
> mon voyage; et si M. de Clèves s'opiniâtre à l'empêcher ou à en
> vouloir savoir les raisons, peut-être lui ferai-je le mal, et à moi-même
> aussi, de les lui apprendre.»[31]

Here, the Princesse's mind proceeds logically from a consideration of Nemours' temperament to a realization of the inevitable
hopelessness of her love; seeing then whither her thoughts have
led her and instinctively recoiling in horror at having so far
forgotten herself, she lists the alternatives of behaviour open to
her and their probable results. In conclusion however she can

only recognize the helplessness of her state, which she is unable to fight. Her emotional condition at this moment and the possible action it may make her take are put clearly before us.

The final important method which Mme de Lafayette uses to reveal her characters to us is dialogue, either reported indirectly, when the conversation is not very important, or more usually directly. In fact, even when the dialogue is not reported, the speakers continue in the same tone and language as the main narrative, as the formality with which Mme de Lafayette tells her tale is preserved in the interchanges between the characters. We would expect this in the snatches of galant conversation, for example, between Nemours and the *reine dauphine*, since these are worldly people who do not want in their speeches to reveal an emotional reality but rather to categorize and embellish it so that what they say may appear elegant and witty, if not particularly true:

> «M. de Nemours avait raison,» dit la reine dauphine en souriant, «d'approuver que sa maîtresse allât au bal. Il y avait alors un si grand nombre de femmes à qui il donnait cette qualité que, si elles n'y fussent point venues, il y aurait eu peu de monde».[32]

We gather little from this type of dialogue about the individuals who are taking part in it. Only very occasionally does Nemours show his inner feelings in what he says, for even when he is speaking to the Princesse, he must translate his passion into conventionally polite phrases which may move without offending her.

> «. . . les grandes afflictions et les passions violentes,» repartit M. de Nemours, «font de grands changements dans l'esprit; et, pour moi, je ne me reconnais pas depuis que je suis revenu de Flandres . . .»[33]

It is in his final scene with her and once or twice before, when his patience is almost exhausted, that the violence of his desire emerges. The dialogue of these secondary characters is also occasionally used to reveal something about the hero and heroine as when the *reine dauphine* says to the Princesse: "Il n'y a que vous de femme au monde qui fasse confidence à son mari de toutes les choses qu'elle sait . . ."[34], thus proving to us both the popular knowledge of the confidence between husband and wife and its exceptional nature.

More surprisingly, the self-consciousness and sophistication of these conversations appear also in the scenes between the Prince and Princesse de Clèves; and yet these scenes are among the most moving of the whole novel. On the whole, they come at chosen times when the relationship between husband and wife is at a crisis so that they must be dramatically revealing; yet at the same time, in order that the dignified tone of the rest of the narrative may not be broken and the essential *bienséances* may be preserved, the couple must maintain a discipline and a formality which could seem out of place. How does Mme de Lafayette succeed in reconciling these two apparently contradictory aims? Primarily, she succeeds because her hero and heroine from the beginning have these two sides to their nature, the violence and the discipline; indeed this is why their hearts are in conflict at all. The Princesse, especially in her final scene with Nemours, but also in the confession scene with her husband and in the scene where she accuses him of betraying her confession, is always afraid of going too far in showing her love for Nemours. She knows it is a guilty love and she has such respect for her husband that any emphasis on it to him would seem to her tactless and hurtful—hence the controlled reticence and deliberate ambiguity of the very terms in which she confesses to him:

> Il est vrai que j'ai des raisons de m'éloigner de la cour et que je veux éviter les périls où se trouvent quelquefois les personnes de mon âge. Je n'ai jamais donné nulle marque de faiblesse et je ne craindrais pas d'en laisser paraître si vous me laissiez la liberté de me retirer de la cour.[35]

The formality of Astrée in her speeches has no such inner cause; there is no reason why her emotions should not appear unrestrained since she is innocent and happy in her love. Her unconvincing rhetorical utterances can only make her into a conventional puppet.

It is especially however in the speeches of the Prince that we find this uniquely moving combination of violent emotion and stern self-control. So far we have used the Princesse as our main illustration of Mme de Lafayette's methods of psychological analysis, for her conflict forms the central theme of the novel, and all the other characters, even her husband, only exist in relation to her. Obviously then it is she who is most usually the subject of the author's straight descriptions, the inner monologues and soliloquies; for the same reason it is the Prince who is primarily revealed by dialogue, the only method of analysis which reveals him to his wife at the same time as to the reader. Apart from the scene immediately after their marriage in which he expresses his disappointment at her indifference to him, the Prince hardly appears in the novel until the confession scene, for it is only then that he becomes involved in the Princesse's conflict. The admission by his wife that she loves another produces in the Prince exactly those two contradictory emotions which are the keynote of all the dramatic dialogue of the work—violent passion and an intense desire to control it. His jealousy is acutely aroused, but his respect for and at least at first his admiration of his wife hardly ever allow him to give it full vent. Very occasionally in his speeches there are outbursts of pure, spontaneous feeling which he cannot control, as when he frenziedly questions his wife immediately after her confession:

> Et qui est-il Madame, cet homme heureux, qui vous donne cette crainte? Depuis quand vous plaît-il? Qu'a-t-il fait pour vous plaire? Quel chemin a-t-il trouvé pour aller à votre cœur?[36]

or later when he breaks out in unrestrained despair at the suspicion that she has seen Nemours alone:

> «Hé! j'ai pu croire,» s'écria-t-il, «que vous surmonteriez la passion que vous avez pour lui. Il faut que j'aie perdu la raison pour avoir cru qu'il fût possible.»[37]

These outbursts make all the more moving by contrast those other moments, far more frequent, when his feelings are disciplined by his reason and sense of decency.

How exactly does Mme de Lafayette succeed in giving such dignity and restraint to her hero's expression of his deepest passions? In the first place, the Prince's formal politeness never forsakes him: he always addresses his wife as "Madame", is ever careful to take her feelings into consideration and never loses sight of the figure he will cut in her eyes. This is how he apologizes for having asked her the name of her lover:

> «Vous avez raison, Madame,» reprit-il, «je suis injuste. Refusez-moi toutes les fois que je vous demanderai de pareilles choses; mais ne vous offensez pourtant pas si je vous les demande.»[38]

Moreover, he never overwhelms the Princesse with declarations of a passion to which she cannot respond: his protestations of love have a discretion and a moderation that cannot but give him great dignity in our eyes—similar to that of Mme de Chartres as she turns away from her daughter to die alone, and typical of the whole atmosphere of the novel. Here are the Prince's last words to his wife:

> Je vous prie que je puisse encore avoir la consolation de croire que ma mémoire vous sera chère et que, s'il eût dépendu de vous, vous eussiez eu pour moi les sentiments que vous avez pour un autre.[39]

Finally, most of his speeches are couched in the same ordered, symmetrical style as the Princesse's inner monologues and the author's objective descriptions, and, because of this deliberate patterning of spontaneous emotional expression, they move us as does classical poetry. The effect, for example, of the Prince's words at the end of the confession scene, quoted above, is a poetic and aesthetic as well as a dramatic one.

This disciplined ordering of reality, which we have noticed so often in our study of Mme de Lafayette's art of psychological analysis, is of course a characteristic of every seventeenth-century work of art, always the product of the conscious, rational mind, moulding and criticizing the basic material. In this lies one of the main reasons why we would never mistake *La Princesse de Clèves* for a work of any period other than its own. Yet the control is combined here with a dramatic relevance, a concreteness and a realism in the psychological analysis that make the work of Mme de Lafayette unique in its time.

K

[1] Marguerite de Navarre, *l'Heptaméron* (ed. by Michel François, Classiques Garnier), p. 75.

[2] D'Urfé, *l'Astrée* (Magendie, analyse et extraits), p. 75.

[3] *Op. cit.*, p. 201.

[4] Mlle de Scudéry, *Clélie* (chez Augustin Courbé MDCLX), p. 1049.

[5] Segrais, *Les Divertissements de la Princesse Aurélie* (Text in Raynal, *La nouvelle française*), p. 15.

[6] Segrais, *Eugénie* (Text in Raynal, *La nouvelle française*), p. 37.

[7] *La Princesse de Montpensier* (Garnier edition).

[8] *Op. cit.*, p. 24.

[9] *Op. cit.*, p. 26. See also chapter 5 for Madame de Lafayette's dramatic exploitation of the seventeenth-century *bienséances* in conversation.

[10] *La Comtesse de Tende*, p. 401.

[11] *Zaïde*, p. 112.

[12] *Op. cit.*, p. 107.

[13] *Op. cit.*, p. 113.

[14] *La Princesse de Clèves* (Harrap), p. 13.

[15] *Op. cit.*, p. 50.

[16] *Op. cit.*, p. 2.

[17] *Op. cit.*, p. 3.

[18] *Op. cit.*, p. 3.

[19] *Op. cit.*, pp. 7–8.

[20] *Op. cit.*, p. 28.

[21] *Op. cit.*, p. 17.

[22] *Op. cit.*, p. 133.

[23] *Op. cit.*, p. 139.

[24] *Op. cit.*, p. 10.

[25] *Op. cit.*, p. 120.

[26] *Op. cit.*, p. 53.

[27] *Op. cit.*, p. 41.

[28] *Op. cit.*, p. 32.

[29] *Op. cit.*, p. 50.

[30] *Op. cit.*, p. 59.

[31] *Op. cit.*, pp. 83–84.

[32] *Op. cit.*, p. 30.

[33] *Op. cit.*, p. 49.

[34] *Op. cit.*, p. 81.

[35] *Op. cit.*, p. 86.

[36] *Op. cit.*, p. 87.

[37] *Op. cit.*, p. 114.

[38] *Op. cit.*, p. 89.

[39] *Op. cit.*, p. 127.

4. THE HISTORICAL SETTING

La Princesse de Clèves is part fact and part fiction: although all the secondary characters, all the public events and many of the briefly described minor intrigues are historical, the character of the heroine and all the central psychological action are pure invention. Since it is in this central action that the interest of the novel lies, why did Mme de Lafayette take such pains to set it on a backcloth so scrupulously accurate? This minute concern for history seems irrelevant to the modern reader. We may indeed find the load of tiny detail rather tedious. What literary attitudes led Mme de Lafayette to pay such attention in all her fictional works to the historical truth of their setting? Was she particularly successful or in any way original in her method of reconciling fact with fiction? These are some of the questions which this chapter will attempt to answer.

As we have seen, the ancestor of the novel is the epic poem, which tells in more or less sophisticated terms all or part of the history of the country in which it is born. More specifically, the ancestors of the medieval romances from which we traced the seventeenth-century novel and *La Princesse de Clèves* were the classical epics, set in Greek and Roman history, or the Celtic epics, set in Cornwall, Wales and Ireland. These had in the first place been historical or semi-historical works but in such medieval reconstructions as *Le Roman d'Énéas* or the *Tristan*, they lost most of their historical associations to become contemporary stories of love and adventure simply set in another time and place. In these settings themselves, moreover, the Middle Ages had neither the desire nor the resources to distinguish what was fact from what was legendary, so that any historical pretentions soon became meaningless.

This was however a tradition which died very hard. Writers clung to their anachronistic settings because they were part of the epic and romance tradition and could not be shelved without a complete transformation of the genre. This only began to happen in the sixteenth century, when for a short time, largely as a result of the sudden and transient emergence of the *nouvelle* as a serious genre with realistic settings, writers were starting to give a modern location to their novels. Medieval short stories had been crude and plebeian in their appeal and had hardly influenced the epic or the romance at all, but the popularity of Boccaccio in particular in fifteenth and sixteenth-century France produced some serious works in this shorter form, with an avowedly contemporary setting. Most of the stories of the *Heptaméron*, the philosophical as well as the comic ones, happen in modern France, Spain or Italy. Many of the briefer sentimental novels written in France between 1590 and 1620 take place in contemporary Paris. Unfortunately a regression soon set in, which made it fashionable once again for all serious romance to be set in a remote historical period, whose only function was to provide a specific framework for a story whose action and atmosphere were in fact entirely modern.

There were three literary influences in the first half of the seventeenth century which determined this particular form of conservatism. Firstly, the action of *l'Astrée*, source and model for much subsequent romance until the middle of the century, takes place not in contemporary France nor even in an indeterminate pastoral setting that could be contemporary, but in a historical period ten centuries or so earlier. It is true that D'Urfé was the first to try to inform himself of the actual details of life under the Druids and the first to choose a period out of the history of France, and not of Spain, Rome, Greece or the Celtic lands of Cornwall and Ireland. Yet what his successors Desmarests, La Calprenède, and the Scudérys copied was not D'Urfé's serious pretentions to historical truth, but simply the literary device of combining a seventeenth-century story with a non-seventeenth-century background. Indeed, even in *l'Astrée*, although it has been called the first truly historical novel in French (and so it may partly have been in intention) the mixture of fact and fiction was not altogether happy. Characters and action were determined largely by D'Urfé's interpretation of a philosophical system or by the appeal to be made to a seventeenth-century audience, and not by any attempted reconstruction of the atmosphere of another time. The battles, for example, may themselves be historical but they are described in so unrealistic and conventional a way that the result is not unlike the narratives of battles in the blatantly romanesque *Amadis de Gaule*.

Secondly, the other favourite models of early seventeenth-century novelists were such classical writers as Heliodorus or

Virgil. La Calprenède, Desmarests and their like, thought they were writing epics similar to the *Aeneid,* and, in order to preserve the authentic flavour of their sources, they thought it wisest to take over wholesale, with the help primarily of Plutarch, the Greek or Roman background and not to follow their models in spirit and principle alone, as would have been safer. Thus they produced novels whose main figures were Augustus, Cleopatra or Ariadne, whose heroes indulged in glorious warlike exploits and in vast journeys across the ocean, which described in fact a heroic, barbaric race quite unlike the French seventeenth century; yet at the same time they embodied their own sophisticated ideals of morality and behaviour in the characters' hearts and words. Here is again, accentuated now by the careless documenta-tion of the authors, that incompatibility we noted in *l'Astrée* between external events and inner motives.

But perhaps the most important cause for novelists' fondness for a historical setting was the influence on early seventeenth-century romance of the theory and practice of the contemporary theatre. M. Antoine Adam has noticed how the decline of pastoral and chivalric romance and the rise of the epic novel ran parallel to the decline of tragi-comedy and the rise of regular tragedy, the change-over happening in each case in the 1630s.[1] Either the one process influenced the other or else both were the result of a development in literary fashion, of a growing desire fostered by theorists for a more academic form of art. Its result anyway was to draw the two genres closer together and we can see from a comparison between the *Pratique du Théâtre* (1657) of D'Aubignac and the *Traité du Poème Epique* (1675) of Le Bossu, how similar the doctrines at least of theatre and novel had become. The historical setting was intended in both genres to add to a seven-teenth-century atmosphere the dignity of remoteness in time and space and the *vraisemblance* of real characters and events, although these could be altered if the truth was likely to be unpalatable to the contemporary audience. By using the same type of back-grounds as the theatre, whose seriousness as a genre was not contested, novelists thought they were raising their own rather despised art to a higher level, giving it dignity, *vraisemblance* and also a general validity, but whereas Corneille and Racine were fully aware that their historical settings should be subordinated to the dramatic unity of the play as a whole, novelists took their historical pretentions more seriously, or so they thought. They multiplied external details of scenery, battles, dress, armour; they developed *ad infinitum* their descriptions of heroic incidents which could only have taken place in the period they had chosen. Indeed they were in a way compelled to give a large place to precise localization by the very genre they had chosen, for, because of its length, the romance called for many details of setting. The incompatibility between background and psychological action was made all the more striking, the absurdity all the more obvious. The theatre allowed for no such particular descriptions; it selected only what was relevant to its universal, moral theme and so avoided the worst incongruities.

The combined influences then of D'Urfé, Heliodorus, Virgil and contemporary dramatic theory and practice ensured that all serious novels written between 1630 and 1660 or so were set in a historical background, usually that of the Roman Empire. The seventeenth century had little idea of relative values and different atmospheres. History for La Calprènede and the Scudérys, even for a historian like Mézeray, consisted entirely of external facts: the facts of certain personalities having lived at a certain time, of certain battles, certain ways of dressing and travelling from one place to another, facts that one could absorb and reproduce with a simple effort of will and no effort of imagination. On the whole, men did not realize the absurdity of using ancient characters and events to embody contemporary ways of thought, since they did not realize their incongruity. The Roman setting, they thought, made a little more real the very unreal tales, in which the leisured audiences of the *salons* delighted.

With *Le Grand Cyrus* (1649) and even more with *Clélie* (1656) the incongruity reached its pitch, as Mlle de Scudéry became less interested in describing external incidents which might conceivably fit in with the historical background, and more interested in sentimental analysis, which in its detailed sophistication and its feminism could only belong to the French seventeenth century. The Roman setting of *Clélie* acted as a thin cover for portraits of Court personalities and intrigues, which it was a favourite pastime of Mme de Lafayette among others to decipher.[2] All serious pretence at historical reconstruction was abandoned, and with this abandonment, it was natural that sensible people should begin to question the necessity for using these settings at all. Both Sorel[3] and Boileau[4] attacked the *invraisemblance* of the long, epic novel, and public taste including again that of Mme de Lafayette,[5] began to prefer works with a more modern realism.

Segrais made a great step forward first by attacking outright in the theoretical discussions of the *Divertissements de la Princesse Aurélie* (1656), the irrelevances and inaccuracies of a Roman setting for what is essentially a seventeenth-century love story, and secondly by boldly locating his tales in the modern world he knew.

> Mais à dire le vrai les grands revers que d'autres ont quelquefois donnés aux vérités historiques, ces entrevues faciles at ces longs entretiens qu'ils font faire dans les ruelles entre des hommes et des femmes dans des pays où la facilité de se parler n'est pas si grande qu'en France et ces mœurs tout à fait françaises qu'ils donnent à des Grecs, des Persans ou des Indiens sont des choses qui sont un peu éloignées de la raison.[6]

In order to mitigate the novelty of his demands, he refers especially to the *nouvelle* but it is obviously the long romance he is attacking, since the short stories of Sorel and Scarron had already employed contemporary if sometimes Spanish settings.

Though important, Segrais' originality in practice is unfortunately less striking. It is true that the plot of *Eugénie* (1656) takes place in seventeenth-century Paris and that the author has mentioned the civil war and siege of Paris in 1648 in order to make this quite clear, but his realism is still too superficial for the setting to provide a firm and credible anchorage to his romantic tale. The few contemporary touches—certain street names, the mention of a church in Paris and one surname from seventeenth-century French nobility (Aremburg)—come in the opening pages of the tale and after this the action could be taking place more or less anywhere. In another tale, *Floridon*, Segrais takes as his setting not contemporary France but contemporary Persia and, whereas the plot of *Eugénie* was entirely fictitious, here describes events that actually took place there between 1623 and 1640— the same events, in fact, that inspired Racine's *Bajazet*. Unlike Racine, Segrais scrupulously follows historical fact,[7] as he had recommended in the preface of the *Divertissements*, and yet, in spite of this apparent care for the truth, the atmosphere of the tale, the motives and words of the main characters are not really much closer to the sensuality of an Oriental harem than are those of *Clélie* to the brutality of the Roman Empire. Once again the realism is purely external, it has very little effect on the moral core of the tale.

Few authors, including Mme de Lafayette, were ready yet to go even as far as Segrais and abandon completely the historical setting, on which the seventeenth century had so far relied to give dignity and *vraisemblance* to its stories. Undoubtedly however his theories were an important factor in the sudden decline in the 1660s of the heroic novel and the rise of the so-called *nouvelle historique*. Writers like Mme de Villedieu, l'abbé de Saint Réal, Préchac, Boursault and Mme de Lafayette found a compromise between the artificial Roman setting of *Le Grand Cyrus* and the contemporary setting of *Eugénie* in a historical period closer both in date and atmosphere to their own. They were especially fond of the French sixteenth century with whose courtly atmosphere they felt familiar and which they could use successfully to cover their revelations of contemporary intrigue. Thus, a certain credibility, a certain unity of tone was maintained. Mme de Villedieu and Saint Réal for example were proud of the basis of serious documentation upon which their tales rested and included in their publications lists of the learned works which they had consulted. Saint Réal in particular, in such tales as *Don Carlos* (1672) and *La Conjuration de Venise* (1674), seems to have seen himself as much as a historian reconstructing actual events as a *nouvelliste*, and these stories contain an abundance of political detail.

Yet neither author had our respect for history as a science, and they mingled freely fiction with fact within their depictions of individual people on the typically seventeenth-century grounds that human nature is the same everywhere. Saint-Réal ascribed invented, usually amorous, explanations to historical incidents, thus altering character as he wished. Mme de Villedieu, even in those stories for which she makes the greatest historical claims, went further. *Les Annales galantes* (1670) and *Les Désordres de l'amour* (1675) are quite openly a seventeenth-century novelist's imaginative interpretation of history. She pays less attention to the details of historical events, military or political, and more to the elaboration or invention of the love intrigue behind them and the dialogue which accompanied them: "si ce ne sont ceux qu'ils ont prononcés, ce sont ceux qu'ils auraient dû prononcer"[8], she says. In the second tale of *Les Désordres de l'amour*, for example, which many have seen as a source of *La Princesse de Clèves,* she took her main characters, Mme de Thermes and Bellegarde, and the political intrigues in the second part, from Brantôme and

Mézeray, but herself provided all the sentimental complications, including Mme de Thermes' first marriage.

These two authors, and others like them, really used historical fact for their own ends, selecting only what might add *vraisemblance* to their modern sentimental tales and yet not jar on the seventeenth-century atmosphere with which the tales were imbued. They wrote, even Saint Réal, for the entertainment to be derived from a complicated political and romantic intrigue, not for instruction on the unique and local flavour of the historical period in which this was set. Thus the history is still really incidental to their aims. It did little more than protect the authors from accusations of indiscreet revelations about their contemporaries. It was inevitable that the short story would soon dispense with it altogether.

Mme de Lafayette was not among the pioneers in this sphere, but still used the convention with more discretion and more success than did her contemporaries. *La Princesse de Montpensier* of 1662 is really the first tale successfully to carry out the spirit of Segrais' injunctions, for Mme de Lafayette was the first to realize how suitable the sixteenth century was as a non-contemporary setting for an intrigue entirely contemporary in atmosphere. An abundance of historical material on the sixteenth century was available, in the works of Brantôme especially, and of Matthieu and Mézeray too, for the period was literate enough and close enough to her own to have inspired and left many assessments of its personalities and events. She must also have realized the similarities between court life under Henry II and Charles IX, and Louis XIV and seen ways of deliberately exploiting them. Moreover, Mme de Lafayette in *La Princesse de Montpensier* was the first novelist to attach much importance to historical accuracy, to take some trouble to inform herself in detail about sixteenth-century characters and incidents, although she did not bother to add to the end of her work a list of her sources as did the later writers, Mme de Villedieu and Saint Réal. So the invented moral drama of her tales rests on a basis of clear, historical documentation. It is she who in practice effected the transition from the inaccuracies and inconsistencies of the long heroic novel to the relative precision and realism of the *nouvelle historique*.

In our more detailed study of Mme de Lafayette's treatment of history, we will hardly speak of *Zaïde*. For, with the exception of the sections concerning Consalve's life at Court and the later battles against the Moors, the plot is entirely invented. In describing the love between Consalve and Zaïde, between Alphonse and Bélasire, and the various intrigues of Alamir, Mme de Lafayette makes no reference to historical figures or events. We know that the novel is set in ninth-century Spain, but in practice the characters move in a timeless world of poetry and romance, which Mme de Lafayette makes no attempt to locate further. Here she departed from her habitual, precise realism and tried her hand at building up a sentimental, fairy tale atmosphere similar to that of medieval romance. She took the general tone, slightly falsified, and some names from the Spanish *Guerras Civiles* of Perez de Hita, a collection of legendary tales and ballads about military and amorous contacts between Spain and the Moors in the Middle Ages, of which three editions had appeared in France in 1660. The work had appealed very much to French taste because of its intrigues both sentimental and political and the chivalric ideals of its characters, and it inspired stories by Voiture, Mlle de Scudéry and Mme de Villedieu, besides Mme de Lafayette herself. Yet it is not really history and so could not form the basis of any serious historical reconstruction. In the narrative of Consalve's life at the Court, Mme de Lafayette followed a more reliable source, whose identity has been variously guessed at by critics. Beaunier suggests Du Verdier's *Abrégé de l'Histoire d'Espagne*[9] and Magne prefers Mayenne-Turquet's *Histoire Générale d'Espagne*.[10] Whichever it may be, Mme de Lafayette uses it in exactly the same way as she uses Brantôme or Mézeray in her sixteenth-century tales, taking from it some important characters and intrigues and weaving about these an invented sentimental plot. What we shall say about her technique in *La Princesse de Montpensier* and *La Princesse de Clèves* will apply equally to this early part of *Zaïde*.

It is clear that the main interest of Mme de Lafayette's tales lies in the psychological dramas that they portray, and that the background descriptions of society are always subordinated to these. First then we must ask whether these central dramas are ever based on an actual historical case or whether they are always entirely invented. Was the author's obsession with the problem of the married woman in love with another man inspired by her reading of history or was it the result of her private thoughts on what she saw around her? First we can say that none of the sixteenth-century originals of her main characters are known to have ever gone through those experiences which they go through in Mme de Lafayette's novels. The Prince and Princesse de Montpensier did exist, and they did marry only after a former engagement of the Princesse had been cancelled. But there is no evidence that the wife fell in love with a former suitor or with anyone else, and the figure of the third lover, Chabannes, is completely invented. Indeed, Mme de Lafayette at the beginning of this work deliberately denies any historical source for her tale:

> . . . le respect qu'l'on doit à l'illustre nom qui est à la tête de ce livre, et la considération que l'on doit avoir pour les éminentes personnes qui sont descendues de ceux qui l'ont porté, m'oblige de dire, pour ne pas manquer envers les uns, ni les autres en donnant cette histoire au public, qu'elle n'a été tirée d'aucun manuscrit qui nous soit demeuré du temps des personnes dont elle parle.[11]

Mlle de Chartres, the Princesse de Clèves, has no sixteenth-century counterpart at all; and there is some confusion about her husband, the Prince de Clèves. Brantôme only gives the Duc de Nevers, M. de Clèves' father, two sons, whereas Mme de Lafayette mentions three, probably following here an *Histoire de la Maison Royale* of 1674 by Père Anselme. He gives to the additional son the Christian name of Jacques and tells us only that he was born in 1544 and died without children in 1564. All that Mme de Lafayette found here was the fact of an untimely death, and she added the story of an unfaithful wife to account for it. The Comte and Comtesse de Tende were both actual people who were married in 1560 but again there is no evidence that their marriage was destroyed by infidelity. Indeed Brantôme depicts the wife as honest and much esteemed. What can we conclude from all this? In her two shorter tales, Mme de Lafayette took as her central characters two married couples about whom very little was known, and ascribed to them emotions and behaviour for which she had no evidence at all. In her longer work, she invented her heroine entirely and married her to someone about whom she knew nothing but that he died young. In this way, then, she protected herself from accusations of slander and allowed herself the greatest possible freedom to develop the psychological drama as she wanted.

Many critics have suggested however that, although nothing similar to what Mme de Lafayette describes is known to have happened to the people whose names she uses, the central plot is still not invented but is inspired by people whose names she deliberately does not use. One hypothesis suggests Anne D'Este as the original of Mme de Clèves.[12] It is true that she was courted by the historical Duc de Nemours while she was married to someone else, although unlike the Princesse she married her lover after the death of her husband, but this suggestion is otherwise difficult to substantiate. Anne D'Este appears in Brantôme as a forceful, energetic, practical woman and her husband the Duc de Guise was an outstanding military leader. The couple bears no resemblance to the innocent, passionate M. and Mme de Clèves. What is much more likely is that Mme de Lafayette became interested in the character of the Duc de Nemours, in describing whom she remains very close to Brantôme, read of his affair with a married woman and decided to use him as the lover, but had no thought of extending this to using Anne D'Este as the wife. More plausible are the suggestions of a seventeenth-century source and our study in a former chapter of the *Histoire d'Henriette d'Angleterre* proves with little doubt that Mme de Lafayette was at least partly inspired by the intrigues of her royal friends. After all, it is clear that, while nominally describing the sixteenth century, she is really commenting on life under Louis XIV. Various seventeenth-century ladies have been designated as the source of the Princesse de Clèves—Mme de Combalet, Louise Angélique de Lafayette, Mme de Montespan even, who is said to have confessed her affair with the king to her husband—but it can by no means be proved that they did anything more than suggest to Mme de Lafayette the frequency and dangers of infidelity in marriage.

As far as we can see then, the central action of none of Mme de Lafayette's tales is historical; she has indeed each time been careful to deny any pretentions to historical validity by taking as her main characters invented or obscure sixteenth-century person-alities. We will find however on studying the social background that the opposite becomes true.[13] Only in her last work, *La Comtesse de Tende*, does she make little attempt to localize the moral drama through reference to actual people or events. The Chevalier de Navarre, the Comtesse's lover, and the Princesse de Neuchatel, her friend and the wife of Navarre, have no obvious counterparts in reality and no historical intrigues, amorous or political, are described to give weight and *vraisemblance* to the drama of husband and wife, which appears quite bare of context.

The background descriptions however of both *La Princesse de*

Montpensier and *La Princesse de Clèves* take up perhaps a third of the total space of the whole work. Almost every character and every intrigue, however unimportant, that is mentioned at all, Mme de Lafayette has taken from one of her sources on sixteenth-century society—from Brantôme's *Mémoires,* Mézeray's or Matthieu's *Histoire de France,* the *Mémoires* of Castelnau, edited and added to by Le Laboureur (these additions consist largely of unpublished texts by Brantôme) or Père Anselme's *Histoire de la Maison Royale* and his summary of Godefroy's *Cérémonial Français.* The trouble Mme de Lafayette took to document herself was immense: she must have worked with these great volumes for ever beside her and referred to them again and again for historical details to incorporate into her tales of love and despair. All the portraits of royal personalities with which *La Princesse de Clèves* opens come directly from one or other of these works—thus Brantôme has supplied data for the king, Mézeray for Catherine de Médicis and Le Laboureur for the *reine dauphine.* Then the descriptions, more or less lengthy, of the main figures at the court—of the Roi de Navarre, Duc de Guise, Cardinal de Lorraine, Prince de Condé, Vidame de Chartres, and of Nemours himself—have also an easily traceable historical source. Even the very minor characters, mentioned once or twice in the rôle of messengers or confidants—Lignerolles, Nemours' intermediary in his courtship of Queen Elizabeth of England, Chastellart, protégé of the *reine dauphine,* Mme de Mercœur, Nemours' sister —really existed and took part in those events in which they take part in the novel. Indeed every single person mentioned in the main body of the tale has an original except Mme and Mlle de Chartres, and in *La Princesse de Montpensier* we find the same scrupulous fidelity to history.

What of the major national events with which both tales are punctuated? Once again these are historical in every detail. *La Princesse de Clèves* begins at the time of the preliminary peace talks at Cercamp between France and Spain, in October 1558. The next important date is the marriage of Claude de France, daughter of the king, to the Duc de Lorraine, in January 1559, and it is to celebrate this marriage that the ball is given at which the Princesse and Nemours first meet. Thus in the three months between October and January, Mme de Chartres, after making various attempts to find a husband for her daughter, has betrothed and married her to the Prince de Clèves. Perhaps Mme de Lafayette has even been here too precise in defining the historical frame-work into which the invented action fits, for much has had to happen in a very short space of time. The next anchoring event is the signing of the peace treaty of Cateau-Cambrésis in April 1559, just before the episode of the letter which finally impels the Princesse to flee to the country and confess her guilty love to her husband. Last comes the death of Henry II at the tournament to celebrate both the engagement of Elizabeth of France, another of the king's daughters, and the marriage of Madame, the king's sister—this all happened in July 1559. By this time, the Princesse and her husband are almost completely estranged and it will not be long before she again flees to the country whither Nemours will follow her, thus indirectly causing the Prince's death. In exactly the same way the moral drama of *La Princesse de Mont-pensier* plays itself out against the background of the religious wars, as they cease for a year and then start up again, for according to these intervals of war and peace Mme de Montpensier lives at the Court in Paris or remains in her country home. The tale ends with the massacre of Saint Bartholomew's Day during which Chabannes is killed. At every stage, Mme de Lafayette has located and made more credible the invented emotional drama of her main characters by connecting it with historical events.

She has occasionally found herself obliged by psychological or dramatic necessity to bring forward or push back a historical date; but these are always minor, unimportant ones and the change is thus easily acceptable. The death of the Duc de Nevers, the Prince's father, is brought forward from 1562 to 1559 so that his objections to his son's marriage with Mlle de Chartres may be effectively removed. In the same way, the marriage of the Prince's elder brother to Anne de Bourbon is moved from 1561 to the end of 1558, to account for the objections of the father to his younger son's less eminent alliance. Then Nemours uses as one of his reasons for ceasing his courtship of Elizabeth of England the fact that if she were inclined to marry, she would certainly marry Lord Courtenay, her admirer for many years—Lord Courtenay had in fact died in 1553. All these three falsifications were made by Mme de Lafayette in order to justify psychologically some action connected with the central moral drama. They involve only a few years, never enough to destroy the air of *vraisemblance* of the tale as a whole.

It seems in fact reasonable to expect that Mme de Lafayette

would see that all details connected with the important events and personalities that she describes were accurate; here she had either to follow a reputable source or not mention them at all. What is more surprising is her scrupulousness as regards the minor characters and incidents, sometimes occupying only a few lines, which she deemed it necessary to include in order to build up in the Court the right atmosphere of agitation and intrigue. The first part of the novel is especially full of brief anecdotes about Court personalities: we are told of the loves of D'Anville and Chastellart for the *reine dauphine*, of the complications caused by the marriage of a daughter of the king by Diane de Poitiers to the son of Montmorency when he had already been promised to someone else. These facts and others like them come straight from Brantôme, Mézeray or other historians.

Out of the four interpolated stories, two are entirely historical and must have involved much extra research on Mme de Lafayette's part, since they cover periods or places other than those on which she was working already. Mme de Chartres' narration of the early stages of the king's liaison with Diane de Poitiers is full of details of personalities and intrigues, and every one of these Mme de Lafayette found in one or other of her sources. For the *reine dauphine's* account of her mother's life and death and of the life of Anne Boleyn, Mme de Lafayette probably had even more difficulty, since she had to consult a completely new set of historical compilations—those on sixteenth-century England—and once again her accuracy is unimpeachable. The same may be said of the secondary intrigues of *La Princesse de Montpensier*: Guise's pretentions to the hand of Marguerite de Navarre and, according to some authorities, her attraction to him, the marriage of Mme de Montpensier's father-in-law to Mlle de Guise and Guise's later liaison with Mme de Noirmoutier.

More relevant to the central action of *La Princesse de Clèves* are Mme de Lafayette's elaborate descriptions of the ceremonies arranged to celebrate the marriage by proxy of Elizabeth of France and the marriage of Madame, and of the circumstances surrounding the king's death and the accession of Francois II. She fills several pages with precise and even technical details on the arrangements for the tournament and its actual procedure, as she had done too for the *jeu de paume* at which the ill-fated letter was dropped by the Vidame de Chartres. Most of this comes from Matthieu's *Histoire de France*, and the details of the wedding preparations from Godefroy's *Cérémonial Français*. Then Mme de Lafayette begins the fourth part of her tale with a description of the regrouping of the Court factions as people rose or fell in royal favour with the accession of the new king, and thus keeps the social background of the novel up to date. Here she found the sort of picturesque details in which she delighted and to which she occasionally added a telling touch. Thus she is careful to include Diane de Poitier's defiant reply to those who tried to depose her before Henry II had actually died.

> Cette duchesse s'enquit si le roi était mort; et, comme on lui eut répondu que non: «Je n'ai donc point encore de maître,» répondit-elle, «et personne ne peut m'obliger à rendre ce que sa confiance m'a mis entre les mains.»[14]

and the bitterness of the now dowager queen when she must give up her place of precedence to her son's wife:

> . . . elle se recula de quelques pas et dit à la reine, sa belle-fille, que c'était à elle à passer la première; mais il fut aisé de voir qu'il y avait plus d'aigreur que de bienséance dans ce compliment.[15]

Almost every fact, every judgment Mme de Lafayette has found in one of her sources; to build up the Court background of her tale she invented almost nothing.

Let us now look at some of those incidents which are directly linked to the central psychological action without being actually part of it. The affair between the Vidame de Chartres and Catherine de Médicis, included partly to bring out more clearly those aspects of the Court mentality which Mme de Lafayette finds most important, and partly simply to engineer prolonged meetings between Nemours and the Princesse, rests on a basis of fact, albeit very slight. Mme de Lafayette found in Le Laboureur mention of the attraction felt by the queen for the Vidame, of his reputation for inconstancy and of his final ruin by the queen herself. On the basis of these hints, she builds up an important episode which has a fitting place in the novel as a whole. She succeeded too in incorporating an odd historical fact in her account of the psychological drama of Nemours and the Princesse de Clèves. For Nemours' pretentions to the hand of Elizabeth of England she also found in Le Laboureur, although she organized his comings and goings as the plot required, for by abandoning these pretentions Nemours gives another proof of how great is his love for Mme de Clèves. Apart from the main plot, the only intrigue described that is entirely imaginary is the story of Sancerre and Mme de Tournon, told to the Princesse by her husband, which plays a definite rôle in the emotional development of the heroine. Sancerre was a common name among the sixteenth century nobility but the tragedy of Mme de Lafayette's Sancerre cannot be identified with that of any historical original.

This analysis shows how seriously Mme de Lafayette took this aspect of her work, how she realized the need for accuracy and precision in order to provide a credible framework to her central tragedy. Why is it then that we feel nevertheless that she has not written convincing sixteenth-century memoirs, that we care not at all for the exact documentation which lies behind both *La Princesse de Montpensier* and *La Princesse de Clèves*? A study of the treatment to which she subjected her sources, consulted in such detail, will perhaps give us the answer.

Mme de Lafayette's view of history was similar in its essentials to that of the seventeenth century in general, to that of her contemporary story writers, Mme de Villedieu, Boursault and Saint Réal. History for her as for them consisted only of external facts, and since she had accumulated a vast mass of facts and used them almost without alteration, she thought she was being faithful to her historical purpose. She did not see any difference between her reproduction of sixteenth-century society and that of Brantôme, just as Mézeray before her had seen no difference between the truth and his seventeenth-century interpretation of the truth. Yet to us, as we compare Mme de Lafayette's descriptions of characters and incidents with those of a contemporary historian, the difference is very apparent. Although she invented nothing in her descriptions, she omits and changes to such a degree that the end effect is really quite different. Brantôme's portraits are usually long and digressive, full of concrete, realistic, even occasionally vulgar detail about people's behaviour and the events of their lives. Mme de Lafayette takes those details which fit in with her image of the character and expresses them in a concise, abstract, elegant and hyperbolic language. She omits most of the more colourful and distinctive traits in which Brantôme delighted and so loses much of the peculiarly sixteenth-century flavour of the society she is describing. Yet although in the end the tone of her portraits of Court personalities has little in common with that of her source, beneath the paler, abstract expressions, they evoke a definite if rather different individuality, not a type or an ideal. Her character is no longer quite the person she found in Brantôme but he is nevertheless a man, particular and unique. This is especially true of the more important people she describes—Catherine de Médicis, the Vidame de Chartres and especially Nemours himself. Both Brantôme and Mme de Lafayette see Nemours as a rake and all the qualities Mme de Lafayette mentions she took directly from Brantôme—his peculiar charm, his popularity, his witty conversation, the elegance of his dress, his attractiveness to women, his physical agility. But because of her technique of generalization and omission, the Nemours which emerges from this description has a refinement and a discretion for which we look in vain in the Brantôme original. Let us compare the end of Brantôme's portrait with a sentence from that by Mme de Lafayette:

> Je luy ay oüy raconter plusieurs fois de ses avantures d'amour, mais il disoit que la plus propre recepte pour jouïr de ses amours estoit la hardiesse, et qui seroit bien hardy en sa premiere pointe, infailliblement il enporteroit la forteresse de sa Dame, et qu'il en avoit ainsi conquis de cette façon plusieurs, et moitié à demy force, et moitié en jouant en ses jeunes ans.[16] (*Brantôme*)
> Il avait tant de douceur et tant de disposition à la galanterie qu'il ne pouvait refuser quelques soins à celles qui tâchaient de lui plaire: ainsi il avait plusieurs maîtresses, mais il était difficile de deviner celle qu'il aimait véritablement.[17] (*Mme de Lafayette*)

The crude reality is hidden beneath a suggestive but consistently refined veneer. Mme de Lafayette has unwittingly created here the sixteenth-century Nemours' seventeenth-century counterpart.

It is not only in the description of personalities, taken straight from a historical work, that Mme de Lafayette modernizes her source. She does it in her whole picture of Court life, by omitting all reference to those preoccupations which belonged specifically to the sixteenth century. Thus she never discusses the great national political and religious issues of the time but always makes a point of including all the love intrigues concerning minor characters for which she can find space. Indeed she hardly mentions a person without relating some circumstance of his amorous career. D'Anville, Chastellart, the Comte d'Eu, Catherine de Médicis, Mme de Mercœur, they have all had their affairs. So Mme de Lafayette increases the appeal of her tale to a society thirsty for sentimental gossip, but quite ignores the demands of historical realism. She picks out and even if necessary invents details of motive and reaction, giving shrewd psychological explanations for known facts. Here again she is writing for an audience which loved above all to analyse behaviour. She spends pages describing the arrangements for the various ceremonies, giving details of people's dress, of the weapons and rules of a fencing tournament, of the fixed rites for the marriage of a royal princess and so on. Indeed the space she thus fills is occasionally excessive and she is here pandering to her own and her public's taste for elaborate ritual and magnificent costumes, instead of concentrating on the main drama.

In spite of Mme de Lafayette's historical accuracy, the society of *La Princesse de Clèves* then is unmistakably that of the Court of Louis XIV, and indeed so it had to be, for the moral tragedy of its heroes and heroine could only have been conceived in the French seventeenth century. It is the product of a refined mentality born of years of discussion on the problems of love and duty, of years of an existence of leisured futility. In 1560, these years were still to come: idealism was a new and strong force, the atmosphere of the Court was not yet so artificial, so demoralizing. We have only to look at Marguerite de Navarre's treatment of a tragedy similar to that of Mme de Clèves in her story of Floride and Amadour to see clearly this difference. Floride remains immune to temptation in her heroic idealism and her resistance to physical love. Here are none of the sophistications of self-inflicted torture and despair of the seventeenth-century masterpiece. The moral drama of La Princesse de Clèves belongs as little to the sixteenth century as does its social atmosphere. The facts alone are historical.

In her attitude to history, then, Mme de Lafayette distinguishes herself little from minor seventeenth-century *nouvellistes*. But in her conception of the historical novel, she shows far more originality and achieves a striking success. Her contemporaries, Mme de Villedieu and Saint Réal, built up their stories simply by elaborating on the lives of more or less famous historical figures on the basis of certain incidents which they had found in one of their sources—thus Saint Réal in *Don Carlos*, thus Mme de Villedieu in *Les Annales galantes*. The result is an inextricable mixture of fact and fiction: some of the scenes depicted are historical, some concerning the same people are imaginary, and it is quite impossible to tell which is which. In comparison with this, Mme de Lafayette has a far more modern respect for the truth. With the exception of the Sancerre episode, all the background of *La Princesse de Clèves*, all the anecdotes and intrigues concerning characters other than the three principal ones, is strictly historical fact, whereas more or less all of the central moral drama, including the figure of its main protagonist, is invented. Mme de Lafayette allows thus the minimum of ambiguity, and keeps her historical pretentions in their rightful place. This indeed is one of the aspects of her novel that her contemporary Valincour, attacks at the greatest length in his *Lettres à la Marquise*, a critical work on *La Princesse de Clèves*, on the grounds that the main plot of a *nouvelle historique* should itself be historical, that Mme de Lafayette is misleading her public in placing invented action and invented characters in a true setting:

> . . . c'est un grand défaut d'introduire dans ces sortes d'ouvrages des personnes qui n'ont jamais été, lorsque ces personnes sont fort remarquables, comme des rois, des princes ou des princesses, ou de leur faire faire ce qu'elles n'ont jamais fait, comme de les marier, si elles n'ont point été mariées.[18]

The critic allows the invention of only secondary details, the likely consequences of known facts, and not of important events. In this he reflects the general practice of other *nouvellistes* of the time. Yet surely Mme de Lafayette shows a greater feeling for history by depicting incidents that are either entirely true or entirely false, and by not ascribing invented causes to a historical happening. She had the good sense and the independence of mind to realize the limitations of the *nouvelle historique* with its emphasis on plot and character, and to remain in her reconstruction of history strictly within them.

Her greatest originality however lies in the particular uses to which she puts her historical setting, the expert way in which she weaves together fact and fiction so that the former supports the latter while still remaining distinct from it. The early seventeenth-century novel, with the possible exception of *l'Astrée*, basing itself doctrinally very much on the theatre, used history primarily as a means of idealization and generalization. This is the idea behind the classical background of *Le Grand Cyrus* and behind the Spanish background of Mme de Lafayette's *Zaïde*—Zaïde and Consalve are unreal, poetic types whose love exists in a more beautiful, unfamiliar world. In *La Princesse de Clèves*, on the other hand, Mme de Lafayette uses her sixteenth-century setting for quite the opposite effect—in order to anchor and particularize her action.

She does not pretend that the moral drama of the Princesse de
Clèves has anything other than an immediate relevance; she is
talking about a certain kind of individual subjected to certain,
specific pressures. To make her point, Mme de Lafayette needed
precise, realistic details of Court life and these she accumulated
from the thousands of trivial facts she found in her several
sources. Because of the minute accuracy of the historical passages,
the non-contemporary settings of her novels have a contrary
effect to that of Zaïde or Andromaque. Hermione, as Racine
presents her, could exist at any time and in any place; the Princesse
de Clèves, as she is presented by Mme de Lafayette, could exist
only within a limited period.

How exactly does Mme de Lafayette achieve this localization?
First of all, as we have seen, external political and social events
provide anchoring dates, in the intervals between which the
Princesse's inner conflict develops and changes. The stages of one
action fit in with the stages of the other. The Princesse lives her
private life and the Court its public life simultaneously and yet
distinctly. The growth of the heroine's helplessness and despair
is punctuated by the various attempts of statesmen to conclude
the peace of Cateau-Cambrésis; her final estrangement from her
husband happens just before and after the king's death. Thus we
are made to feel the passage of historical as well as emotional
time—time as it is marked in regular months and years by public
events, and as it moves faster or more slowly according to the
state of the heroine's heart. Furthermore external events not only
proceed parallel to the moral agitation of the Prince and Princesse;
they also help to stimulate the crises or slow them down. At the
beginning, Nemours returns to the Court in order to be present
at the celebrations for the marriage of Claude de France, sister
to the king, and thus sets the whole tragedy in motion; he shows
his devotion to the Princesse by abandoning his courtship of
Elizabeth of England; the Prince finds out the name of his rival
by including him in a list of Elizabeth of France's escort to Spain
—this escort actually existed. In the same way, the Princesse de
Montpensier's sojourns in the country and the absences of her
husband correspond both to the various stages of the religious
wars, and to the various stages of her affair with Guise.

As well as major national events, the trivial, social round is
linked to the central moral drama, and this linking is perhaps even
more significant than the other since it is through this daily

routine that Nemours and his love are continually present to the Princesse until her own passion can be hidden no longer. Nemours, as the epitome and representative of all the dangerous sophistication that characterizes Court life, must appear most often in a social context and only rarely and after the damage has been done as a private person. He first offers himself to the young Princesse's eyes at a ceremonial ball; her love for him is increased by his magnificent appearance and his accident at the *jeu de paume*; he first directly reveals his love for her at a public sitting for her portrait, and again and again she either hears him spoken of or watches him in person at the daily gatherings in the apartment of the *reine dauphine*. Indeed Nemours is not alone in availing himself of the social round to precipitate the Princesse's submission to him; she uses it first when she refuses to go to the ball of the Maréchal de Saint André, because he will not be there, hoping unconsciously that he will understand her motives. Then later she takes advantage of the rules of *bienséances* not to meet him face to face and alone, and of the upheaval caused by the king's death to flee from him into the country. The tragedy of her husband and herself is determined by and inextricably linked to the social and often historical events of the court within which they live.

In this way, the relative rôles of fact and fiction in Mme de Lafayette's works are beautifully balanced and contrasted; scenes of factual description alternate with scenes of mental crisis, the former often containing in them the seeds of the latter. Even in the second half of *La Princesse de Clèves*, when the psychological action speeds up as a result of the Princesse's confession, the long descriptions of the tournament, the king's death and the resulting reshuffle of Court factions come to interrupt it. The reader's attention is held all the time; when the emotional tension becomes unbearable for him and for the heroine herself, when the situation reaches a deadlock, the narrative switches to the more leisurely recital of external happenings. We have time to regain our strength and interest; the Princesse is given a temporary respite from her suffering. There is no similarly successful balance between the historical and sentimental parts of their tales in the works by Mme de Lafayette's contemporaries. Mme de Villedieu is too interested in her invented intrigue to spend long on setting the scene. Saint Réal is more preoccupied with political minutiae and he does not always link these effectively to his sentimental plot. Thus both authors eventually bore us, the one with her succession of meaningless incidents, the other with his list of factual details. Mme de Lafayette only bores us when her system breaks down, when perhaps she spends too long introducing the Court personalities to us (this was the opinion of Fontenelle) but these occasions are very rare: indeed for many readers they may not occur at all.

What emerges then in conclusion to this study of the historical setting of Mme de Lafayette's tales? There is no doubt that her idea of history was largely the conventional idea of her century, that she used it as a background to her novels because she felt bound to it by tradition. Yet, through her honesty and scrupulousness, she not only avoided the convention's worst absurdities, she even succeeded in making it appear relevant and useful through her skill in combining the setting with the more essential parts of her work.

NOTES TO PART II, CHAPTER 4

[1] see *Histoire de la Littérature française au XVIIe siècle*, Antoine Adam (Éd. Domat), vol. 1, p. 402.

[2] *Correspondance* (ed. by André Beaunier), vol. 1, letter 58.

[3] Sorel, *Le Berger extravagant*.

[4] Boileau, *l'Art poétique*.

[5] *Correspondance*, letter 26.

[6] Segrais, *Les Divertissements de la Princesse Aurélie* (see Raynal), p. 12.

[7] for example Floridon's (Atalide's) easy compromise after the death of Bajazet.

[8] Madame de Villedieu, Preface to *Annales galantes*.

[9] Beaunier, *L'amie de La Rochefoucauld*, p. 120.

[10] Magne, Introduction to *Romans et Nouvelles de Madame de Lafayette*, Classiques Garnier, p. xxii.

[11] *Op. cit.*, p. 3.

[12] see Valentine Poizat, *La véritable Princesse de Clèves*, Paris, La Renaissance du Livre, 1920.

[13] The material for what follows is taken from: Revue du XVIe siècle, Chamard et Rudler:

> *Les sources historiques de La Princesse de Clèves.* 1914.
> *Les épisodes historiques dans La Princesse de Clèves.* 1914.
> *La couleur historique dans La Princesse de Clèves.* 1917.
> *L'histoire et la fiction dans La Princesse de Clèves.* 1917.

[14] *La Princesse de Clèves*, p. 109.

[15] also p. 109.

[16] quoted by Chamard et Rudler.

[17] *Op. cit.*, p. 3.

[18] Valincour, *Lettres à Madame la Marquise sur le sujet de La Princesse de Clèves* (ed. by Cazes, Bossard, p. 138).

5. FORM AND STYLE

The dramatic effectiveness of the form of *La Princesse de Clèves* accounts to a great extent for its success. Before Mme de Lafayette, the novel had not been sufficiently mature as a genre to fit itself to any deliberate formal pattern. Its structure was episodic, following the twists of the intrigue as they occurred to the author. The epic romances of La Calprènede and Scudéry, it is true, attempted to obey the rules of composition laid down by theorists of the theatre: all action should take place within a year and all secondary episodes be related to the main plot; but these laws, originally devised for the drama, had necessarily to be so reinterpreted to fit the novel that writers hardly felt bound by them at all. Besides, they could rarely be reconciled with the structural features of the other models which these authors followed—the epic poems of Virgil and Tasso, the romances of Heliodorus, the action of which takes much longer than a year and includes numerous incidents only incidentally attached to the central plot. In practice it is these works, and not classical drama, that *Polexandre* and *Le Grand Cyrus* imitated. The story opens *in medias res* and its various opening threads are described in interminable flashbacks, full of the conventional disasters which had become part of the genre—shipwrecks, kidnappings, battles etc. The point of these reminiscences lay obviously not in their often devious connection with the central plot, which proceeds indeed as episodically and as wordily as they do, but in the entertainment to be derived from them in themselves.

In the overall structure of *Zaïde*, it is this convention that Mme de Lafayette followed, probably under the direction of Segrais, who says of the work:

> Il est vrai que j'y ai eu quelque part, mais seulement pour la disposition du roman, où les règles de l'art sont observées avec grande exactitude.[1]

—by which he means that he uses the traditional formal devices of the epic romance. Indeed Mme de Lafayette would probably have had neither the professional skill nor the imagination to spin out her work to such lengths on her own, and as we have seen most critics have ascribed to her only certain of the shorter episodes, notably the love affairs of Consalve and Alphonse, and to Segrais the linking of these into a coherent whole and the provision of the banal central love story. The novel begins *in medias res* with the meeting between Consalve, who has fled from the Court of Léon, and Alphonse, already living in retirement, and the shipwreck on their shores of the mysterious Zaïde. The first episode tells the story of Consalve's reasons for flight, the second those of Alphonse, the third continues the first, the fourth describes Zaïde's origins, the fifth the early experiences of her rival suitor, Alamir, the sixth links up the fourth and fifth, and in between, the main intrigue is gradually unfolded. Moreover the initial situation and its final solution depend on a number of coincidences and *coups de théâtre*. Yet *Zaïde* is more tightly constructed, moves faster and is somewhat shorter than its predecessors and models. Public taste was already beginning to change, and the authors of *Zaïde* could not but conform to it, even in a genre to which different rules applied.

What was it that the public now required of its novelists? Had it realized the formal awkwardness of the romances in which it had delighted and was it now demanding the dramatic relevance here that it found in contemporary theatre? Unfortunately no. Men and especially women still sought in the novel the obvious entertainment to be derived from a series of exciting incidents only superficially linked to each other. All it asked for now was that these incidents should be narrated more concisely, and that the work as a whole should be shorter. This concentration alone was of course a great advance. It laid bare any defects in narrative technique and forced authors like Mme de Villedieu, Boursault or Saint Réal to keep the interest of the reader at full pitch all the time. Thus various devices to give the story new and interesting twists were freshly exploited—coincidences, disguises, confrontations; the main intrigue was supported by secondary complications told in a more rapid, concise style which bears one along with it. Mme de Villedieu was especially skilled in the art of story-telling and produced lively, dramatic tales of love and adventure. This tightness, this relevance was, however, never more than superficial: the action still proceeded along an arbitrary course; it simply proceeded rather faster. The stories show little true sense of design; they have no all-embracing theme, and no unifying formal pattern. Either the central plot moves along in episodic jerks or else it is continually interrupted by irrelevant flashbacks.

In *La Princesse de Montpensier* and particularly in *La Princesse de Clèves*, Mme de Lafayette does more than simply tell a story. The form of *La Princesse de Clèves* springs from its very core, from the moral conflict of its hero and heroine. The incidents, the descriptions obey the logic of their passions as they rise, explode and burn themselves out. Mme de Lafayette does not let the psychology of her characters follow the requirements of an exciting external intrigue; it is the psychology which imposes its own pattern on the plot, a disciplined pattern which is aesthetically satisfying as well as dramatically necessary. The novel remains in our minds not only as a moving experience but also as a beautifully balanced composition.

We find some of this harmony, this relevance, already in *La Princesse de Montpensier*, whose overall form is also the inevitable, not the incidental result of its psychological theme. The tale has one definite point to make, on the tragedy of love in a Court society, and to this all the incidents and all the characters must be related. The passion of Guise and the Princesse first reawakens when they meet in the country; it is given opportunity to flower through the lovers' conversations at the royal Court in Paris; when they are back in the country, they attempt to cross the limits of the *bienséances* and their love receives its death-blow. Thus the *nouvelle* is composed in three parts, corresponding to the various changes in the characters' circumstances and to the inner developments of their hearts, each set of changes depending on the others.

As yet however Mme de Lafayette has not integrated as perfectly as she will later the external action of the tale and its moral theme. The intrigues of love and ambition at the Court which involve the lovers, the Duc d'Anjou and Madame, are described at a greater length than their relevance to the central love affair would demand, since their only function is to provide occasions for Guise and the Princesse to persuade each other of their passion. In giving so much space to such incidental complications Mme de Lafayette has omitted to analyse in great enough detail the psychological changes in the main characters for which they are really the excuse. Thus we are often presented with a long narrative of external events, followed by a too quick, unmotivated moral change. The last scene of *La Princesse de Montpensier* too, the final catastrophe, in which Chabannes in place of Guise is discovered by the Prince in his wife's bedroom, is not the inevitable result of the development of the characters. Like Nemours, in trying to visit Mme de Clèves at Coulommiers at night, the lovers are courting disaster in arranging a meeting in the Princesse's chamber, but the disaster itself happens by pure chance as the Prince de Montpensier is awakened by a noise and so surprises them. The catastrophe in *La Princesse de Clèves*, the death of the Prince, is the logical final stage of his increasing jealousy. In one work the husband brings on his own disaster; in the other he merely submits to it. The reader has the feeling too that Mme de Lafayette partly engineers the last scene of *La Princesse de Montpensier* for its melodrama, just as she prolongs the Madame-Anjou affair unnecessarily to flatter the taste of her public for complicated intrigue. The discretion she shows in her handling of the end of *La Princesse de Clèves*—Nemours does not even enter the Princesse's room—is one of her later novel's most effective originalities.

The form of *La Princesse de Clèves*, the working out of a moral conflict in action, is both more complex and more perfect than that of *La Princesse de Montpensier*. The novel divides naturally into five parts, corresponding perhaps to the exposition, peripateia, crisis, catastrophe and dénouement of a classical play. The first establishes the initial situation from which the whole drama will emerge. After the introductory description of the Court and the appearance of Mlle de Chartres, it tells of the complications leading to her marriage with the Prince de Clèves, her first meeting with Nemours, the awakening of her love for him, and ends dramatically with her mother's death and her flight to the country. It contains two critical scenes, each of which seriously changes the state of the Princesse's heart: the ball at which she first falls in love, and the death scene when her love is first clearly brought home to her. The narrative is briefly interrupted by Mme de Chartres telling the story of the king's liaison with Diane de Poitiers. The second part opens with another interpolated story, that of Sancerre and Mme de Tournon, and then describes the gradual growth of Nemours' and the Princesse's passion, which culminates in the important incidents connected with the Vidame de Chartres' letter, the complex emotions it arouses in Mme de Clèves and her second flight to the country. This part is interrupted by the story of Anne Boleyn, by lengthy passages on preparations for the *jeu de paume* and by the sentimental complications which surround the letter incident. Events now move more quickly, and the crisis and turning point occurs at the beginning of the third part, as the Princesse confesses her love to her husband and is overheard by Nemours. From now on, we are shown the development no longer only of the Princesse's passion, but also of M. de Clèves' jealousy and of their hostility, as he discovers the identity of her lover and as they each suspect the other of having told a third person of the Princesse's confession. At the end of this section Mme de Lafayette leaves her hero and heroine in order to describe preparations for the tournament, the tournament itself, the death of the king and the subsequent realignment of Court factions. The fourth part tells of the final estrangement between the Princesse and her husband, the attempt of Nemours to see his mistress after her flight to the country, and the resulting catastrophe of M. de Clèves' death. It only remains in the fifth part to describe the Princesse's final supreme conflict, her long interview with Nemours, her renunciation and her death. The first two parts are well rounded off by the temporary respite afforded to the Princesse's struggle as she takes refuge from the Court in her country home at Coulommiers. After the crisis, as emotions gather momentum, tragedy pursues her here too and Coulommiers ceases to be a refuge; catastrophe is now inevitable.

These suggested divisions coincide almost but not quite with the divisions made by Mme de Lafayette herself. Each time she either stops short of what seems to us a natural pause or else goes a little way beyond it. Her first section ends just as the Prince is about to begin the story of Sancerre, her second in the middle of Chartres's story explaining the origin of the letter, and the third immediately after the death of the king and before the description of the new Court. It is difficult to see why Mme de Lafayette should have thus broken the natural stages of the drama—possibly so that her readers should be kept in suspense at the end of one part and want to read on to the next—but the closeness of her divisions to the ones we have suggested shows that she deliberately aimed at a pattern more or less identical. It emerges from this analysis that the structure of the novel is determined almost entirely by the logical development of the psychological conflict, and not by any unmotivated external twists. Every scene, every description serves to change the characters' state of mind, to however slight a degree, to bring them one step nearer to a crisis and a catastrophe. Even the interpolated stories, whose length was so much criticized by Valincour, have their rôle to play in the preparation of the dénouement. In including them, Mme de Lafayette was partly following in the tradition of epic romance with its flashbacks and episodes. A seventeenth-century audience liked to have its interest diverted and renewed by fresh intrigues interrupting the central plot. Yet just as she exploited with original effectiveness the conventional historical setting, Mme de Lafayette also gave to these secondary episodes a function, a relevance that they had not had before. They all occur in the first two parts of the novel, those parts on whose accumulation of detail the rapid action of the third and fourth is to rest. That is, Mme de Lafayette uses them not as they are used in *Zaïde* to describe the past but rather to prepare the future, and thus she gives them a dramatic significance in the present. Except for the story of the Vidame de Chartres, which is however the only one which is necessary to the plot, they are all told to Mme de Clèves herself, by the *reine dauphine*, by her mother and by her husband, and effect, it is implied, some alteration in her state of mind which will precipitate a crisis. This is most obvious in the case of Sancerre's story, in telling which the Prince is moved to expatiate on the virtues of absolute sincerity between husband and wife, thus causing his wife untold inner shame, and preparing the reader for her eventual confession to him of her guilty love:

> Ces paroles firent rougir Mme de Clèves, et elle y trouva un certain rapport avec l'état où elle était, qui la surprit et qui lui donna un trouble dont elle fut longtemps à se remettre.[2]

The other tales also affect the Princesse indirectly, although less overtly. Through hearing all the details of Diane de Poitiers' liaison with the king, and the story of the tragic life and death of Anne Boleyn, Mme de Clèves learns early on of the sufferings caused by jealousy and inconstancy, unavoidable even in those most highly stationed. So she will later realize the inevitable consequences of her own passion more clearly and her conflict will be more lucid and more poignant. Indeed, in the final part of the novel, we see how well she has learnt her lesson. These stories thus play their part in building up the atmosphere of intrigue and dissimulation which is the necessary context for the

Princesse's tragedy. In this respect the tale of the Vidame de Chartres is perhaps more important than any other, since its subject is the double and even triple dealing of its narrator. This is how Mme de Chartres points the moral of them all:

> «Si vous jugez sur les apparences en ce lieu-ci,» répondit Mme de Chartres, «vous serez souvent trompée: ce qui paraît n'est presque jamais la vérité».[3]

The Princesse must learn of this hidden corruption and be on her guard.

In spite of the analogies of its structure with that of a five act play, and although in moral seriousness it resembles more the plays of Racine than the *nouvelles* of Mme de Villedieu, *La Princesse de Clèves* is truly a novel and not a play in novel form. For the work's detailed description of the external setting as it determines the inner drama belongs to the genre of the novel by definition. No classical play had the scope for such a portrayal— its action is purely psychological, the result of eternal human failings. Mme de Lafayette had the task of embodying a universal message in a particular localized case.

It is indeed a task in which on the whole she succeeds most remarkably, although just occasionally her fusion of social and psychological, outer and inner, is not always quite happy. The narrative switches from dynamic analysis to static, historical description; thus the monotony of the one relaxes the reader from the tension of the other, and the alternation between the two gives the novel a rhythmic swing which is aesthetically as well as dramatically satisfying. So long as the change is not too sudden or too extreme, its effect is rather to add a new dimension to the central plot than to divert one's attention from it. Mme de Lafayette wishes to draw the parallel courses of M. and Mme de Clèves' public and private lives, showing how little each was allowed to impinge on the other, how fatally and painfully unbreakable was the wall which separated them. Thus we leave Mme de Clèves in great anguish in order to read of the incidents concerning the death of the king, only to return to her still in the same anguish, thinking not of the public consequences of this national event but only of how she can make use of it for her own ends, employ it as a cover for her real emotions and give it as a pretext for a further flight to the country:

> La cour était trop occupée pour avoir de l'attention à sa conduite et pour démêler si son mal était faux ou véritable.[4]

Just occasionally Mme de Lafayette's sense of proportion apparently deserts her and she goes too far in pandering to the taste of her audience for complicated details of social conspiracies and royal ceremonial. At the beginning, the novel is rather slow-moving. The opening lengthy portraits of Court personalities and intrigues are meant largely to establish the context of the Princesse's conflict but are probably partly included also for their documentary, historical value. Similarly, Mme de Lafayette breaks off her narrative for too long in order to describe the preparations for the tournament and the tournament itself, to give us every detail of the rituals and the costumes which accompany it. After the death of Henri II and the advent of François II, the new appearance of the Court is also told us in great detail—again partly because Mme de Lafayette is trying to localize her novel. Sometimes she is too concerned not about the historical background of her tale but about its moral atmosphere, placing perhaps unnecessary difficulties in the way of the Princesse's marriage to the Prince de Clèves, and insisting too much on the complicated sentimental intrigue around the letter addressed to the Vidame de Chartres. Both these episodes have an indirect relevance to the central drama; the first reveals much that will be important about the Prince de Clèves' character, his unflinching love and his respect, and about the values generally consulted in the arrangement of marriages. The second helps to build up the atmosphere of duplicity and corruption in which the Prince and Princesse move, but perhaps their relevance is a little too indirect for the space they occupy.

Most of the time, however, that fusion between the external and the psychological which can only really exist in a novel is here most successful—especially on the occasions when the public incidents are trivial in themselves, but are important for the dramatic support they give to the central moral theme. Then the reader is not distracted from the psychological action but is rather made to see it on another level or from another angle. Most important among these are the various scenes depicting the social calls which the Princesse or Nemours pay on the *reine dauphine* or the queen, where, in apparently casual irrelevant conversations by third persons, references are made to the heroine's state of mind: thus the *reine dauphine* remarks to Mme de Clèves: "il n'y a que vous de femme au monde qui fasse confidence à son mari de toutes les choses qu'elle sait",[5] when talking of the Vidame de

Chartres' letter. Then the Princesse and especially Nemours take advantage of trivial events to hide or reveal their passion, Nemours by stealing a picture of the Princesse during a public sitting for her portrait, the Princesse by not attending the ball of the Maréchal de Saint André and by the expression on her face as she watches the *jeu de paume*. So the crises in the heroine's heart are the result of many small public incidents as well as of her own private self-torture and the incidents themselves become significant and moving. On such occasions as these, Mme de Lafayette has interwoven perfectly her characters' private and public lives, has succeeded in reconciling the two views of her novel as a social document and an individual case history, the two influences of the contemporary *nouvelle* and contemporary drama. *La Princesse de Clèves* has the moral seriousness and dramatic logic of the theatre but these are filled out with the external incidents and detailed descriptions of a novel, and only very occasionally does the balance go wrong.

*   *   *

The literary standards of the seventeenth century to which we owe the concise balance of the form of *La Princesse de Clèves* determine also the qualities of its style. For this period attempted in its works of art not an imitation of reality, an approximation to experience such as we find in Virginia Woolf or, on another level, John Braine, but a recreation of reality in the special medium of literature. Just as the Prince's and Princesse's conflicts are ordered and controlled within a firm, formal framework, so they are intellectualized and explained in a clear, rational language.

Throughout the sixteenth and seventeenth centuries, language had been an important civilizing factor, first as with cultural expansion came vast new spheres of knowledge and experience, and second as this knowledge was codified and disciplined in words. In the seventeenth century indeed its influence spread beyond this and not only scholars and literary men but the cultured nobility too paid great attention to the formation and definition of the rapidly changing French language. The endless conversations carried on in the *salons* and in the Court contributed as much to this as the treatises of the grammarians, while people strove for greater and greater elegance and precision of expression. Did not Vaugelas, one of the linguistic authorities of the century, take as his criterion "l'usage des gens de la cour"? Language was regarded even by the unliterary *honnête homme* as

M

something artificial, to be used with deliberation in describing even the smallest circumstance. It is no wonder then that works of literature with any pretentions to seriousness should have an excessively artificial, conscious style, since the experience they were describing was so much more worthy of definition in language, than the experience of the ordinary people of the Court. Thus too this artificiality is found in the novel not only in the direct narrative by the author but also in the dialogues and soliloquies. Mme de Lafayette's characters express themselves with as much formality and clarity as she, the author.

Writers' methods of achieving this intellectual domination of reality through language changed as the century advanced. Men writing under Louis XIII inherited from the sixteenth century a vast vocabulary of new, picturesque words and a loose meandering sentence structure; they could only attempt to discipline such a language by cutting out some of the more obviously unnecessary neologisms and by linking each part of a sentence logically and obviously to the one before. Thus the letters of Guez de Balzac are written in long, involved periods which in Mlle de Scudéry, who has less sense of language, become awkward and overloaded:

> Pour moy, luy dis-je, je suis persuadé que la trop grande prudence est bien souvent inutile en l'amour, sans considérer tout ce que vous considérez; je ferois diverses choses, car je combattrois ma passion autant que je le porrois, et si je ne la pouvois vaincre, je chercherois à me persuader tout ce qui la poirroit flatter; et je n'oublierois rien de tout ce qui me pourroit tromper agréablement.[6]

In reaction to the ambiguities, the looseness of sixteenth-century style, every connection was made clear, every idea explicit—hence the abundance of relative pronouns and conjunctions. People were beginning to regard language as an important instrument whereby reason controlled imagination but at the same time, by depriving it of its simpler, cruder words and substituting periphrases, they made it seem unnatural and contrived.

Mme de Lafayette, however, followed the taste of the second half of the century, although Valincour accused her of an occasional ambiguity, tautology or grammatical irregularity.[7] Long complex sentences were now out of fashion and language was to achieve rational control of experience not by explaining it in every detail but by pinpointing the essentials. Reality and language, the content and the form must fuse perfectly, so that none of the experience be allowed to escape but no unnecessary parts of it be dwelt on for too long. The sentences are shorter, less circumstantial, the vocabulary simpler, more precise and the effect is more natural and more pleasing. This is basically the style of La Rochefoucauld, of La Fontaine, of Boileau and of Mme de Lafayette, whose writing becomes increasingly laconic in *La Comtesse de Tende*, and then in the *Mémoires de la Cour de France*.

Indeed this linguistic control is doubly meaningful in *La Princesse de Clèves*, since self-control is of the essence of its plot. Even if the novel had been written in another century when different literary standards prevailed, any lyricism or exaggeration on the part of the author would have been out of place, since the characters themselves refuse to let themselves go:

> Je lui dis que tant que son affliction avait eu des bornes, je l'avais approuvée, et que j'y étais entré; mais que je ne le plaindrais plus s'il s'abandonnait au désespoir et s'il perdait la raison.[8]

Thus the Prince answers Sancerre's excessive cries of distress, and on various occasions the same attitude appears—in Mme de Chartres at her death, in the Prince again immediately after his marriage, in the Prince and Princesse at the confession scene, in the Prince at his death and in the Princesse in her final interview with Nemours. Controlling their passion and despair in their words may help them to control it in their hearts.

Let us examine certain characteristics of the language of *La Princesse de Clèves,* stylistically as well as psychologically the greatest and most characteristic of Mme de Lafayette's works, and estimate which of these are typical of the late seventeenth century and which are peculiar to the author. The most important quality of the work is probably its combination of concision and clarity, its way of saying all that needs to be said in the minimum of space. The psychological analyses of *La Princesse de Clèves*, whether spoken by Mme de Lafayette herself or by her hero or heroine, are particularly good examples of this; every word in them adds something to the reader's knowledge, none is there for a solely aesthetic purpose or as part of a cliché not genuinely relevant here. Mme de Lafayette gives us bald statements of the facts of a certain emotional situation, never enlarging on them unless the situation has a critical importance in the drama. Her work should be read slowly for it is easy to miss an important detail. She rarely makes any effort to catch the attention of a reader by a surprising image or turn of phrase. Here is how she describes the first occasion on which the Princesse successfully masters her desire to see Nemours. It happens when her husband is ill:

> Elle exécuta enfin la résolution qu'elle avait prise de sortir de chez son mari lorsqu'il (Nemours) y serait; ce fut toutefois en se faisant une extrême violence. Ce Prince vit bien qu'elle le fuyait, et en fut sensiblement touché.[9]

No more is said but the plot has taken a step forward.

This concision does not mean however that Mme de Lafayette never uses long, even complex sentences. She can write involved periods, like those of Mlle de Scudéry, but always gives to each subordinate phrase in them an important rôle to play. The action of *La Princesse de Clèves* results from the accumulation of small details which must all be expressed but which are not significant enough to be given the weight of a whole sentence: thus

> Il (Nemours) revint le lendemain du bal, il sut qu'elle ne s'y était pas trouvée; mais comme il ne savait pas que l'on eût redit devant elle la conversation de chez le roi dauphin, il était bien éloigné de croire qu'il fût assez heureux pour l'avoir empêchée d'y aller.[10]

There are as many relative pronouns here as in a typical sentence of one of the earlier romances, but here each clause that they introduce is relevant and tightly linked to another; only very rarely do they sound awkward.

Mme de Lafayette often shows great brevity and clarity in the narrative describing external action too. The following sentence for example could not be more laconic, although it describes the starting-point of the whole novel:

> Cette héritière (Mlle de Chartres) était alors un des plus grands partis qu'il y eût en France; et quoiqu'elle fût dans une extrême jeunesse, l'on avait déjà proposé plusieurs mariages. Mme de Chartres, qui était extrêmement glorieuse, ne trouvait presque rien digne de sa fille; la voyant dans sa seizième année, elle voulut la mener à la cour.[11]

Five salient points are included: Mlle de Chartres' high rank, her youth, her domination by her mother, Mme de Chartres' pride, and her decision to take her daughter to the Court: all of this is important for what is to ensue.

The clarity and concision that we have been illustrating implies a very deliberate use of language on the part of Mme de Lafayette —a spontaneous style would be more confused. This deliberateness is especially obvious in the ordered structure of her sentences, which are logically and aesthetically effective. The author frequently uses antithesis and repetition, preferring balanced symmetrical sentence forms, which correspond to the hopelessly even balance in the heroine's heart between her love and her loyalty, her shame and her desire. The sentiments often appear in pairs, either contrasting or complementary:

> Tout ce qu'il eût pu souhaiter, eût été une conversation avec elle; mais il trouvait qu'il la devait craindre plutôt que de la désirer.[12]

Or whole sentences are related to each other in twos or even threes:

> «Ce n'est pas la gloire, Madame,» reprit M. de Clèves, «qui vous fait appréhender que M. de Nemours ne vienne avec moi. Le chagrin que vous en avez vient d'une autre cause. Ce chagrin m'apprend ce que j'aurais appris d'une autre femme, par la joie qu'elle en aurait eue. . . .»[13]

Here, "chagrin" and "gloire" are played off against each other, as are then "chagrin" and "joie".

Or else phrases of a similar structure are accumulated for the space of half a page, as the author follows the logic of her characters' minds:

> Il dit aussi que, quand on n'est point aimé, on souffre encore davantage de voir sa maîtresse dans une assemblée; que, plus elle est admirée du public, plus on se trouve malheureux de n'en être point aimé; que l'on craint toujours que sa beauté ne fasse naître quelque amour plus heureux que le sien. Enfin il trouve . . .[14]

In this minute analysis of the variety of feelings behind Nemours' unwillingness to allow his mistress to go to a ball, the author shows clearly her training in the contemporary *salons*. Nemours' desires here, however, are not really important, dramatically or psychologically, so the rigid analysis is not unsuccessful. On other more critical occasions, such a regard for an artificial order, balance and symmetry may destroy the emotion which its purpose is to reveal. Again it is in Nemours' speeches that this danger is the greatest, since he must always disguise his feelings beneath a sophisticated wit, and since he anyway finds it difficult to discard completely the conversational elegance he has so long cultivated. In this next passage, he is trying indirectly to convince Mme de Clèves of his love in a speech which rises almost too well to a fitting dramatic climax:

«Les femmes jugent d'ordinaire de la passion qu'on a pour elles,» continua-t-il, «par le soin qu'on prend de leur plaire et de les chercher; mais ce n'est pas une chose difficile pour peu qu'elles soient aimables; ce qui est difficile, c'est de ne s'abandonner pas au plaisir de les suivre; c'est de les éviter, par la peur de laisser paraître au public, et quasi à elles-mêmes, les sentiments que l'on a pour elles. Et ce qui marque encore mieux un véritable attachement, c'est de devenir entièrement opposé à ce que l'on était, et de n'avoir plus d'ambition, ni de plaisir, après avoir été toute sa vie occupé de l'un et de l'autre».[15]

"Ce n'est pas" is followed by the contrasting "ce qui est . . . c'est" then again "c'est" and finally "ce qui marque . . . c'est". Thus the paragraph follows a symmetrical, accumulative pattern.

A second characteristic of seventeenth-century styles in general and of that of *La Princesse de Clèves* in particular is their disciplined restraint. Here is another way by which an experience can be controlled by a form which suggests but does not insist upon its intensity. This restraint is especially obvious in the dialogue of the novel, where it is most moving as it corresponds to the tragic self-control each character must exercise in order not to embarrass the others with his unreciprocated and misunderstood desires; it is emphasized too by the formality of address even between husband and wife. The Prince often uses simple, almost banal vocabulary in his efforts not to encumber his wife with his irksome devotion. Thus he asks her pardon for his repeated pleas to know the identity of her lover in what is perhaps the most moving sentence of the whole novel because it is the most violently controlled.

«Vous avez raison, Madame,» reprit-il, «je suis injuste. Refusez-moi toutes les fois que je vous demanderai de pareilles choses; mais ne vous offensez pourtant pas si je vous les demande.»[16]

In the same way, the negative phrase Mme de Clèves uses to describe her infidelity to her husband, "Je vous demande mille pardons si j'ai des sentiments qui vous déplaisent",[17] adds to rather than detracts from the overpowering effect of her sincerity.

Mme de Lafayette is as discreet and suggestive in her narrative of events as the characters are in their professions of loyalty or despair. She too leaves many of the important things unsaid, leaving the reader to guess at the violence of feeling beneath the quiet words. This is how she describes Mme de Chartres' dismissal of her daughter on her deathbed:

Elle se tourna de l'autre côté en achevant ces paroles et commanda à sa fille d'appeler ses femmes, sans vouloir l'écouter davantage.[18]

Here it is one of the characters who hides her grief at having to leave her daughter alone, when she feels her to be helpless and in danger. In the following passage describing Mme de Clèves alone at Coulommiers, it is the author who refuses to lay bare emotions which convention believes are best left hidden. Yet how suggestive are these small details of appearance and behaviour!

> Il faisait chaud, et elle n'avait rien, sur sa tête et sur sa gorge, que ses cheveux confusément rattachés. Elle était sur un lit de repos, avec une table devant elle, où il y avait plusieurs corbeilles pleines de rubans; elle en choisit quelques-uns, et M. de Nemours remarqua que c'était des mêmes couleurs qu'il avait portées au tournoi. Il vit qu'elle en faisait des nœuds à une canne des Indes, fort extraordinaire, qu'il avait portée quelque temps et qu'il avait donnée à sa sœur, à qui Mme de Clèves l'avait prise sans faire semblant de la reconnaître pour avoir été à M. de Nemours. Après qu'elle eut achevé son ouvrage avec une grâce et une douceur que répandaient sur son visage les sentiments qu'elle avait dans le cœur, elle prit un flambeau et s'en alla, proche d'une grande table, vis-à-vis du tableau du siège de Metz, où était le portrait de M. de Nemours; elle s'assit et se mit à regarder ce portrait avec une attention et une rêverie que la passion seule peut donner.[19]

The kind of vocabulary used here is rare in *La Princesse de Clèves*. Instead of imbuing such conventional and abstract words as "inclination", "infortune", "trouble", with a vital weight of meaning, Mme de Lafayette suggests the Princesse's passion through apparently innocuous concrete phrases: "il faisait chaud, sur sa gorge, confusément rattachés, un lit de repos, faisait des nœuds, grâce, douceur sur son visage, un flambeau, regarder avec une attention et une rêverie . . ." and the result is exactly right. We are made aware that this is a special, unlooked-for moment, the only moment when Mme de Clèves gives way completely to her feelings, by the style changing to fit in with the change in the heroine's behaviour: yet the effect is obtained through words so simple and restrained that they do not jar on the controlled abstractions of the rest of the novel.

Here Mme de Lafayette can use the action to imply the emotions beneath. Occasionally however at times of profound feeling which there is no action to reveal, she does find difficulty in conveying the full drama of the moment. Her training in analysis and control leaves her unable to convey the spontaneous lyricism which at these rare moments is called for, and her colourless, usually meaningful but here inadequate vocabulary cannot rise to the occasion. Nemours' and Mme de Clèves' first and last encounter alone is thus rather clumsily introduced:

> L'on ne peut exprimer ce que sentirent M. de Nemours et Mme de Clèves de se trouver seuls et en état de se parler pour la première fois.[20]

The author's embarrassment passes as soon as the characters themselves regain their control:

> Ils demeurèrent quelque temps sans rien dire; enfin, M. de Nemours, rompant le silence: «Pardonnerez-vous à M. de Chartres, Madame,» lui dit-il, «de m'avoir donné l'occasion de vous voir et de vous entretenir, que vous m'avez toujours si cruellement ôtée?»[20]

Mme de Lafayette shows the same restraint on quite another occasion, in her description of the death of Henriette d'Angleterre in the *Histoire d'Henriette d'Angleterre*. Very few hints of the grief she undoubtedly felt are allowed us; it would have been improper to intrude her private emotion on a scene so solemn. The tragedy seems the more awful for being told us in such simple, matter-of-fact terms. Mme de Lafayette never digresses for one moment from the scene before her, never embellishes her account with rhetorical flourishes, never indulges in such solemn generalities on fame and death as make of Bossuet's sermon on the same subject so powerful but so elaborate a piece of writing. Mme de Lafayette was watching her friend die. The facts were terrible enough on their own:

> M. de Condom lui parlait toujours, et elle lui répondait avec le même jugement que si elle n'eût pas été malade, tenant toujours le crucifix attaché sur sa bouche; la mort seule le lui fit abandonner. Les forces lui manquèrent, elle le laissa tomber et perdit la parole et la vie quasi en même temps. Son agonie n'eut qu'un moment; et, après deux ou trois petits mouvements convulsifs dans la bouche, elle expira à deux heures et demie du matin, et neuf heures après avoir commencé à se trouver mal.[21]

Certain critical moments in the drama of Mme de Clèves and her husband are made especially moving by the rhythm of their speeches. Emotion is then expressed not only through vocabulary and syntax but also through the very sounds of the phrases, as the poetic cadences enhance the simple, restrained words. Mme de Lafayette uses the well-known rhetorical devices—antithesis, accumulation, repetition—not here to make her style more

elegant nor even more ordered, but more poignant. Here is
M. de Clèves:

> . . . je n'ai que des sentiments violents et incertains dont je ne suis
> pas le maître. Je ne me trouve plus digne de vous; vous ne me
> paraissez plus digne de moi. Je vous adore, je vous hais, je vous
> offense, je vous demande pardon; je vous admire, j'ai honte de vous
> admirer. Enfin il n'y a plus en moi ni de calme ni de raison. . . . Je
> vous demande seulement de vous souvenir que vous m'avez rendu
> le plus malheureux homme du monde.[22]

The passage begins quite calmly, but as the speaker proceeds his
anger and despair rise; the phrases become shorter and more
contradictory until their climax and resolution in, "Enfin il n'y
a plus en moi ni de calme ni de raison". Later and perhaps most
moving of all comes the last sentence of the whole speech with
its long falling cadence expressive of the Prince's sad resignation,
contrasting with the short sharp rhythms which came before.

And here is Mme de Clèves:

> Songez que, pour faire ce que je fais, il faut avoir plus d'amitié et
> plus d'estime pour un mari que l'on n'en a jamais eu; conduisez-moi,
> ayez pitié de moi, et aimez-moi encore, si vous pouvez.[23]

First she justifies herself in a long firmly rounded sentence; then,
suddenly dropping her dignity, she pleads openly with her husband in three brief, balanced phrases which contrast with the
preceding phrases and do not end abruptly but which rather fade
away apologetically, "aimez-moi encore, si vous pouvez". At
these moments, the dramatic clarity of the rest of the work
becomes something greater: the prose becomes poetry, the order
music.

In extent and kind, Mme de Lafayette's vocabulary resembles
that of the late seventeenth century in general. It is firstly almost
entirely abstract in its exposition of character: there are very few
picturesque details of appearance which might distract the reader
from analyses of inner conflicts. After the initial rudimentary
portraits which tell us that Mme de Clèves is beautiful—fair haired
and white-skinned—that Nemours is handsome and well-made,
the author seems unaware of her characters' bodies beyond their
conventional blushing or going pale. In descriptions of their
emotional state, all the weight is taken by abstract nouns and not
by adjectives or verbs, for the hero and heroine are rarely allowed
to show their feelings in their appearance or behaviour; they must
keep them locked in their minds and hearts:

> Elle passa toute la nuit, pleine d'*incertitude*, de *trouble* et de *crainte*, mais enfin le *calme* revint dans son esprit. Elle trouva même de la *douceur* à avoir donné ce témoignage de fidélité à un mari qui le méritait si bien.[24]

By skilful selection of abstract nouns—here "incertitude, trouble" and "crainte" all complement each other and contrast with "douceur" and "calme"—Mme de Lafayette gives such passages of grievous conflict vitality and meaning. She succeeds perhaps less well however in descriptions and professions of love, where she has no choice but to use trite, traditional vocabulary, the vocabulary which was vivid a century ago but from which all solid reality had now gone:

> M. de Nemours se jeta à ses pieds et s'abandonna à tous les divers mouvements dont il était agité. Il lui fit voir, et par ses paroles, et par ses pleurs, la plus vive et la plus tendre passion dont un cœur ait jamais été touché.[25]

The vocabulary of this sentence is not characteristic of the novel in general: it is more exaggerated and less abstract, "se jeta, s'abandonna, agité, paroles, pleurs, la plus vive et la plus tendre passion". Nemours is here acting as the typical romantic lover and thus he can only be described in typically romantic terms. Neither M. de Clèves nor Mme de Clèves ever act typically, so the language which describes them or in which they express themselves is always clear and meaningful. How lifeless because so fulsome are Nemours' words in contrast with his companion's frank simplicity!

> «Vous ne vous êtes point flatté,» lui répondit-elle; «les raisons de mon devoir ne me paraîtraient peut-être pas si fortes sans cette distinction dont vous vous doutez, et c'est elle qui me fait envisager des malheurs à m'attacher à vous.»
> «Je n'ai rien à répondre, Madame,» reprit-il, «quand vous me faites voir que vous craignez des malheurs; mais je vous avoue qu'après tout ce que vous avez bien voulu me dire, je ne m'attendais pas à trouver une si cruelle raison.»
> «Elle est si peu offensante pour vous,» reprit Mme de Clèves, «que j'ai même beaucoup de peine à vous l'apprendre.»
> «Hélas! Madame,» répliqua-t-il, «que pouvez-vous craindre qui me flatte trop, après ce que vous venez de me dire?»[26]

The speeches of Nemours are full of artifice and flattery: he pretends to be unable to answer Mme de Clèves', "je n'ai rien à répondre", then refers unworthily to what she has just said of her love for him. She takes no notice of his artifice but replies simply and truthfully. He answers her with a rhetorical question, unnecessary and exaggerated, and the scene continues in the same vein.

Seventeenth-century *bienséances* also imposed on Mme de Lafayette's style a certain refinement, prevented her characters from stating directly a truth which might offend the delicate ears of their listeners. So reality is suppressed beneath yet another mask; a vague periphrasis takes the place of the plain word, and the social decencies are preserved:

> J'étais amoureux de Mme de Thémines; mais, quoiqu'elle m'aimât je n'étais pas assez heureux pour avoir des lieux particuliers à la voir. . . . Je savais bien aussi que j'avais un commerce de galanterie avec une autre femme moins belle et moins sévère que Mme de Thémines . . .[27]

The same attitude lies behind Mme de Clèves' attempts to wipe out her guilty love by refusing to speak of it again to her husband after her confession. She seems to feel that so unworthy an emotion should not be given the consecration of language:

> Mais trouvez bon que je ne vous parle plus d'une chose qui me fait paraître si peu digne de vous et que je trouve si indigne de moi.[28]

The style of Mme de Lafayette's novels then bears many of the same qualities as most literary works of the second half of the century—it is concise, ordered, restrained, abstract, refined. Occasionally it is also dull and conventional, but it rises as often to heights of poetry and drama only equalled by the greatest contemporary dramatists.

NOTES TO PART II, CHAPTER 5

[1] *Segraisiana.*
[2] *La Princesse de Clèves*, p. 41.
[3] *Op. cit.*, p. 23.
[4] *Op. cit.*, p. 108.
[5] *Op. cit.*, p. 81.
[6] Mlle de Scudéry, *Clélie*, p. 228.
[7] Valincour, *Lettres à Madame la Marquise*, 3rd letter.
[8] *La Princesse de Clèves*, p. 42.
[9] *Op. cit.*, p. 52.
[10] *Op. cit.*, p. 30.
[11] *Op. cit.*, p. 7.
[12] *Op. cit.*, p. 104.
[13] *Op. cit.*, pp. 93–94.
[14] *Op. cit.*, p. 29.
[15] *Op. cit.*, p. 50.
[16] *Op. cit.*, p. 89.
[17] *Op. cit.*, p. 87.
[18] *Op. cit.*, p. 35.
[19] *Op. cit.*, p. 118.
[20] *Op. cit.*, p. 133.
[21] *Histoire d'Henriette d'Angleterre*, p. 265.
[22] *La Princesse de Clèves*, p. 114.
[23] *Op. cit.*, p. 87.
[24] *Op. cit.*, p. 90.
[25] *Op. cit.*, p. 139.
[26] *Op. cit.*, pp. 136–37.
[27] *Op. cit.*, p. 70.
[28] *Op. cit.*, p. 92.

SELECT BIBLIOGRAPHY

Texts of Madame de Lafayette's work:

For a detailed bibliography of the texts, see:

H. ASHTON: *Mme de Lafayette, sa vie et ses œuvres* (C.U.P., 1922).

C. DÉDÉYAN: *Mme de Lafayette* (Société d'Enseignement Supérieur, Paris, 1955).

Recommended editions:

MME DE LAFAYETTE: *La Princesse de Clèves:* Preface by Anatole France (Paris, Conquet, 1889).

MME DE LAFAYETTE: *Mémoires, précédés de La Princesse de Clèves* (Flammarion).

MME DE LAFAYETTE: *La Princesse de Clèves:* ed. by Cazes (Paris, Belles Lettres, 1934).

MME DE LAFAYETTE: *Romans et Nouvelles:* ed. by É. Magne (Classiques Garnier).

MME DE LAFAYETTE: *Correspondance* (2 vols.): ed. by A. Beaunier (Gallimard, 1942).

MME DE LAFAYETTE: *La Princesse de Clèves:* ed. by P. Nurse (Harrap, 1970).

Books and articles on the novel (in chronological order):

SEGRAIS: *Nouvelles françaises, ou les Divertissements de la Princesse Aurélie* (1657).

HUET: *Traité de l'origine des romans* (1670).

ANDRÉ LEBRETON: *Le roman au XVIIe siècle* (Hachette, 1890).

G. REYNIER: *Le roman sentimental avant l'Astrée* (Colin, 1908).

G. DULONG: *L'abbé de Saint Réal, étude sur les rapports de l'histoire et du roman au XVIIe siècle* (Paris, 1921).

JEAN CAZENAVE: *Le roman hispano-mauresque en France* (Revue de littérature comparée oct.–déc. 1925).

MARJORIE CHAPLYN: *Le roman mauresque en France de Zaïde au dernier Abencérage* (Nemours, 1928).

M. A. RAYNAL: *La nouvelle française de Segrais à Mme de Lafayette* (Paris, Picard, 1926).

M. MAGENDIE: *L'Astrée* (Grands événements littéraires, 1929).

M. MAGENDIE: *Le roman français au XVIIe siècle de l'Astrée au Grand Cyrus* (1932).

DOROTHY DALLAS: *Le roman français de 1660 à 1680* (Lib. Univ., Gamber, Paris, 1932).

ALBERT CAMUS: *L'intelligence et l'échafaud* (Problèmes du roman: Confluences, Lyon, 1943).

ALEXIS FRANÇOIS: *De l'Heptaméron à La Princesse de Clèves* (R.H.L.F., 1949).

C. E. MAGNY: *Histoire du roman français depuis* 1918 (Paris, Éditions du Seuil, 1950).

G. POULET: *Études sur le temps humain* (Plon, 1950).

Books on Mme de Lafayette's life and works:

VALINCOUR: *Lettres à Madame la Marquise sur le sujet de La Princesse de Clèves.* 1678 ed. by Cazes (Boissard, 1925).

JEAN-ANTOINE DE CHARNES: *Conversations sur la critique de La Princesse de Clèves* (Paris, Barbin, 1679).

COMTE D'HAUSSONVILLE: *Mme de Lafayette* (Paris, 1891).

LUDOVIC LALANNE: *Brantôme et La Princesse de Clèves* (Paris, 1898).

ANDRÉ BEAUNIER: *La jeunesse de Mme de Lafayette* (Flammarion, 1921).

ANDRÉ BEAUNIER: *L'amie de La Rochefoucauld* (Flammarion, 1927).

H. ASHTON: *Mme de Lafayette, sa vie et ses œuvres* (C.U.P., 1922).

VALENTINE POIZAT: *La véritable Princesse de Clèves* (Paris, La Renaissance du livre, 1920).

HENRI BORDEAUX: *Amours du temps passé. Les Amants d'Annecy* (refutation of Poizat's thesis; Paris, Plon-Nourrit, 1921).

A. VIOLLIS: *La vraie Mme de Lafayette* (Paris, Blond et Gay, 1926).

ÉMILE MAGNE: *Mme de Lafayette en ménage* (Paris, Émile-Paul Frères, 1926).

ÉMILE MAGNE: *Le cœur et l'esprit de Mme de Lafayette* (Paris, Émile-Paul Frères, 1927).

M. A. RAYNAL: *Le talent de Mme de Lafayette* (Thèse, Toulouse, 1927).

F. STYGER: *Essai sur l'œuvre de Mme de Lafayette* (Affoltern au Albis, 1944).

C. DÉDÉYAN: *Mme de Lafayette* (Société d'Enseignement Supérieur, 1956).

B. PINGAUD: *Mme de Lafayette par elle-même* (Écrivains de Toujours, Éditions du Seuil, 1959).

MARIE-JEANNE DURRY: *Mme de Lafayette* (Mercure de France, 1962).

HELEN KAPS: *Moral Perspective in La Princesse de Clèves* (University of Oregon Books, 1968).

Articles on Mme de Lafayette's life and works:

FONTENELLE (Mercure, mai 1678).

SAINTE-BEUVE: *Portraits de Femmes.*

TAINE: *Essais de Critique et d'Histoire* (1858).

COMTE D'HAUSSONVILLE: *Mme de Lafayette et Ménage* (Revue des deux mondes, 1890).

C. SALOMON: *La doctrine morale dans La Princesse de Clèves* (Revue Universitaire, II, 1898).

F. BALDENSPERGER: *À propos de l'aveu de la Princesse de Clèves* (Revue de philologie française, 1901).

J. LEMOINE: *Mme de Lafayette et Louvois* (Revue de Paris, 1907).

CHERBULIEZ: *L'âme généreuse* (Revue des deux mondes, 1910).

CHAMARD ET RUDLER: *Les sources historiques de La Princesse de Clèves* (Revue du *XVIe* siècle, t.2, 1914).

CHAMARD ET RUDLER: *Les épisodes historiques de La Princesse de Clèves* (idem).

CHAMARD ET RUDLER: *La couleur historique dans La Princesse de Clèves* (idem, t.5, 1917).

CHAMARD ET RUDLER: *L'histoire et la fiction dans La Princesse de Clèves* (idem).

ANDRÉ BEAUNIER: *Mme de Lafayette et Madame Henriette* (Revue hebdomadaire, jan. 1921–fév. 1921).

ANDRÉ BEAUNIER: *Mme de Lafayette et ses bons amis les savants* (Revue des deux mondes, mars 1921).

ANDRÉ BEAUNIER: *Les dernières années de Mme de Lafayette* (Revue des deux mondes, sept. 1924).

ANDRÉ BEAUNIER: *Mme de Lafayette et Madame Royale* (Revue de Paris, 1926).

H. ASHTON: *The confession of the Princesse de Clèves* (Modern Language Notes, 1919).

C. GAZIER: *La conversion de Mme de Lafayette* (Cahiers Catholiques, juillet 1921).

C. GAZIER: *Les dernières années de Mme de Lafayette* (Correspondant 320, sept. 1930).

E. HENRIOT: *Mme de Lafayette et l'Histoire de Madame Henriette d'Angleterre* (Le Temps, mars 1926).

E. HENRIOT: *Ménage et Mme de Lafayette* (Le Temps, août 1926).

M. LANGLOIS: *Quel est l'auteur de La Princesse de Clèves?* (Mercure de France, nov. 1939).

B. MORRISSETTE: *Marcel Langlois' untenable attribution of La Princesse de Clèves to Fontenelle* (Modern Language Notes, 1946).

ARMAND HOOG: *Sacrifice d'une princesse* (La Nef, juillet 1949).

JEAN FABRE: *L'art de l'analyse dans La Princesse de Clèves* (Mélanges de Strasbourg, vol. 2, Études littéraires, 1945).

JEAN FABRE: *Bienséance et sentiment chez Mme de Lafayette* (C.A.I.E.F., mai 1959).

J. W. SCOTT: *Criticism and La Comtesse de Tende* (Modern Language Review, Jan. 1955).

J. W. SCOTT: *Le 'Prince' de Clèves* (Modern Language Review, July 1957).

J. W. SCOTT: *The "digressions" of La Princesse de Clèves* (French Studies, Oct. 1958).

J. W. SCOTT: *Quelques variantes de La Comtesse de Tende* (R.H.L.F., avril–juin 1959).

B. PINGAUD: *Les secrets de Mme de Lafayette* (Pensée française, déc. 1958).

B. PINGAUD: *Le mythe de La Princesse de Clèves* (Médecine de France, no. 99, 1959).

SERGE DOUBROVSKY: *La Princesse de Clèves: une interprétation existentielle* (T. R., juin 1959).

CLAUDE VIGÉE: *La Princesse de Clèves et la tradition du refus* (Critique, 1960).

MARC CHADOURNE: *Isabelle ou Le Journal amoureux d'Espagne* (T.R., 1960).

B. MORRISSETTE: *Compte rendu de 'Isabelle ou Le Journal amoureux d'Espagne'* (T. R., fév. 1962).

CLAUDETTE SARLET: *Le temps dans La Princesse de Clèves* (Marche Romane, avril–juin 1959).

CLAUDETTE SARLET: *Les jaloux et la jalousie dans l'œuvre romanesque de Mme de Lafayette* (R.S.H. 115, 1964).

CLAUDETTE SARLET: *Style indirect libre et 'point de vue' dans La Princesse de Clèves* (Cahiers d'analyse textuelle, no. 6, 1965).

JULES BRODY: *La Princesse de Clèves and the myth of courtly love* (University of Toronto quarterly, Jan. 1969).